EAST AND WEST

EAST AND WEST

China, Power, and the Future of Asia

CHRISTOPHER PATTEN

TIMES BOOKS

RANDOM HOUSE

Grateful acknowledgment is made to the following for permission to
reprint previously published material:

Harcourt Brace & Company and Faber and Faber Limited: Excerpt
from "Little Gidding," in *Four Quartets.* Copyright © 1943 by T. S.
Eliot and copyright renewed 1971 by Esme Valerie Eliot. Rights out-
side of the United States are controlled by Faber and Faber Limited.
Reprinted by permission of Harcourt Brace & Company and Faber and
Faber Limited.

W. W. Norton & Company, Inc.: Excerpts from *The Analects of Confucius,* translated by Simon Leys. Translation copyright © 1997 by
Pierre Ryckmans. Reprinted by permission of W. W. Norton & Company, Inc.

Princeton University Press: Nine lines from "Things Ended," five
lines from "Wise Men Are Aware of Future Things" (a poem by C. P.
Cavafy based on lines by Philostratus, *Life of Apollonius of Tyana,* VIII,
7), twenty-eight lines from "In a Large Greek Colony, 200 B.C.," and
nine lines from "Waiting for the Barbarians," from *C. P. Cavafy: Collected Poems,* translated by Edmund Keeley and Philip Sherrard. Translation copyright © 1975 by Edmund Keeley and Philip Sherrard.
Reprinted by permission of Princeton University Press.

The Society of Authors: Eight lines from XXXV from *A Shropshire
Lad,* by A. E. Housman. Reprinted by permission of The Society of Authors as the literary representative of the Estate of A. E. Housman.

Library of Congress Cataloging-in-Publication Data
Patten, Christopher.
East and west : China, power, and the future of Asia / Christopher
Patten.
p.   cm.
Includes index.
ISBN 0-8129-3232-3
1. Hong Kong (China)—Politics and government.   2. Pacific Area—
Politics and government.   I. Title.
DS796.H757P39   1998
951.25′04—dc21   98-24150

Frontispiece:
Hong Kong handover ceremony, June 30, 1997.   COURTESY OF THE AUTHOR

FOR LAVENDER

CONTENTS

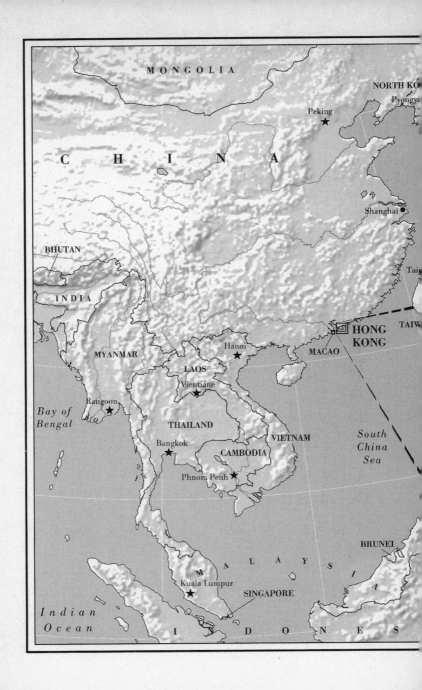

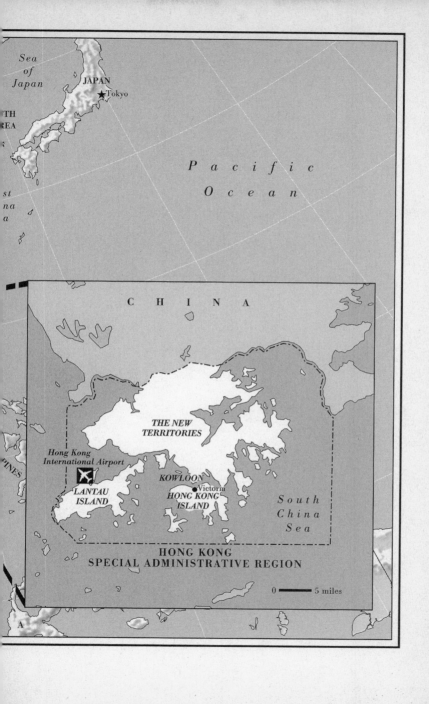

Sea
of
Japan

JAPAN
★ Tokyo

TH
REA

st

na

a

P a c i f i c

O c e a n

C H I N A

*THE NEW
TERRITORIES*

Hong Kong
International Airport

*LANTAU
ISLAND*

KOWLOON
● Victoria
*HONG KONG
ISLAND*

PINES

*South
China
Sea*

HONG KONG
SPECIAL ADMINISTRATIVE REGION

0 ▬▬ 5 miles

"CAVEAT EMPTOR"

A WORD TO THE WISE: I would not wish you to start this book
under false pretenses. I had better confess right away what it is not.

First, this is not a book of memoirs. There may be a case for the giants of politics to write their memoirs, and even for the rest of us to buy
and, conceivably, read them. They provide a slab of stone for historians
to attack with their chisels, a doorstop for all but the most intrepid
reader. Hulking self-justification is, however, rarely an interesting literary form. For those who have served in the political infantry, never rising to the greatest commands, the case for writing one's memoirs is
slight indeed. So you are spared my modest journey from happy child-
hood to happy middle age.

Second, I kept a diary of much of my time in Hong Kong. I hope my
family will be entertained by its accurate indiscretions when I am long

gone. I have drawn on it occasionally to jog my memory in writing this book. But this is not a long and detailed account of my governorship of Hong Kong, the most important and interesting job I have ever done. Others have written and will write their own accounts, more or less accurate, of those years. It would be unfair of me to do more for the time being than outline my experiences there in order to draw some general lessons—unfair to those who worked with me and certainly unfair to Hong Kong. I sometimes doubt as well whether anyone would believe the whole unvarnished story, so that is not for now.

Third, I do not want to contribute another volume to the temporarily discontinued library of books puffing Asia. Tiger virtues, tiger values, tiger miracles, tiger futures, have been so recklessly celebrated that we now find ourselves, boom to bust, told that all the tigers are skinned and stuffed. What has happened in Asia has been remarkable; once exaggerated, it is now belittled. I hope this book provides some middle ground in this important debate about Asian development.

Fourth, this is not an economic textbook about Asia. It does contain information as well as argument. You will occasionally scrape your shins on GDP statistics. But if you want to know the savings rate in Indonesia or the health-care cost projections in the Philippines, you must search elsewhere.

So that's what it's not.

I have tried to draw on my experiences as Governor to develop a number of arguments about Asia, about the conduct of economic policy, about the components of good governance, and about the relationship between political freedom and economic liberty. Five years in Hong Kong gave me an extraordinary opportunity to see what was happening in Asia, and particularly in China. It obliged me to deal with China on issues that reveal much of the worst side of the present Chinese leadership; they are issues as well that comprise the most sensitive facets of China's relationship with the rest of the world. As Governor, I experienced the vitality of life in a booming and free Asian city, saw routinely the best and worst aspects of human nature, and was made to revisit some of the principles in which I have always believed but to which I had rarely given much thought previously. In the darker hours of occasionally fretful nights I found myself face-to-face with the moral dimensions of political action to a greater extent than I had ever been before. I also had to reexamine some of my instincts, two of the most important of which are reflected in the quotations at the beginning of this book. While it is true that Yokohama is definitely not the capital of Japan, "Up to a point, Lord Copper" has been my invariable response to the clattering certainties of much political debate and analysis. If I had to name my own party, Up to a Point might be the best title for it, which is perhaps why I have always been, and remain, a liberal Tory.

But there are some occasions when "Up to a point" does not apply. There is a difference between right and wrong; some of the things, for example, that the Chinese government has done and still does have been and are iniquitous. Criticizing the Chinese Communist party does not make one anti-Chinese. The only person in the Deng Xiaoping era to be the vilified subject of a nationwide criticism campaign was the writer Bai Hua, who argued that patriotism and loving the Communist party need not be the same thing. The point should not require making. Totalitarian systems, even when they are starting to break down, always insist that there is a perfect and comprehensive symmetry between the national interest and that of the system; country and party become ideologically interchangeable. No one else should be obliged to sign up to this insulting, demeaning nonsense. I greatly admire Chinese culture and many of China's achievements—including the 1980s opening of the economy. I have many Chinese friends and several Chinese heroes. But I do not admire or look up to the Chinese Communist party any more than of old I admired the Soviet Communist party.

There is one further absurd footnote to this argument that dislike of the Communist party and all its works is one and the same as hostility to China. I always refer to Peking, not Beijing. This is not an insult. It is because there is a word in the English language for China's capital. I refer similarly to Rome, not Roma; Brussels, not Bruxelles; Lisbon, not Lisboa. I am not told when I do so that I am being anti-Italian, anti-Belgian, or anti-Portuguese.

The events on which I have drawn in writing this book took place at a time when the Asian economies seemed to be climbing like rockets; I began writing against the background noise of the rockets crashing to earth. My views have remained much the same throughout. This unorthodox consistency meant that I used to be criticized for declining to go along with the then-fashionable hyperbole about Asia and its prospects. I guess some will now criticize my disinclination to write Asia off. I regard what has happened in Asia, despite the recent setbacks, as on the whole exciting, unique, and good for the region and the world. It has not been a miracle. It can be explained—above all, as an example of the benefactions of free trade and technological advance. It cannot be attributed to some continent-based value system. "Asian values" has been a shorthand for the justification of authoritarianism, bossiness, and closed collusion rather than open accountability in economic management. Values are universal. So, too, is the case for market economics, which works everywhere better than any other economic system, and free and open economies perform most effectively in plural societies. Liberal economics and liberal democracy go hand in hand. Freedom, democracy, the rule of law, stability, and prosperity are found most frequently in one another's company. The relationship between these aspects of the good and open society will be tested in all parts of Asia, but most fiercely in China, whose die-hard leadership is intent on demonstrating that Leninism and capitalism can happily coexist. The emergence or suppression of civil society in China will be affected by Hong Kong's return to Chinese sovereignty; the China that evolves in the next generation and the way that evolution takes place will more than any other imaginable development determine whether we are more successful in the next century in preserving free markets and liberal democracy than we were in much of this one.

American power and leadership have been more responsible than most other factors in rescuing freedom in the second half of this century. America has been prepared to support the values that have shaped its own liberalism and prosperity with generosity, might, and determination. Sometimes this may have been done maladroitly; what is important is that it has always been done. Now the United States has to continue, unthanked, to stand up for these values in Asia, not eschewing engagement with China and those in the authoritarian camp, but ensuring that the engagement is principled and emphatic, not flaccid. It will have to contend with lobbyists who claim with only vestigial evidence that China will refuse access to a so far largely illusory cornucopia to those who do not, in Peking's view, behave in a politically correct way. Washington will have only spasmodic support from European countries, whose pretensions to a common and honorable global policy are, alas, regularly turned inside out by China's facility at playing off the uninformed greed of one against the unprincipled avarice of another. For all the difficulties of the next few years, I remain on balance optimistic about the economic and political outlook in Asia. With Mr. Salter's caveat, I believe a process has likely begun that is irreversible and which will ensure that the next century belongs not to Asia or America or any other continent but to those values which best combine decency and a good life. A hundred years ago, A. E. Housman's "steady drummer" beat a warning of death and misery to come. Today, on the threshold of another century, the omens seem better. Eastward as well as westward, the land is bright.

I have dedicated this book to my wife. This is more than a marital formality. She has been my best friend and my constant support, to an extent that only she and my daughters know. Dame Shirley Oxenbury bought a magnifying glass to read my writing and typed the manuscript at truly heroic pace. Freda Evans typed my Hong Kong diary (on which I have drawn) from whistling tapes. They have been great friends to me and terrific personal assistants.

I also wish to pay tribute to my British editor, Stuart Proffitt, who was brave and honest when others were not. Any inadequacies in the book are, naturally, my own responsibility, but Stuart Proffitt and my literary agent, Michael Sissons, helped ensure that the book appeared in the form I wished. We all took part in a small drama, starring Rupert Murdoch and one of his publishing companies, that miserably epitomized some of the things about which I have written.

In other circumstances, I might have dedicated this book to the people of Hong Kong, with whom I had the pleasure of living for five years and for whose well-being I was responsible. They are good and brave people, with the customary proportion (or perhaps less than is customary) of those whom Confucius would have regarded as pigheaded. They taught me a lot, and Hong Kong's superbly led, loyal, and professional civil service, and the leaders of the city's democratic and civil liberties movement, made me think harder than ever before about why I went into politics and what I believe. It will always be the greatest regret of my public life that though Britain governed these Chinese men and women very well in many ways, leaving behind a rich and free society, it fell below the highest standards of its colonial record in the very last of its significant colonial responsibilities. The Empire story of the most humane and well intentioned of the colonial powers—a story that at its best encompasses scholar-administrators who knew and loved the distant lands they governed more than the country in whose name they served, the dissemination across tropical jungles and icy wastes of the impartial clemencies of the rule of law, the usually peaceful preparations for the independence of scores of new countries (sometimes successfully) as free and plural societies—ended one hot and wet night on the dazzling shore of Hong Kong's harbor. It could have ended worse. But (as I will argue) Hong Kong deserved better—deserved better of Britain. The way we in Britain have done things, the sort of people we have tried to be, tells us that bluntly. It was a sad way to go. And I fear that the people we left behind know it.

PART ONE

Governing

That things in the Colony aren't what they should be
no one can doubt any longer,
and though in spite of everything we do move forward,
maybe—as more than a few believe—the time has come
to bring in a Political Reformer.

But here's the problem, here's the rub
they make a tremendous fuss
about everything, these Reformers.
(What a relief it would be
if they were never needed.) They probe everywhere,

question the smallest detail,
and right away think up radical changes
that demand immediate execution . . .

. . . as they proceed with their investigation,
they find an endless number of useless things to eliminate,
things that are, however, difficult to get rid of.
And when, all being well, they finish the job,
every detail now diagnosed and sliced away,
and they retire (also taking the wages due to them),
it's a wonder anything's left at all
after such surgical efficiency.

Maybe the moment hasn't arrived yet.
Let's not be too hasty: haste is a dangerous thing.
Untimely measures bring repentance.
Certainly, and unhappily, many things in the Colony are
absurd,

But is there anything human without some fault?
And after all, you see, we do move forward.

—from "In a Large Greek Colony, 200 B.C.," by C. P. Cavafy

Preceding page: Christopher Patten in Legislative Council.   COURTESY OF THE AUTHOR

1

The Last Governor

The Mountains are at their loveliest
and court cases dwindle,
"The birds I saw off at dawn
at dusk I watch return,"
petals from the vase cover my seal box
the curtains hang undisturbed.

—Tang Xianzu, "The Peony Pavilion"

Colonial governors, like the Sumatran rhinoceros, the Florida manatee, and the Politburo of the Chinese Communist party, are an almost extinct species. The sun has set on Europe's nineteenth-century empires. For Britain, trumpeted Last Posts have echoed back over continents and seas. The Royal Instructions and Letters Patent, which carried the smack of benevolently authoritarian governance to distant tribes and lands and cultures, have been filed away. All that is left is the sovereign responsibility over a handful of rocks and islands whose people are too few or too presently secure to allow us to slip off home. In Britain, we don the remaining hat rack of ostrich-plumed topees with resignation, not enthusiasm.

Hong Kong is where the story of Empire really ended, but it was a curious footnote to a tale already largely told. I was the Last Governor (a title invariably given capital letters to denote, I suppose, its historic significance) of what was one of Britain's greatest colonies and certainly its richest. But my job was different from that of all those governors who had lowered the Union flag elsewhere. They had been charged with the duty of preparing their communities for independence. Coming from what Nelson Mandela among many others has called "the home of parliamentary democracy," British governors were required to provide those they ruled with the means, intellectual and institutional, to take their destiny in their own hands. Empire was to be dissolved from the top down.

No one today would seek to justify reverting to imperial rule, one country governing the whole or part of another, or to defend the injustices and humiliations of colonial history. And most of us can refrain from the temptation to speculate about how much less freedom there is today in some formerly colonized countries now that they are "free." But apologists for Britain's record are surely entitled to claim that by and large no empire has been wound up so peacefully and with such benign intent. There were mistakes; there was blood—tragically, far too much of it in India. There was sometimes procrastination, though the speed of departure, once the decision to go had been made, was usually extraordinarily swift, too swift for comfort in some cases. Overall, nevertheless, it is not a bad story—men and women infused with the values of nineteenth-century liberalism trying to do their best, installing democracy, training civil servants, policemen, and soldiers, establishing independent courts, entrenching civil liberties. In one country after another, the whole constitutional module was wheeled out one sultry southern night, mounted on its launching pad, and as the midnight hour struck and the brass bands played a baptismal anthem, it was blasted off into outer space. Sometimes the satellite went satisfactorily into orbit; sometimes it crashed embarrassingly to earth; but the enterprise was usually well managed and well meant.

Colonial rule in Hong Kong was to end differently. Only a part of Hong Kong had been granted to Britain in the nineteenth century by China; the majority of the land was held on a lease, due to expire in 1997. While it would have been theoretically possible to retain the territory held by grant—a course of action urged on Britain in the early 1980s by some of those local Chinese advisers to the British Governor who subsequently (such is politics) became cheerleaders for China— this would have been neither politically judicious nor administratively feasible. Hong Kong island and the Kowloon peninsula—the land ceded outright by grant—depended on the hinterland of the New Territories and beyond for food and water. For Britain to have made a last imperial stand on the shores of the South China Sea would have risked local calamity and international obloquy. But the alternative was hardly palatable. It was to hand a free Chinese city back to a totalitarian Chinese state. This was inevitably a rip-roaring story for the global media—the last British colony was to be surrendered to the last Communist tyranny. A good audience for the show was guaranteed.

The situation was entangled in political complexity, economic uncertainty, and human frailty. It had sapped the energy of British administrators and bored the British political classes into indifference. It brought out the very worst in British sophistry and the best in our traditions of public administration. It made quiet heroes of the overwhelming majority of the people of Hong Kong. It was capable of almost any outcome—from economic collapse to urban riot, from mass emigration and capital flight to civil breakdown and blood on the streets. Before I went to Hong Kong as Governor, one newspaper editor told me he thought that the odds were evenly balanced as to whether I would leave by royal yacht or by air force helicopter from the ballroom roof of Government House.

While I thought this decidedly far-fetched, it was the more credible impossibilities of the job that attracted me to it. After five years running the Conservative party's Research Department, I had become a Member of Parliament in 1979, one of the beneficiaries of Margaret Thatcher's landmark victory that year, and I remained in the House of Commons for thirteen years. From 1983 to 1992 I had been a British Minister, a member of the Cabinet for the last three of those years. But in 1992, while Chairman of the Conservative party, I lost my own Bath seat in a general election that the Conservative party won. The proffered possibilities of staying in British politics were then unattractive. Elevation to the House of Lords would, in my judgment, have ruled out my holding any of the most senior and most interesting jobs in government, like the Foreign Office and the Treasury. I did not believe those who told me otherwise, and thought they were allowing their friendship for me to overwhelm their political sense. A by-election was equally unappealing. Parachuting senior party figures into understandably wary constituencies has a calamitous track record—bones are broken and careers wrecked. I was particularly averse to subjecting my long-suffering (though willing) wife and family to another bruising encounter with my political ambitions. Politics seemed a closed door domestically, yet I still wanted to work in public service and was drawn to the prospect of spending some time abroad, which would save me from becoming one of the wallflowers of Westminster, pining for the next dance. When the Prime Minister, John Major, generously suggested on the morrow of his victory and my defeat that I might be interested in becoming Governor of Hong Kong, I leapt at the offer, regarding the hazards of the enterprise as among its main selling points.

"It's an impossible job," an American friend, Professor Nelson Polsby, told me, "which you'll have to make look possible as long as you possibly can." Not everyone took this view. I was strongly counseled against accepting the job by one former diplomat and politician (who has made a career out of resigning from careers) on the grounds that there was nothing left to do in Hong Kong. All had been settled, and I would find myself coping with an enervating climate and dull people who talked about nothing but money. The job wasn't impossible; it was all too possible. It consisted simply of being transported along already laid tram lines to a known destination five years hence. The petals would certainly gather on my seal box.

There was also a strongly held view in some diplomatic quarters that to appoint a politician as Governor was to run a number of unconscionable risks. First, a politician would not by definition have been soaked in the orthodoxy of the Foreign Office mandarinate on China and Hong Kong. The apostolic succession of Hong Kong governors, ambassadors to China, and leading policy makers on Hong Kong had shuffled a handful of people around the senior posts in this important area of public policy. They were not all cut from the same timber. For example, Sir Edward Youde (who was Governor from 1982 until his death in office in 1987) had been a strong-minded and immensely popular Governor, fiercely loyal to Hong Kong, and perhaps as a result was regarded in the Foreign Office's private historic assessment of its custodianship of Hong Kong as a tad awkward. The same officials had moved conscientiously and honorably from chair to chair, but their political ministers (and—in some cases—masters) had come and gone, particularly at the junior levels, with all the casual frequency of British political life. The notion of a politician arriving in the job with, conceivably, his own questions and his own ideas was bad enough; what was worse was to have a politician senior enough to have a direct line to the Prime Minister and the Foreign Secretary. With a former cabinet minister as Governor, policy was clearly more likely to be initiated in Hong Kong than in London or Peking.

It has sometimes been said that the Chinese themselves wanted this, seeing it as the best way to speed up decision making in the last few years of transition. I never saw any evidence for this, or for their concern to expedite the business of government. What is true is that Chinese harassing and harrying of my predecessor, particularly over the plans to build a new airport, undermined him politically. They made a decent and intelligent man seem weak when in fact what he was attempting to do, believing it to be in Hong Kong's interest, was to win Chinese understanding and consent for his policy initiatives. So Chinese policy resulted in exchanging a scholarly diplomat for a well-connected Westminster politician. I doubt whether subsequent events made Chinese officials think this was a good bargain.

In any event, I did not accept that my background disqualified me from taking the post. While no sinologist myself—a point that some regard as a reproof and others as an accolade—I was not as wholly unfitted for the governor's plumes as a few critics subsequently suggested. True, my arrival in the job owed more to the propensities of the people of Bath than to the experiences gained in the foothills and on the mountain slopes of a conventional diplomatic career. But I always felt, with regular twinges of embarrassment, that it was rather more to the point that no one in Hong Kong had had anything to do with my appointment.

However, I could point to as much experience in handling Asian issues as any minister is likely to acquire in British politics. I had visited Hong Kong on three occasions, the first in 1979 as a young back bencher. The main purpose of that visit was to see at first hand how Hong Kong was dealing with an influx of Vietnamese boat people. We went to many of the makeshift camps, seeing the families who had braved the storms and the pirates to sail in usually overcrowded and leaky boats from Communist Vietnam to the capitalist haven of Hong Kong. The colonial government was doing its best to cope with tens of thousands of migrants, to whose claims for refuge the local Chinese community was generally hostile. With the colleagues who accompanied me I was also able to discuss other aspects of Hong Kong's life. At the end of that visit, two of the delegation in particular—a very likable

Labour MP, Ted Rowlands, and I—pressed the Governor and his ministerial superior to introduce democracy in local government in Hong Kong. This modest suggestion reflected our genuine bafflement that in a city so sophisticated and with such a rapidly growing young professional middle class, political lobbying for democracy and civil liberties was still regarded as dangerously radical.

From 1986 to 1989, I was Minister for Overseas Development, responsible for Britain's aid program and for our concessional, soft-loan financing of industrial projects in developing countries. I visited most Asian countries during this period, admittedly getting to know South Asia (where Britain had its biggest aid programs) better than the Southeast Asian or Eastern Asian countries. China was an exception to this. I had two long visits to China, and negotiated a large concessional financing agreement with Chinese officials; at the time, it was the largest such agreement that we had signed with anyone.

The second of my two visits came at a particularly tumultuous moment in China's history. I attended the annual meeting of the Asian Development Bank that began in Peking at the beginning of May 1989. Before the meeting had commenced, it had been thought that the main interest would be the way that China handled Taiwan's attendance at it. But we arrived in Peking at the outset of the Tiananmen Square demonstrations. We found ourselves in a city bubbling with excitement and intoxicated with hope. Each day we witnessed the audacious enthusiasm of a great political carnival. Driving from our hotel to the meeting place for the conference in the Great Hall of the People, we passed impromptu political meetings at road junctions and flyovers. Young people cheered and sang in Peking's spring sunshine. Everyone smiled, including the police. "Notice," said the Ambassador, Sir Alan Donald, one of the most amiable and experienced of "old China hands," "that the police are wearing brown sneakers. You don't wear sneakers if you're going to stamp on people." He went on to explain to us that we were witnessing a sophisticated Chinese drama in which everyone knew his part and in which tradition and shared national ambition would help to secure an accommodation in which all would be able to save face. With his arms making great sweeping movements through the air, he explained that the authorities would enfold dissent rather than confront it, as though following some military maneuver from Sun-tzu's two-thousand-year-old classic text *The*

Art of War. I recall a few journalists at an impromptu press conference in the embassy garden offering a sourer opinion of the probable turn of events.

As the international bigwigs in town, we were able to meet Chinese leaders despite their other preoccupations. We met the sprightly old President, Yang Shangkun, the ploddingly unimpressive Premier, Li Peng (surveying us suspiciously from beneath the canopy of his huge black eyebrows), and the Party Secretary, Zhao Ziyang. Zhao met seven or eight of the visiting Western ministers one warm afternoon, sufficiently warm for us to be slightly startled by the sight of his long johns protruding below his pale gray trousers when he crossed his legs. He was an attractive man, with an enchanting smile that had somehow survived the dangerous decades of his rise to the top through the cadres of the Chinese Communist party. Zhao answered charmingly and intelligently as we asked him about rural electrification, public health, child mortality statistics, and all the other matters that crowd the agenda of aid ministers. Discreet, none of us quite dared ask about the only thing we had really discussed in private and the issue that was plainly at the top of his own mind—the milling, churning throng outside his window, their ambitions and their manifestations of raw popular power. Eventually, toward the end of the meeting, I apologized for changing the subject and asked if he would care to tell us what was happening all around us as we discussed development economics in Asia. With an almost audible sigh of relief, he produced from his pocket a card covered in headings and embarked on a long reply. He told us he was confident that legal and democratic avenues would be found to resolve the students' demands. The students' concerns about corruption and graft were shared by the Party and the government. Zhao was articulate and convincing. He was also throwing down the gauntlet at the feet of the Party hard-liners. When this "speech" was reported on the evening news, the students in the square applauded. Zhao's more mule-headed comrades presumably began to sharpen their knives.

I left Peking for Hong Kong a few days later convinced by the meeting with Zhao, by the sight of his dour antagonist Li Peng, and by the ebullience of the public mood in the capital that the demonstrations would end peacefully and well. I believed I had witnessed a peaceful revolution in the making. The subsequent experience made me rather more circumspect in my future predictions about Chinese politics.

That was not the end of my Asian experiences. As Britain's Environment Secretary in 1989–90, I was involved in some of the earlier bouts of environmental diplomacy between developed and developing countries. In particular, in 1990, I chaired the London Conference, which sought to tighten up implementation of the Montreal Protocol on chlorofluorocarbons. We managed to cobble together an agreement despite some bitter arguments about technology transfer and what is invariably seen in poorer countries as hypocritical bossiness by those who have already grown rich partly through polluting their own environment. I worked in the margins of that conference closely with Japanese officials with whom I have invariably had good and cooperative relationships down the years.

As far as Asian experience was concerned, then, the "Last Governor" was not wholly a tyro. What was the city like that I was to govern? Hong Kong, with all its flash and dash, has a partiality for parading its uniqueness. Statistics of biggest and best crowd the page. This self-conscious vanity, a manifestation in part of a neurotic search for assurance, should not blind observers to the fact that Hong Kong really is one of a kind: chop sui generis. No other place has quite the same blend of East and West, ancient and modern, spectacular and humdrum. It is a great Chinese maritime city, crowding down to and soaring above its magnificent natural harbor. Perhaps the most absurd of all the controversies during my years in Hong Kong surrounded the proposal that Elton John should hold a concert in our main sports stadium just before the handover. Local politicians and residents' associations blocked the idea on the grounds that the singer would make far too much noise; the concert might be allowed to go ahead only if the audience listened to the unamplified music on headsets and clapped politely in cotton gloves. Yet Hong Kong is nonstop noise: clanking jackhammers, bleeping pagers and cell phones, clacking mah-jongg sets, roaring traffic, clanging trams, hooting ships. The sounds of commerce constantly serenade the visitor unless he or she is well informed enough to know that you can escape to some of the finest hill walking anywhere, in emerald highlands from whose elevations you occasionally catch the sight of a distant shore or skyscraping office block.

Hong Kong swishes and stirs most of the better ideas that have been adduced for explaining the nature and causes of economic growth. It supports the proposition that growth is essentially an urban phenomenon, the unplanned consequences of one bright spark's energies animating the prospects for other less talented citizens. The economists call this, rather dourly, the "externalities" of growth. Both Adam Smith and Milton Friedman would find much to celebrate in Hong Kong's record. At a time when it was politically and bureaucratically fashionable in the postwar years to plan, subsidize, intervene, and control, Hong Kong's special fortune was to be blessed with a small team of colonial administrators eccentric enough to believe in free markets and cussed enough to stick to their guns despite efforts to get them to see social democratic sense. It is a mark of the extent to which the sovereign power, Britain, left Hong Kong to its own devices, guaranteeing its autonomy in domestic matters, that while the home country flirted with many of the famously well known ways of impoverishing a nation (nationalization, high taxation, rigid labor markets, excessive public spending), it allowed its colonial dependency to practice the ancient economic virtues with conspicuous success.

Natural entrepreneurial flair, randomly and sometimes brutally suppressed at different times in China's long history, also contributed its vitality to the Hong Kong economy, and this quality was given an especially fleet-footed audacity by the fact that Hong Kong is essentially a refugee community, not rootless but markedly able to dig up and put down roots at high speed. Those who had once made fortunes in Shanghai (in textiles, for instance) only to see them stolen in the name of Marxism-Leninism remade fortunes in Hong Kong. Those who had starved elsewhere in China, especially in the southern provinces that formed the Colony's hinterland, came to Hong Kong to make a fortune for the first time.

The Hong Kong story is at its most remarkable in the years after the Second World War. Broken-backed by war and ruthless occupation, attempting to reestablish the institutions of government and to rebuild its modest fortune as a trading center in the bleak days of the Korean War's embargo on China, Hong Kong found itself having to provide a home for wave after wave of refugees from the turbulent events of modern Chinese history. They fled from the brutalities of war and revolution, from the famine spawned by the Great Leap Forward, from the insane cruelties of the Cultural Revolution. Sometimes they climbed over barbed-wire fences to get into Britain's Chinese colony; sometimes they cheated the sharks in Hong Kong's waters and swam; sometimes they clung to the bottom of railway carriages or hid in baskets of fruit and vegetables. They came by the hundred thousand. I remember giving lunch one day to a retiring civil servant; I always invited those at senior levels who were about to retire to join my wife and me for a meal with a group of their friends. On this occasion, the civil servant and each of his half dozen or so colleagues around the table were all postwar refugees. One ran a newspaper; another, a conservatory. Another was a banker; another, a very successful businessman; and two were high-ranking civil servants. For each one of them it was a story of rags to riches, of destitution to opportunity and success. Their families had prospered. Their children were away at universities. At least half of them had foreign passports, just in case they needed to dig up their roots again. Only one of them had arrived in Hong Kong with any money—fifty pounds, which had been stolen by a British Sikh policeman at the border. Each of their lives had been a triumphant adventure, a grand slam for the human spirit. How could a community that was built by, with, and on these men and women fail to be a success?

And the story continued in a smaller way in much the same fashion. Sitting one year next to a tuxedoed young official, recently graduated, at the annual Civil Service Association Ball, I was told that his father, who spoke little Mandarin and no Cantonese (Hong Kong's native dialect) or English, had fled northern China for Hong Kong during the Cultural Revolution. Some years later, he had managed to get permission for his wife and family to join him in Hong Kong, where he had gotten a regular though menial job. He had sent his wife enough money to buy one ticket on the slow train south, and she had sat day after day on the hard railway seat with a baby son on each knee. One of those sons was now studying medicine; the other was the first young man from his school to get a prestigious place in the administrative class of the civil service. His parents were buying their own apartment; they still spoke no English, and little Cantonese. It is a story that would resonate around the great refugee cities of America.

But what did these refugees find in Hong Kong, and how or why did they prosper? They arrived in China's only free city; it was indeed (in the words of the Chinese journalist Tsang Ki-Fan) "the only Chinese society that, for a brief span of one hundred years, lived through an ideal never realized at any time in the history of Chinese society—a time when no man had to live in fear of the midnight knock on the door." Hong Kong had a competent government, pursuing market economics under the rule of law. It was a government that fully met the Confucian goal—"Make the local people happy and attract migrants from afar."

During my governorship, I frequently found myself asked to explain in speeches and articles the secret of Hong Kong's success. I was never able to do better than return to two paragraphs from Alexis de Tocqueville's *Journeys to England and Ireland*. I first read Tocqueville while at university. What was then an obligation in order to pass my preliminary examinations became a pleasure as I discovered that he is the wisest, most perceptive, and most practical minded of political philosophers. The paragraphs that I used to quote were those I had first inserted, twenty years before, in the introductory argument of a political pamphlet entitled "The Right Approach," in which Margaret Thatcher set out, as the then Leader of the Opposition, the broad political program of the party she was shortly to lead into government.

"Looking at the turn given to the human spirit in England by political life," Tocqueville wrote, "seeing the Englishman, certain of the support of his laws, relying on himself and unaware of any obstacle except the limit of his own powers, acting without constraint; seeing him, inspired by the sense that he can do anything, look restlessly at what now is, always in search of the best; seeing him, like that, I am in no hurry to inquire whether nature has scooped out ports for him, and given him coal and iron. The reason for his commercial prosperity is not there at all; it is in himself.

"Do you want to test," he continued, "whether a people is given to industry and commerce? Do not sound its ports, or examine the wood from its forests or the produce of its soil. The spirit of trade will get all these things, and without it, they are useless. Examine whether this people's laws give men the courage to seek prosperity, freedom to follow it up, the sense and habits to find it, and the assurance of reaping the benefit."

Good government, the rule of law, and market economics transformed the battered and beggared community of the postwar years into one of the greatest trading centers on earth, the economic capital for the Chinese diaspora, and the most secure base for international investors keen to do business in China. While most journalistic attention focused on the indices of wealth, the fortunes of tycoons, and the consumption patterns of the middle class, social progress was in its way just as remarkable. Successful market economics paid for a general improvement in the overall quality of life. Where people had once wheezed and coughed and died of epidemic disease in shanty settlements, there were now soaring new estates of apartment blocks whose inhabitants lived longer and healthier lives than any in Asia except in Japan; their health statistics were indeed better than those of many OECD countries. The range and quality of welfare services—homes for the aged, kindergartens for the young, training for those with disabilities—expanded as dramatically, if not so visibly, as the communications infrastructure. Educational standards soared, with up to a quarter of young men and women entering undergraduate institutions. Over half of these students came from public-housing complexes, and very few of them—perhaps one in twenty—had a parent whose education had extended beyond secondary school. It was a real social revolution.

Social and economic progress had helped to reinforce the stability of a community made up of the potentially restless—just arrived and, with bags ready to pack, prepared to depart again. One good indicator of stability is crime. Crime figures had peaked in the 1980s and fell through the 1990s. According to Interpol, the figures were about on a par with those of Singapore, sometimes a little better (in 1992 and 1993, for example), sometimes a little worse (in the following two years). Hooligans in Hong Kong were not thrashed; drug pushers were not hanged; gum was not banned from the increasingly healthy teeth of Hong Kong's teenagers. But the streets were pretty safe, and Hong Kong—as my wife and I were to discover—was an easier place to bring up our youngest, teenage daughter than most European or North American cities. The precise relationship between crime and economic and social advance is impossible to gauge. Human wickedness is not circumscribed by economics, and it is of course ridiculous to behave as though there were some exact equation between, say, unemployment and deprivation on the one hand and crime on the other. It is a calumny on the virtuous poor. My experience in Hong Kong, however, convinced me that it is ludicrously counterintuitive to argue that unemployment and poverty have nothing to do with crime levels.

Hong Kong possessed all the institutions and culture of civil society, at least all those bar one. There were churches, active in the social and educational as well as in the spiritual life. There were professions, custodians of the interests and standards of their callings. There were nongovernmental organizations providing many of the social services that would have been run by the state elsewhere—kindergartens for infants, hostels for the handicapped, "sheltered" homes for the elderly, hospices for the dying. There were more newspapers per head of population than anywhere else in the world, proof of Hong Kongers' interest in current affairs as well as in gambling on the horses. So a free society lived and breathed—up to that boundary line beyond which a governing class wrestled with the arduous choices of politics. There was freedom of a substantial sort. But there was no freedom to choose those who would be wholly responsible for even the most mundane of public services.

It was not as if Hong Kongers had been politically lobotomized, though this was frequently argued. The Cantonese, who make up the majority of the population, are noisily argumentative and take a natural and articulate interest in political debate. Nor can it be convincingly claimed that the Chinese as a whole are uninterested in politics. The history of the past century suggests otherwise. The reasons for blocking the development of democracy in Hong Kong were not cultural; they were political. This was the sovereign power's greatest failing, allowing colonial habits of mind to survive for too long and denying Hong Kong the chance to grow its own self-confident political culture at a steady and irreversible pace.

Naturally, there were always reasons why the time was not quite right for democracy. The postwar Governor, Sir Mark Young (1941–47), had unveiled ambitious plans for beginning the same process of democratization that was being triggered at the time in other British colonies. After his departure, and for three decades to come, the development of representative government was buried in a permafrost of official disapproval. Some of the reasons for this made passing sense. The flood of refugees into Hong Kong, and the social and economic demands they made, created administrative priorities other than political reform. There were worries that free elections would see the community polarized between supporters of the principal mainland political identities, the Communists and the Kuomintang. And there was the brooding and minatory presence of China. Treat Hong Kong like other British colonies, senior Chinese officials including Premier Zhou Enlai warned, and the territory may be deluded into thinking that it will one day share their destiny and achieve independence. Not for the last time, the Chinese Communist party's shadow was allowed to blot out the sun.

To be fair, until the late 1970s there was no great pressure for change; people were too occupied making their way in the world—earning a living, getting a roof over their head, putting their children into school, finding the security that stormy times had so far denied them—to worry too much about democracy. When the government got too far out of touch with common feeling, a riot soon redressed the balance. But in fact this rarely happened. Without politicians, so it was argued, Hong Kong managed its affairs conspicuously well. Proconsuls ordained; officials administered; buildings rose; trade flourished; bank accounts burgeoned.

Yet there were, of course, politicians—politicians who rose and fell on the tide of gubernatorial rather than popular approval. Hong Kong created a class of appointed politicians, a regiment of the sometimes great and the often good, drawn mainly from business and the professions, bound together by patronage, by honors, and by a mutual interest in the preservation of the existing way of doing things. It was very colonial, and the ranks of the Order of the British Empire in every class were full of those who had made this more or less benevolent system work.

It would be churlish to belittle the immense amount of public service undertaken by many people over many years. There were some fine public servants in the ranks of those selected to help run Hong Kong. But it is shortsighted to overlook the deficiencies of this system, which at best added a local dimension to official decision making and at worst provided no more than a veneer of consultative respectability for benign authoritarianism. For a start, those who shared in government were on the whole representatives of the better-off sections of society, with a leavening of priests, social workers, and housing activists to help authenticate the whole process. It is difficult to believe that some of Hong Kong's present social and economic problems—for example, the control of property development by a small group of the mega-rich—did not partly result from this. Certainly, representatives of business became so accustomed to being able to get a sympathetic hearing at the highest levels that they regarded any democratic challenge to the system with the most profound suspicion. They even came to believe that it would be impossible to gain approval for their views about free enterprise in a democratic assembly, an eccentric belief given that there is hardly anywhere in the world more naturally receptive to the prospects and disciplines of capitalist economics than Hong Kong.

Needless to say, when governors and ministers and the panjandrums of British public life asked these appointed advisers and those from whose ranks they were largely drawn for their views on democratic development, they gave the answers that might have been expected. No one in Hong Kong, came the pat reply, was really interested in politics; business came first—it was not a political city.

By the late 1970s, this self-serving argument had begun to sound a little tinny. Education, prosperity, and travel had produced the same effects in Hong Kong as elsewhere. Those young men and women brought up in Hong Kong, and increasingly born there too, who, at universities at home—or in Britain, Canada, or the United States—had been encouraged to read Locke, Hume, Paine, Mill, and Popper, those who had been examined in the histories of Britain's and America's struggles for freedom, could hardly be expected to accept that in Britain's last colonial redoubt the full panoply of civil liberties they had been taught to cherish should be denied them. Where were the honor and the honesty in that? At precisely the moment that Hong Kongers were starting to notice that the return to the motherland was only just around a not so distant corner, the city saw the beginnings of serious and responsible pressure for democracy, sufficient to be noticed but not sufficient to do more than thaw the outer edges of the political frost. Faced with signs of political unease in Hong Kong, a Labour government in Britain in the 1970s concluded that the right response was social progress—above all, the construction of cheap rented housing—rather than democratic reform. Hong Kong's democratic campaigners were left to fend very politely for themselves, a job-creation program for those members of the Police Special Branch who could be persuaded that these lawyers, teachers, and social workers with impeccably British accents and opinions represented a seditious threat.

This argument is worth elaborating because of its long-term effects. First, the political class that Britain created had the virtues and the failings of Archbishop Abel Muzorewa, Zimbabwe's never-to-be-elected Premier, in permanent waiting. It had no deep roots in the community; it was full of befeathered chiefs attended by very few Indian braves; its loyalties were to a colonial power, not to a set of political principles. What is more, civil liberties and the values of freedom became so associated with opposition to British colonialism that when the departing colonial sovereign eventually changed its tune, a few of those who had previously attacked it for its political obduracy found it impossible to pardon the offender so late in the day. Their antipathy to British colonialism had become greater than their enthusiasm for democracy and civil liberties. So both Muzorewaites and some of the readers of Paine and Popper found themselves, as the transfer of sovereignty loomed, deserting en bloc from one colonial power, Britain, to another, China.

The suppression of open politics also led to a political climate from the 1970s onward in which it often seemed easier to believe in conspiracy rather than coincidence, screw-up, or even what you could see with your own eyes. The passage of so much politics between the calculatedly secretive officials of the Chinese government and the culturally secretive officials of the British Foreign Office made conspiracy theories ever more exotic. Chinese officials learned to play on this mood with the virtuosity of keyboard maestros.

For all this denial of Hong Kong's emerging and homegrown political identity, the city enjoyed a real sense of its own nature. Hong Kongers knew who they were. They were . . . Hong Kongers. Their sense of Britishness was choked off by the British government's decision in 1981 (which, as a young Member of Parliament, I alas supported) to redefine the rights that possession of a Hong Kong British passport imparted. While Hong Kong's counterparts in Britain's other colonies in Gibraltar and the Falklands retained the principal entitlement of citizenship—that is, the right of abode in the country whose passport a citizen carries—Hong Kongers were left with a second-class document that only allowed them access to British consular protection and easier travel across international frontiers. The clear intention was to avoid, in the populist parlance, a flood of Hong Kong Chinese immigration into Britain once discussions with China about the uncertain future had gotten under way. This may have been "realistic," to use the adjective customarily applied when one country attempts to prevent immigration, by a group that is ethnically different, from another country. But it was hardly edifying, and it gave the distinct impression that Britain cared less about its colonial subjects than they deserved. Nothing much changed this impression subsequently, despite the decision in 1990 to give a full British passport to 50,000 families who might otherwise have emigrated in the wake of the Tiananmen murders and the decisions in 1996 and 1997 on visa-free access to Britain and on the nationality status of the small but important South Asian community in Hong Kong. If the average Hong Kong citizen thought of himself as a Hong Kong Britisher, this was despite the efforts of British politicians to prove him wrong. The cynicism of Britain's approach to this question of nationality was made manifest within months of the transition to Chinese sovereignty, when the new Labour government promised full British passports to the residents of the remaining handful of British colonies.

The temptation for Hong Kongers to think of themselves as Chinese first and foremost was regularly thwarted by the behavior of the Chinese government and its agents. What was the relationship to Hong Kong of those who incarcerated dissidents, of those who locked up bishops and their flocks, of those who shot demonstrators, of those who hectored and bullied in the language of 1950s and 1960s Maoism? What is more, a majority of those who lived in Hong Kong had themselves fled Communist China or were the offspring of families that had done so. They were in Hong Kong because of their experiences in China. The real dividing line in Hong Kong was less between those who believed in democratic values and those who did not than between those who trusted China and those who did not. Proximity to 1997 eventually made some impact on this issue as more people tried to shrug off their elementary instincts and face up realistically to a future from which there was no escape. Yet overwhelmingly, the Chinese citizens of Hong Kong were to think of themselves as just that: Hong Kongers first and foremost—Hong Kongers who were Chinese and who had benefited, albeit for historic reasons that few would seek to justify, from the pluralism provided by temporary British sovereignty over their city.

If Britain was to deny any moral obligation to Hong Kong that raised issues of race (and this was the real purport of its policy on nationality and passports), it clearly recognized its duty to defend Hong Kong's bonds to the economic and political values that had shaped it and that defined its difference from the rest of China. From the outset in 1982 of its negotiations with China on Hong Kong's future, Britain made plain its commitment to the maintenance of capitalism and freedom in the territory. Margaret Thatcher argued strongly for this. And the Chinese responded with what some have always regarded as improbable alacrity and generosity of imagination. Deng Xiaoping, whose clout continued to extend, almost until his death, well beyond what was latterly his only honorific position as president of the All China Bridge Federation, offered a convenient catchall formula for landing a successful negotiation. In return for an unambiguous transfer of sovereignty from Britain to China, Hong Kong was offered the guarantees of a protocol probably devised even more with Taiwan in mind. There would be one country, he said: China, but two systems—China's and Hong Kong's. Some, like Milton Friedman, shook their heads in disbelief; others pored over the history books to try to find examples of this formula ever working before. They did not find them, yet here it was: "one country, two systems." The diplomats of both sides set out to put flesh on its bones.

The negotiations were long and difficult; they covered important issues of principle; they involved leaps of faith and comprehension. At the end of the day, they resulted in the Joint Declaration of 1984, a detailed treaty that sought to guarantee in every whit and particular that the way of life enjoyed by Hong Kong would survive for fifty years after China's five-starred flag was first raised over the territory. China promised to retain not only Hong Kong's capitalist system and its autonomy to run its own affairs but also its rule of law and the freedoms associated with it—of speech, assembly, religious practice, and belief. While Hong Kong was to continue to have an executive-led government—a subjective term, though more or less understandable—that government was to be accountable to a legislature constituted by elections. Hong Kong's flight path to democracy, so long denied, was at last formally accepted by both the present and the future sovereign powers.

Some have argued subsequently that such a commitment to elections had nothing to do with the introduction of democracy. It is not easy to believe that when the then British Prime Minister, Margaret Thatcher, or her Foreign Secretary, Geoffrey Howe, were presented with the text of the agreement, they were told that the elections were not to be democratic, or that they were to be the sort of elections with which the Chinese rather than the British would feel comfortable, the sort of elections that for example produced the Central Committee of the Chinese Communist party or the members of China's National People's Congress.

When the Joint Declaration was displayed before an admiring world, the democratic underpinnings for Hong Kong's autonomy and civil liberties were themselves highlighted as a principal achievement of the negotiations and as a reason for having confidence in their outcome. "We may have denied you passports," Hong Kong was told, "and we may have no alternative but to hand you over to Communist China, but we have given you the chance of a voice in your own affairs, which you can raise to defend your liberties." The world also was invited to applaud. "Where are your criticisms now that we have, albeit rather late in the day, secured Hong Kong's free and democratic future?" Nowhere was the message put more clearly than in the British Parliament, where it was possible to detect a little squeamishness about what was happening. Indeed, a former Prime Minister, Edward Heath (who was subsequently to sing from a different song sheet), admonished the government to press ahead with democratic reform. Ministers seemed to envisage a slower process than was desirable. This was, he argued, invariably the mistake made in Britain's colonial past, yet the young people of Hong Kong were quite capable of running their own affairs. In the debates on the Joint Declaration and its aftermath, many parliamentarians made a similar point. Their arguments were put with the greatest clarity by a Labour MP, George Robertson, later to become the Defense Secretary in Tony Blair's Labour administration in 1997. Criticizing an "unduly cautious" approach to democratic development in the Colony, he went on to argue, "the danger now is not of Chinese overreaction to democratic reform but of insufficient time before 1997 in which to create a strong, viable, locally based system which will withstand the inevitable pressures and tremors as 1997 advances." To which ministers in both houses of Parliament gave the unequivocal reply that they "fully accept[ed] that we should build up a firmly based democratic administration in the years [before] 1997."

Should there be the smallest doubt about the importance of this point, the democratic development of Hong Kong was loaded with even weightier responsibilities. During the negotiation of the Joint Declaration, some in Hong Kong, including the senior member of the governor's main circle of advisers (his elite Executive Council, the majority of whose members represented the leading business and professional interests in the community), had fretted that there was no real guarantee that the Chinese would stick to it. Perhaps there should be some form of binding arbitration, some international jury that could be summoned to adjudicate in such circumstances. A British cabinet committee itself reviewed the argument and, while doubtless also concluding that it would be well-nigh impossible to get the Chinese to accept such an arbitral clause, asserted that there was no need anyway for any such fallback mechanism because Hong Kong was now launched on the path to democracy and could speak and stand up for itself if the Chinese were ever tempted to break the terms of the agreed treaty. So the claims about democracy were not some trivial sideshow—cakes for the public, ale for the press: They appeared central to the government's understanding of its own purposes and to its claims about its good intentions.

There was one unfortunate side effect of this failure to build arbitration into the Joint Declaration (to be closely followed, it should be added, by the slipping and slithering away from the promises on democracy). The extent to which people could really depend on the implementation of the Joint Declaration by China became a matter for prayer and aspiration, accompanied in more bracing moments by advice to worried questioners that they should grow up and live in the real world. It may be the case that in that "real world" there is little that one country can do to make another do what it has agreed to do in a third place far across the sea, especially now that gunboat diplomacy is happily a thing of the past. But this was not quite how the situation was explained to Hong Kong. Not for the first time, British spokesmen wanted to have their cake and eat it, too. They announced that the people of Hong Kong could depend on the continuance of their liberties because this was promised in the Joint Declaration. And what if the Joint Declaration were to be breached? Well, naturally (so the argument always ran), we would not answer hypothetical questions, but were this to happen, we would presumably take our cue from King Lear—"[We] will do such things,—What they are yet, [we] know not: but they shall be The terrors of the earth. . . ."

And so it played. Whatever China was subsequently to do between the signing of the Joint Declaration and 1997, no one would ever quite be able to say it had actually breached the sacred document, because to do so would invite the question "So what are you going to do about it?" "What are we going to do about it? That's a very interesting question: 'such things, such things as . . . The terrors of the earth.'" The Emperor—or, more precisely, the Governor of Hong Kong, the British Foreign Secretary, and the British government—had no clothes.

As the Chinese in the 1990s continued the habit they had started earlier of breaking with enthusiasm one of the main undertakings they had given in the Joint Declaration—namely, to cooperate with the British sovereign power in the good government of Hong Kong (over issues both major and trivial, from the building of Hong Kong's infrastructure to the modernization of its laws to the final detailed plans for the transition)—I never felt able to seek recourse in one answer about Chinese broken promises that had been provided in my initial briefing. In response to a question on what we would do if the Chinese went back on their word, I was advised to answer, as others had before me, that this would not happen because the Chinese always did what they had promised. Having recently read several histories of China, including histories of Tibet, which had been the grateful recipient of its own Joint Declaration from China, I decided it might be a shade unwise to use this answer, and I never did so. I tended to argue, if pressed, that it would be in China's long-term interest to keep its word, which was true but not very convincing.

Within months of the signing and proud public display of the Joint Declaration, the trouble started. As the Chinese side turned the screw, what had understandably been regarded as something of a British diplomatic triumph was rapidly followed by the painstaking and secretive search by intelligent and decent men for ways to ensure a quiet life with China. Defeat was painfully extracted from the jaws of victory. The first Chinese assault was on what was quaintly called "the three-legged stool": They furiously contested the notion that there was a political entity called Hong Kong that could be represented in any official way in the discussions with the two sovereign powers about its future. For the Chinese, it was a question of two legs good, three legs unacceptable. The argument about the participation of Hong Kong representatives in talks about the Colony rumbled on for the best part of a decade. There may have been some in the British Foreign Office who would not have been too fussed about this. There had, after all, been a serious attempt to freeze the Hong Kong Governor's senior advisers out of the consultative circle during the negotiation of the Joint Declaration, which had been seen off by the vigorous protests of the Governor, Sir Edward Youde.

The next Chinese offensive should have raised everyone's hackles in London. Chinese officials made it quite clear that they wished to exercise as much control as possible over Hong Kong before 1997, particularly over its political development. The battlefield was to encompass almost every aspect of Hong Kong's social and economic life, but the struggle was joined most fiercely over democratic reform and the protection of civil liberties.

Within a year, the argument had concentrated on one single Chinese demand, a reversal, in effect, of the notion of Chinese cooperation in the good governance of Hong Kong under British stewardship. The Chinese insisted that the British should cooperate in ensuring that Hong Kong became what they wished it to be in 1997. They would describe what Hong Kong's constitutional and legal arrangements were to be in 1997, and the British would ensure that Hong Kong converged with this model. There was an obvious answer to this. Hong Kong was Britain's responsibility until 1997; Britain would govern Hong Kong according to the terms of the Joint Declaration; it would expect China to cooperate with this; China would then build on whatever had evolved in Hong Kong within the terms of the Joint Declaration when it became the sovereign power—but to say this would have led to a row, and the Chinese would have threatened to stop Britain's clock and start their own in 1997. Yet there were rows in any event, and, if this answer had been given, China would have been bound—at the very least in presentational terms—by the Joint Declaration in whatever it did; Hong Kong would have developed at its own pace institutionally and according to its own requirements, which would have made it more difficult to replace whatever was established; and Britain would have remained where the notion of sovereignty suggested it should be—namely, in the driver's seat.

Those arguments, if they were ever put, were rejected. In the late 1980s Britain accepted the notion of convergence and all that went with it.

It should not have been difficult for Britain's intelligent and experienced sinologists to see what this was all about. China's Communist party chief in Hong Kong at this time, Xu Jiatun (who fled to California after Tiananmen), stated the obvious in his memoirs, published in 1994—"The Chinese Government resolved to adopt the 'convergence' strategy in a bid to contain the pace of political reform," he wrote; and Peking did just that. Once China had a foot in the door there was to be no closing it. Britain lost authority, moral and political; it lost the initiative; it placed itself in the position in which it was subsequently obliged to give a sort of tacit blessing to the plans for the post-1997 arrangements produced by China (the so-called Basic Law) even when they had a distinctly questionable relationship to the promises given in the Joint Declaration. From that moment on, Britain was on a slippery slope. For the next dozen years, all one could hear diplomatically was the squeak and squelch of British boots trying to find a footing in the mud.

What were the Chinese to conclude from all this? They did not require to be led in their negotiations by intellectual titans to know that if they pushed hard enough, the British would give. This did not always happen, which must have confused and exasperated the Chinese. Where was the consistency in Britain's position? When Napoleon had left Moscow, he had made for Paris as fast as he could go. Why did Britain keep on digging in on unlikely terrain, claiming when doing so that it was because of a concern for Hong Kong? The trouble was that because Britain's bottom line was so often abandoned, the Chinese assumed that it would always be abandoned.

The British case for this initiative-sapping retreat can best be seen by looking at the most considerable Chinese political victory of all. In 1984, Britain had promised to implement the Joint Declaration by putting in hand the democratic development of the Colony. This proposal concentrated on the pace and extent of the introduction of direct elections to the Colony's Legislative Council, and the electoral arrangements made for those seats that were not directly elected. While there are always devils in the details, there is no need to examine at this point the astonishing arcana of Hong Kong's electoral arrangements in order to grasp the main features of the tale. By 1987, the issue had boiled down to this: Should directly elected seats be introduced in the 1988 elections, or should direct elections be delayed until 1991? China's position was clear. There should be no direct elections until China had laid down the nature and pace of Hong Kong's democratic development in its Basic Law, which was to be adopted in 1990. The British and Hong Kong governments' positions were equally clear. The people of Hong Kong should be consulted and progress would reflect their wishes.

What then happened has been the subject of much speculation and several books, newspaper articles, and television documentaries. Before the consultation process was completed, the Chinese believed they had a secret deal with Britain: If it was concluded at the end of this public debate that direct elections were not to be held in 1988, then the Chinese would include a commitment to direct elections in their own Basic Law. They were sufficiently receptive to British sensitivities to keep this under wraps. For their part, the British did not believe they had made an actual deal, but they did think there was an understanding that if Hong Kong opinion appeared not to favor direct elections in 1988, then the Chinese would make the Basic Law commitment. No deal, as far as Britain was concerned, just an understanding between friends: a secret understanding. And then, happy chance, the people of Hong Kong rose on cue to the challenge. The results of the "consultation process" that took place were officially interpreted to mean that Hong Kongers did not want direct elections in 1988, despite the fact that this is what a majority of them appeared to favor in the government's own survey and in every independent survey carried out at the same time. The statistical contortions required to arrive at this outcome, which satisfied both the British and Chinese governments, have been admirably and regularly exposed over the years. Whether one of the American authors who has performed this service—William McGurn—was justified in calling his book *Perfidious Albion* is a matter of judgment.

We come to the case for this policy. It clearly would have been possible to argue that Hong Kong's best chance of democratic development was to tie China down to some arrangements that could be made as acceptable as circumstance and Chinese nervousness about political control would allow. Even though these arrangements might not be what Hong Kong, British, or international opinion would regard as tolerable, at least they would stand a chance of surviving 1997 more or less intact. Hong Kong might think otherwise, but Hong Kong would be wrong. A wise sovereign power knew best.

This case would have been just about morally understandable, even though I do not myself agree with it. What is impossible to defend is so-called realpolitik (though as I shall shortly argue I do not believe that is an adequate description) masquerading as openness and public consultation. Without being accused of hypocrisy, no one can argue at one and the same time both that Britain was trying to do what Hong Kong wanted by introducing direct elections reasonably briskly and that it was also settling realistically for whatever China would allow to happen in its own time and at its own pace.

What, anyway, of realpolitik? Were "practical politics" served by postponing direct elections and allowing China to get its own way? Rather than postponing the elections and allowing China (hardly the best judge of these matters) to interpret what democracy might mean, it would surely have been better to allow the elections to go ahead in 1988, putting pressure on China, through the use of the ballot box, to define the electoral process in an acceptable way. Those who enjoyed a popular mandate in 1988 would have been well placed to take the argument to China as the drafting of the Basic Law reached its final stages in the following two years. Beyond this, a more genuinely democratic legislature in 1988 would have had almost a decade to establish its personality, its credentials, and its public support before the transition. It would also have been well placed to lead and channel public anxieties in Hong Kong in 1989 after Tiananmen. This outcome, not perfect but more attractive than any alternative, was not to be, thanks apparently to the wishes of the people of Hong Kong—or, rather, to what their wishes were determined to be by honorable men with fine minds who had been trained over many years to know what was best for those they ruled.

2

Hong Kong's "Fatal" Years

Zilu stayed for the night at Stone Gate. The gatekeeper said: "Where are you from?"
Zilu said, "I am from Confucius' household"—"Oh, is that the one who keeps
pursuing what he knows is impossible?"
—The Analects of Confucius, 14.38

The Master said: "A gentleman would be ashamed should his deeds
not match his words."
—The Analects of Confucius, 14.27

Having the time to tune up for a new job is rather unusual in British politics. When government changes at an election, politicians are catapulted overnight from the Opposition benches, where they struggle to get their sound bites on the evening news bulletins, to ministerial office, where decisions have to be made from the moment new incumbents arrive. Between elections, ministerial reshuffles send politicians from one job to another at a moment's notice. I recall my first cabinet promotion, leaving the subcabinet portfolio of Overseas Development for the post of Environment Secretary. Within twenty-four hours I had to answer for the government in a major debate in the House of Commons on the spectacularly unpopular poll tax. I spent the whole night trying in vain to master the details of local government taxation before parading my ignorance before my peers.

Hong Kong was different. Between leaving the chairmanship of the Conservative party and departing for my new job on July 9, 1992, I had over two months to do my homework. I was given a small office, previously a waiting room, on the ground floor of the Foreign Office, an admirable private secretary (a folk-singing diplomat some distance, as most diplomats turn out to be, from the usual caricatures), and piles of briefings. Previous custodians of the holy scripts of Hong Kong policy nervously came and went to discover whether I was likely to be "sound." Great figures from Hong Kong itself took me in alongside the other attractions of London's summer season. The Colony's ubiquitous press corps trailed my every step and photographed my photogenic daughters. The files moved each day from the tray on the left to the tray on the right.

They contained much good news. They told me that while inflation was too high, the Colony's economy was otherwise in pretty good shape. It had recovered steadily from the currency crisis of 1983 and had weathered the storms of 1987. The link between the Hong Kong and U.S. dollars, the so-called peg, was strong and provided a firm foundation during times of occasional market turbulence for sustained economic growth. There were worries about violent crime, much of it run from across the border, which had led to gun-toting robberies and shoot-outs on the street, and the theft and smuggling of luxury cars had reached epidemic proportions. Yet the underlying position was pretty stable, with a highly professional police force clearly able to cope with the cross-border threat. The return of over 50,000 Vietnamese economic migrants from Hong Kong camps to their own country under the auspices of the United Nations High Commissioner for Refugees remained a wearisome problem, but the mechanism for dealing with them was now in place. People in Hong Kong seemed pretty content with their lives; they had recovered from the shock of Tiananmen, despite the menacing intransigence of Chinese officials and the inexplicable decision of the British government in the wake of the killings to turn down a cross-community demand, embraced by liberals and many conservatives, for the introduction of direct elections for half the Legislative Council seats. The Hang Seng Index ticked up nicely; the tourists came and spent their money; the tills rang; Hong Kongers rushed cheerfully under their umbrellas from subway station to office building as summer rains hammered down from leaden skies. If this was colonial oppression, it did not appear too onerous or calamitous.

The problems were predictable, and as always happens, they looked at their most formidable on file; muddling through is not an option ever advocated in briefing folders. The Chinese, represented by a highly intelligent hard-liner in Hong Kong, Zhou Nan, and a politically weak career bureaucrat in Peking, Lu Ping, were immobilized by the politics of transition and of post-Tiananmen nervousness. With no one daring to take a risk, they had fallen back on what came most easily and naturally to them—struggle diplomacy. Every issue was turned into a long and debilitating fight, hand-to-hand combat from dawn to dusk and on to dawn again. On every front, a gallant team of young British and Hong Kong negotiators was beleaguered. Progress on all the problems that needed to be solved before the transition was imperceptible. A snail was later to be taken as the motif on our negotiators' ties, though not without some debate about how fair this was to the athletic ability of gastropods.

In particular, haggling about the building of Hong Kong's new airport was consuming vast quantities of time and effort. The existing airport, Kai Tak, had long been saturated; moreover, as any who have used it will know, to arrive there from the west is an experience that can drive even atheists to prayer. Hong Kong had been fortunate that there had been no major accidents; those who lived under the flight path in Kowloon, however, had endured an intolerable noise blight for years. In the aftermath of Tiananmen, Lord Wilson, my predecessor, had proposed the building of a new airport on reclaimed land off an island to the west, with associated bridges, tunnels, roads, and railways, as a morale booster for the community and a shot in the arm for the economy. China had seen the fact that any money borrowed for the project would have to be repaid after 1997 as an opportunity for interfering. But it was not China's money; it was Hong Kong's—and there was plenty of it. Threats by China not to stand behind the repayment of loans by the future Hong Kong government, however, rendered borrowing impossible. The Chinese regarded this mega-project, the biggest civil-engineering project in the world, as a way of exercising political control over Hong Kong. It became clear that they would trade cooperation over the airport for good behavior elsewhere, and on their terms. Every decision that was required on the airport would be used to tweak strings that would remind Hong Kong's government of the identity of its future masters.

The promise of cooperation over the airport had already been used to lure the British Prime Minister, John Major, to Peking. In 1991 he became one of the first senior foreign leaders to set foot in Tiananmen Square since the killings two years before, trapped into inspecting a guard of honor there beside a beaming Li Peng. He should never have been advised to go. He saved his own bacon politically by raising the issue of human rights with Chinese leaders, though his senior foreign policy adviser told the traveling press corps not to take any of this seriously. He did not secure the airport. A memorandum of understanding was signed by the British and Chinese premiers which, it was claimed, would clear the way for rapid planning and construction of the airport. The memorandum's exact meaning was still, unfortunately, the subject of debate four years later. Hardly had it been signed than Chinese officials were offering imaginative interpretations of what it really meant. This was another clear example of the Chinese not honoring the agreements they made.

On the three main issues that were to dominate much of the debate during my governorship, there was either a standoff or battle had not yet been joined. First, negotiations about Hong Kong's future judicial arrangements had produced in 1991 an agreement on the composition of a Court of Final Appeal (the Colony's senior judicial body), which had then been rejected by the legislature. The agreement had been negotiated in secret, as ever, but once its terms had become public, they had been roundly condemned by the legal profession and by the Legislative Council; the necessity of gaining the legislature's approval seemed to have been overlooked by the negotiators. This defeat was a serious setback. One of the obvious lessons from it—namely, the perils of trying to negotiate about Hong Kong's future behind its back—did not yet seem to have been taken on board.

The second issue was the requirement to bring Hong Kong's statute book into line with the Bill of Rights that had been introduced in 1991, again as a post-Tiananmen morale-steadying move, and which applied to the territory the provisions of the International Covenant on Civil and Political Rights (the codification in treaty form of the Universal Declaration of Human Rights). Chinese suspicions about this appeared to be the result of a nervousness that the repeal of antiquated and potentially repressive colonial legislation would make Hong Kong ungovernable. The truth is that no Governor in the 1990s (certainly not the Last Governor) could conceivably have used some of the powers theoretically available to him without provoking protest in Hong Kong, Westminster, and well beyond. It was indefensible to accept the application of the covenant to Hong Kong as the Chinese did, but not accept the necessity of aligning Hong Kong's laws with it. We were living in constant danger of legal challenge. This whole agenda of change had so far been postponed on the grounds that the time was not yet right for legislation; this was the usual formula for putting off an argument with China. It never worked, and merely left unfinished business piling up.

Third, though the electoral calendar was rapidly catching up with the government, there had not yet been any agreement on the exact arrangements for the 1994 elections for Hong Kong's local government and for the 1995 elections for the Legislative Council. Here we were in the middle of 1992 and there was no plan in Hong Kong or London, or any agreement with China save that there should be twenty directly elected legislators from geographically based constituencies in the 1995 legislature, thirty members drawn from functional constituencies (which were supposed to represent the main interest groups in the city), and ten from a so-called election committee, whose precise composition was unknown. Most political speculation in Hong Kong concentrated on how I would handle this question, which was scarcely surprising in view of the past history of twist and turn on democracy in the Colony. I was advised at every level in the clearest terms that, provided I did not seek unilaterally to increase the number of directly elected legislators or change the balance between the other blocs in the legislature, there was a free and open canvas on which to sketch. I have checked the weekly diary that I kept at this time recording all my meetings (an aide-memoire which turned into a full daily diary by the time of my last year as Governor), and this was the advice I was given by every senior official in London and Hong Kong to whom I spoke, as well as by my political colleagues. I took it as my brief, and a very reasonable if demanding one at that, to try to produce electoral arrangements within the existing parameters that would be regarded as fair.

For my overall guidance, I assumed that the Joint Declaration should provide the tablets of stone. No one sought, in public, to resile from it or from that assumption. It was the description of what had been, what was, and what should be in Hong Kong. My government had signed it; I would abide by it. Naturally, I assumed that the words of the Joint Declaration meant what they said: literally, and in English. I did not believe that we could allow another gloss to be put on phrases like "free speech," "a high degree of autonomy," and "the common law." The meaning of these words was not a matter for negotiation, let alone for interpretation by Chinese officials. As for the Basic Law, since the intention to draft it was included in the Joint Declaration, I was bound to recognize that it would form the future Hong Kong constitution, and I was resigned to the necessity of ensuring that as far as possible Hong Kong's institutions and way of life were capable of docking with this constitutional settlement in 1997. But it was not *my* Basic Law, or the British government's. Britain had tacitly, and with a degree of deserved embarrassment, given it a distant blessing, but we had not been party to it and we were not legally, politically, or morally bound by it. There were parts of it, for example its provisions on subversion, that I did not like and had some difficulty reconciling with the Joint Declaration and the common law.

Before I left with my family for my inauguration in Hong Kong, I tried to work out my priorities and strategies for the five years ahead. First, I was determined that I would stay for the full five years whatever the blandishments to return home and whatever the criticisms and brickbats I might face. It would be unfair to leave someone else with a fag-end job, and the suspicion that I might do this would undermine the authority of my administration in Hong Kong and of Britain as the sovereign power. If I was to stay for five years, it seemed important to set out from the very first exactly what I intended to do. People needed to know my program right across the board: A clear blueprint would help to give the administration a sense of direction and purpose throughout my term. When I met Lee Kuan Yew, Singapore's senior minister, in that city on the way to Hong Kong, I was interested that he himself gave the same advice, adding that much firmness and patience would be required.

The idea of having a clear plan and giving a firm and clear lead corresponded in any event to my idea of political leadership. In any community, people need to know what their government is trying to do: They need articulate and coherent messages, directions, justifications, and explanations that correspond to the goals the government has set. Popular perceptions of political leaders do not allow for many different snapshots or many different shades of gray. This sort of leadership may not be successful: Chopping and changing, keeping the show on the road, getting through until lunchtime may sometimes be a more successful short-term formula or a more obvious political requirement. But any community in flux, facing more change and uncertainty, surely needs a firm and unhesitating steer, and politicians are unlikely to gain or convey much sense of direction if they are constantly having to consult their officials, public opinion surveys, or focus groups to find out what they wish to do.

A five-year program, in my view, had to encompass both the economic and the social life of Hong Kong. I needed to give targets for the development of social and educational programs while keeping the economy buoyant. Any economic problems, let alone another financial or property crash close to the transition, would be politically disastrous and would risk social upheaval. Lee Kuan Yew had warned me that I was likely to lose control of the law-and-order situation the closer we got to 1997. I was determined to avoid this at almost any cost.

I knew that the biggest test would come in the political arena, and here I had a hand of pretty low cards. Any moves on elections and civil liberties that satisfied the democratic majority in Hong Kong would annoy China, and the reverse was equally true. Whenever people had the opportunity of a fair and free vote, most of them supported democratic candidates; they wanted people who would stand up for them against China. But while they wanted leaders who would do this, they also wanted a quiet life. It is not unusual for electorates to want contradictory things, and politicians often make promises accordingly. Squaring political circles is less easy when one is a colonial governor rather than an elected political leader. Precisely because of the lack of a democratic mandate, or of the ability to appeal for a fresh mandate, there is less room for maneuver. I was clear in my own mind that while I would do what I could to satisfy China and dampen down red-hot Chinese suspicions, there might not in practice be very much that I could do on either of these matters, and there was a price for success that I simply could not pay. I was not prepared to do China's dirty work by curtailing Hong Kong's freedom and democratic development. This would court local and international obloquy, plunge Hong Kong into partisan debate at Westminster, and risk political uproar with the last years and months of British colonial rule being dominated by a bitter argument with democratic politicians and civil libertarians. Hong Kong's politics could easily have become chaotic as we ran down to the handover. No one should have required an overdramatic imagination to foresee that. It would have been a disaster for Hong Kong and for Britain—and, I believe, for China too.

The only route through this jungle seemed to me to involve sticking firmly to the Joint Declaration. I needed to be as open as possible about what I was doing, to take people into my confidence, to try to develop and encourage the self-confidence of Hong Kong, and to refuse to chloroform Hong Kong or international opinion about the city's future. The more that Hong Kong could be allowed to make the decisions about its destiny, the better. Yet for all this, I knew that I could not satisfy all the demands that would be made on me in Hong Kong, demands that had been nurtured by promises made in the past and sharpened by the secretive way in which those promises had been reinterpreted. When I set off for Hong Kong, I was genuinely unsure about whether I would have more trouble from Communists or from democrats. In gloomier moments I reckoned that, trying to steer a middle course, I would as like as not find myself attacked on all sides.

It would be a grotesque distortion to claim that the whole of my time in Hong Kong was spent dealing with China-sensitive issues—elections, civil liberties, international support, the rule of law, autonomy. Much of my day, every day, was spent being in effect the Mayor of Hong Kong, running the civil service that managed the affairs of a rich and sophisticated city. There were three particular pleasures about this that never left me. First, the team that I led was outstandingly good. My two senior officials—the Chief Secretary and the Financial Secretary—were initially expatriate, Sir David Ford and Sir Hamish Macleod. They were both exceptional colonial civil servants and complemented each other remarkably well—Ford, politically shrewd and subtle; Macleod, clearheaded and direct. Through the most tempestuous months that followed my arrival, they were both like rocks; I cannot recall a moment when they were other than intelligently and strongly supportive, in public and in private. Their retirement from the Hong Kong government marked the final stage in the localization of the civil service. Two first-class Chinese officials, Mrs. Anson Chan and Sir Donald Tsang, took their places. Mrs. Chan was a strong-minded, highly principled, and decisive leader; Tsang was equally attractive, cheerful, clever, and decent. They led a mainly Chinese civil service, which withstood the political buffetings of the following years with character and confidence. It also met my ambitious requests that it should become more open and receptive to the public. We implemented an imaginative program of public service reform, which transformed the image of what had previously been regarded as a rather closed colonial service. One conclusion I reached from working with the Hong Kong civil service was that if you want the best people to go into government, you have to pay them decently, and Hong Kong certainly did that. I am in favor of small government and good government. Good government requires good people, which in turn requires good money.

The second satisfaction for a European politician was to find oneself in a world where one had to make fewer difficult decisions about resources—spending on one priority program did not require cuts in the money spent elsewhere. Provided we kept the overall growth in spending in line with the trend rate of growth in our economy, we were otherwise able to spend sensibly as we wished. Since the economy had grown without check for three and a half decades, there was usually enough money for the things we wished to do.

Third, an efficient government machine, an entrepreneurial culture, and a booming and self-assured Asian city meant that the decisions I took about public programs—for instance, major infrastructure projects—were rapidly implemented. One of the excitements in public life, usually denied to its participants as the electoral or personal cycles take their toll, is seeing bright ideas turn into conference centers, hospitals, welfare facilities, schools, roads, and so on before their own eyes. To see something through from the drawing board to the tape-cutting ceremony is a great treat. When I arrived in Hong Kong, the first work on our great airport had only just begun. Despite all the hassle with China, it was nearly completed by the time I departed. When I was Britain's Environment Secretary, responsible for land-use planning, one of the many controversies in my in-tray concerned the (probably ill-judged) proposal to build a new, fifth, terminal at London's Heathrow Airport. Shortly after I returned to Britain from Hong Kong, seven years after my term in the Environment Department, I recall hearing a discussion on the radio about the necessity of getting on with the building of that fifth terminal. Hong Kong was a good place to be a young civil engineer. It was an excellent place to be a politician and public administrator.

By the time I left, the administration had notched up a record that would have provided a good basis for an election campaign in any Western democracy. Sustained growth had lifted our GDP by about a quarter in real terms, and we had managed in every budget for five years to increase spending on our social and educational priorities, to cut taxes (both corporate and personal), and to increase the amount in our reserves. Inflation had fallen to about half its previous figure, though at just over 6 percent it was still too high. Unemployment had peaked in 1995 at just over 3 percent but had fallen back to between 2 and 2.5 percent by mid-1997. The Hang Seng Index stood below 6,000 when I arrived and over 15,000 when I departed. Corporate profits soared, and so did directors' and executives' remuneration. Those in business who shook their heads over the alleged importation of politics into Hong Kong did not appear to have been ruined by it.

The face of Hong Kong underwent yet another transformation. We spent massively on the improvement of our infrastructure—the program was so large that, try as we might, we were rarely able to spend all the money we allocated annually. Nevertheless, progress was remarkable. Land was reclaimed—at one time we were employing almost half the world's dredging fleet. Bridges, hospitals, roads, health and welfare centers, training colleges, new towns were built; tunnels were dug; and we laid plans (delayed a little partly by the need to consult China) to develop our railway system. The new airport emerged from the waters off the island of Lantau, a vast enterprise more or less paid for out of the public purse as we went along. But our main investment in environmental infrastructure fared less well—a massive scheme for rebuilding Hong Kong's sewage system and cleaning up the filthy waters off our shores went ahead, but too slowly. Our efforts to clean up Hong Kong's air were resisted by some legislators in thrall to the diesel-driven taxi industry, and our gallant attempt to reclaim the initiative in land-use planning in what had once been the countryside of the New Territories, dealing as we did so with the unsightly dumping of containers, construction equipment, and clapped-out cars, made all too little headway. At least we were just about able to preserve the main ornithological pit stop between Siberia and Australia, the bird sanctuary on the marshes of Mai Po, though development encroached from every side. For a former environment minister and environmental enthusiast, however, the record was, alas, distinctly mixed.

Crime during my five years fell pretty steadily and by 1997 was lower than it had been in the early 1980s. We got on top of the cross-border robberies and of the theft and smuggling of luxury cars. Had it not been for crime by illegal Chinese immigrants, the figures would have been even better. There remained among the very rich a nervousness about their own safety, based partly on rumors of what happened in China and what they feared might start to happen in Hong Kong. Several tycoons employed squads of bodyguards in a city where I regarded my own team of amiable tough guys as friends and colleagues rather than a potential imperial guard. For most people, the police seemed more than adequate for the task of securing their streets and homes. The police force had been riddled with corruption in the late sixties and early seventies. This had been vigorously stamped out, and while there were some isolated incidents in the 1990s, Hong Kong's force was—with Singapore's—the cleanest in Asia. Hong Kong's police were well trained, well led by their commissioner, Eddie Hui, and well noticed in public places. I always took high police visibility to be a factor in Hong Kong's success against crime. We employed far more officers than most cities of our size; seeing police regularly as one goes about daily life is good for morale, provided you are not a criminal. The police also played their part, along with the prison service, in handling the difficult issue of the Vietnamese migrants. Despite the occasional problems thrown in our path by the doubtless well-meaning efforts of American politicians to double- and triple-check that the migrants were not political refugees, and despite the difficulties of dealing with Communist officials in Vietnam, by mid-1997 we had reduced the number of Vietnamese in our camps to just over a thousand. Over 200,000 Vietnamese in all passed through Hong Kong in under twenty years. The majority settled abroad; the others mostly returned home. This was thankless work conducted on the whole humanely, subject—such is a free society—to the ever-present attentions of civil-liberties lawyers. We did our duty with no thanks from anyone.

The only crime figures that really worried me were those for drug abuse, especially among the young. Given Hong Kong's geographical position, its port, and its status as a great international city, I was concerned that the steady increase in abuse that had started to show up by the early 1990s could easily get out of hand as it had in so many other cities. We launched a high-profile campaign—"Beat Drugs"—involving police, schools, parents, health and welfare services, and community groups, to tackle the problem, strengthening enforcement, increasing public education and research, and broadening remedial treatment and care. The first indications suggested that we had managed to stabilize and then reduce drug abuse.

One of my earliest impressions was that Hong Kong's economic vitality and strength were not matched by adequate social welfare and educational provision. Services for the disabled were thin on the ground, and Confucian values did not seem to have led to the establishment of adequate services for the elderly, of whom there were a growing number. In the past, Hong Kong had concentrated, understandably enough, on increasing the quantity of education, expanding higher education rapidly. Too little attention had been paid to the quality of schooling at the primary and secondary levels. Language skills, for example, were too low for an international business center. Training and our labor-market institutions were insufficiently flexible and not really plugged in to the needs of employers and would-be workers. I was convinced that we could spend more money on all these areas without fiscal imprudence. The ambitious spending programs we launched were denounced as "socialism" by some business people and, perhaps more surprisingly, by some Communist officials. But public spending continued to take less than a fifth of what Hong Kong made each year, and in my last year as Governor this proportion was lower than it had been in the early 1980s.

I was particularly keen to do more for people with disabilities before the transition, because I was not convinced that this would necessarily receive the priority it deserved if left until afterward. We broadened services (rehabilitation, training, accommodation), supported legislation against discrimination, enlisted the support of the public transport companies in improving transport for the disabled, and made an initial if small impact on the reluctance of employers to take on staff with a disability. We did more for the elderly, not least in the area of sheltered housing, and they benefited with other needy groups from our overhaul of the benefit system. We introduced a scheme of mandatory private provision for retirement that would cater to the longer-term needs of Hong Kong as the population ages (as in most of the rest of Asia).

Our greatest failings in the social field were in housing. Perhaps the problems we encountered were in the short term simply insuperable. We allocated more money to the Housing Authority, led with enormous political skill by Dame Rosanna Wong, and it continued to build more than a hundred apartments a day. More families became home owners for the first time, many with government help. Yet Hong Kong continued to suffer from three interrelated problems. The price of home ownership remained extremely high in relation to real incomes, which were nevertheless rising. Public-housing rents were so low in proportion to household income as to deter tenants from trying to move into their own property. Too many of the really poor waited for too long in substandard accommodation for rehousing in better and cheaper public apartments. Housing was the area of Hong Kong's life where market forces had the least chance to operate. We suffered from the worst eccentrically combined effects of monopoly capitalism and municipal socialism.

Our ability to apply the radical free market solutions that were required was limited by proximity to the transition. Any convincing attack on the monopoly effectively enjoyed by a few extremely rich property developers in Hong Kong making grotesquely large profits could have had a serious effect on market confidence at a sensitive time. The stock market could have plummeted and the property market collapsed. While property prices rising too quickly causes political problems, my recent experience during the British recession suggested that falling prices, which leave many mortgaged home-owners with negative equity, cause a great deal more trouble. This could be especially marked in a city nervous about the future, with so many members of its middle class holding foreign passports and a large proportion of their savings in property. They could reckon that the money for which they could sell even a small apartment in Hong Kong would buy them a mansion in Vancouver (or Hong-couver as it came to be called as the size of its community of Hong Kongers grew in the 1990s). When in 1994 we successfully took measures to damp down speculation and surging apartment prices, we had to move with great caution and were always worried lest a step too far were to kick the supports away from under the property market. Another radical measure that I would have liked to take was to abandon the government's established high land price policy and sell off more land for lower-cost home ownership schemes. But this again was stymied by the Chinese government's obsessive concern about the size of Hong Kong's reserves, and any financial measure that overlapped 1997 could be blocked by the implied or explicit refusal by Chinese officials to endorse it. They were always worried that even if we did not take all Hong Kong's cash with us, we would fritter it away before we departed.

In the public sector, radicalism was hampered not only by China's nervousness about our disposing of the family silver before our departure (that is, letting tenants become home owners at knockdown prices) but also, paradoxically, by the limited extent and duration of democratic politics in Hong Kong. A great deal of politics had been channeled into housing activities, and since elected politicians were responsible for so little from left to right, they tended to articulate tenant grievances rather than apply themselves to the fundamental causes of those problems. The construction of public housing had been regarded as a substitute for, or an alternative to, the introduction of democratic politics. As I shall argue later, I believe that mature democratic institutions are more likely to make difficult social and political decisions than authoritarian structures and that the housing problems in Hong Kong were partly the result of the public not being involved in running its own affairs.

Homes, schools, roads, hospitals, factories, high-tech centers, universities, training colleges, kindergartens—such were the pleasures, as it were, of the mayoralty. I got out and about as much as I could. I wanted my administration to be as open as possible and I therefore needed to give a lead from the top. This had been one of the reasons for my initial decision not to wear the traditional gubernatorial dress on formal occasions—in summer, brocaded whites beneath a pith topee topped by ostrich plumes, looking rather like a recently deceased hen; in winter, the blues and reds of a Ruritanian marshal. With the informal permission of the Queen, I dressed like everyone else, relieved that I was not going to be required, medium-size and usually overweight as I am, to look ridiculous. Vanity buttressed my political instincts.

Wherever I went as "Mayor" for five years, I was pursued by the same questions. Visit a school or hospital, talk of disability or training, what really interested the media was always the same. I would stand outside some welfare center that I had opened talking about the needs of the elderly and observe the pens of the attending press corps still poised unmoving in their hands; nor was there any sign of interest from the TV crews. Then, the first question and we were off and running—running always over the same ground: democracy, freedom, China. A one-issue media would daily drag the "Mayor" back to the main problem of his governorship and would then accuse him of never talking about anything else.

Even before I left London, I had been invited to make an early visit to Peking to share my thoughts on the way forward for Hong Kong with Chinese officials, and in particular with Lu Ping, the head of the department in the Chinese government that covered both Hong Kong and the Portuguese colony Macau. It was suggested to me, not least by an emissary from Lu (a ubiquitous Hong Kong businesswoman called Nelly Fong, whose regular and self-advertised presence in what appeared to be the inner chambers of Chinese policy making inevitably raised questions with all who knew her about the seriousness and understanding of those in Peking who were helping to determine the future of the Colony), that if I were to tell Lu what he wanted to hear about political development, he would give me good news about the airport. I pointed out to Ms. Fong that everyone talked to me about Chinese "face," but there was also such a thing as British "face." The politics of going to Peking before I had arrived in Hong Kong and appearing (not least since the Chinese would leak their side of any meeting) to sell out Hong Kong's freedom and democracy for agreement on an airport would ensure that when I did arrive in the territory, I would be the lamest ever of lame ducks. She left our meeting looking thoughtful.

But I did not give up the idea of an informal exchange with Lu. While it would be impossible for me to go to Peking before I had set foot on Hong Kong's tarmac, and equally difficult for me to go before delivering my first policy address in early October, I suggested to Lu that we should meet in Hong Kong—for example, we could arrange a private meeting at Fanling, the Governor's country lodge within a mile or two of the Chinese border at Shenzhen. It would almost certainly have been possible, as we explained, to fly Lu in by helicopter unseen if that was how he wanted to do things. This offer was declined.

However, we did not give up hope of improving communications between the two sides and of letting the Chinese have some inkling of our overall approach. I had discovered during a dinner at the Chinese embassy in London just before I left for my new job that the Ambassador had never been to Hong Kong. I duly invited him to come and see us on his way home to Peking for his summer leave. Ambassador Ma was a silkily tough diplomat, whose cheerful charm ensconced qualities sufficiently rugged to have enabled him to survive for some years as a Foreign Ministry spokesman during the Cultural Revolution.

During his visit to Hong Kong, I took the Ambassador and his wife on a nighttime helicopter tour of Hong Kong and then landed on Cheung Chau, one of the outlying islands, where we boarded the handsome old gubernatorial yacht, *The Lady Maureen*, for a buffet dinner at sea. I had a long private conversation with Ma before dinner. I told him that I needed a Chinese official in Hong Kong to whom I could talk frankly; everyone knew that the then-senior Chinese official in Hong Kong, Zhou Nan (the combative head of the New China News Agency), did not fall into this category. I pointed out that since I had arrived in Hong Kong, I had behaved exactly as I advised him I would do before I left London. I said that I wanted to go to Peking as soon as I had made my policy speech to the legislature, that it was impossible to do so beforehand (not least because the Chinese had begun to lay down preemptive political demands, such as the public insistence by their spokesmen during June and July that no democratic member of the Legislative Council should be appointed to the Governor's separate advisory Executive Council). There had been plans for me to visit Canada, home to the largest part of the Hong Kong Chinese diaspora, in October, but if invited to Peking I would postpone this trip; it was important that China should be the first country I visited. I wanted to develop a close personal relationship with Lu Ping. I intended to have a strong and broadly based Executive Council, which I would separate from the Legislative Council—that is, I would put no elected politicians, whether democratic or not, on my body of top advisers. As far as elections to the legislature were concerned, I would work within the existing agreements, but I could not be seen to be rigging the polls, and the arrangements must be fair, open, and acceptable to the people of Hong Kong. It would be in no one's interest if the last years of British colonial responsibility were marked by political turmoil. Nor would it be helpful in Hong Kong and beyond if I were to be seen as a puppet of Peking. I would naturally be prepared to lobby in Washington in favor of "most favored nation" (that is, normal) trading status for China when the issue came before Congress the following year. I complained about the slow progress we had made in the Joint Liaison Group (which dealt diplomatically with transitional issues on China's insistence but had become China's institutional device for trying to put an armlock on the Hong Kong government). I added that any attempt to establish linkage between the airport and political matters was clumsy and doomed to failure. I concluded by telling Ma that we would be setting out my governmental agenda for five years in my policy address in October, that we would look forward to discussing it—including the political elements—with Chinese officials when I went to Peking, and that we would ensure that the main outlines of my speech were passed on to senior Chinese officials beforehand. Ma listened politely and courteously. I am sure that, being a competent and experienced diplomat, he did not keep all this to himself.

I have already indicated the rough framework of the economic and social program that I was to set out in my speech to the Legislative Council in early October. There were two main political questions to be resolved. First, I had to decide what to do about the composition of my Executive Council. This council was an odd feature of the colonial constitution and its position inevitably became increasingly anomalous as the legislature became more democratic. It consisted of so-called official members—that is, senior civil servants—and unofficials—men and women from outside government representing the community as a whole. The council was chosen by the Governor of the day. In the years before Hong Kong took its first democratic steps, when both the Executive and the Legislative councils were appointed, there was often cross-membership. The Executive Council formed a sort of Senior Common room with prominent legislators among its members. This cross-membership began to look distinctly anomalous once some of the legislators were elected. Should the Governor continue to appoint senior legislators regardless of whether they were elected, or should only those who had a democratic mandate be chosen? It was a messy constitutional consequence of sunset colonialism. The council—Exco, as it was known for short—advised the Governor in the exercise of his executive responsibilities. Before elections began, it had been particularly valuable in conferring a local legitimacy on colonial government. This was specially marked during the negotiations over the Joint Declaration. By definition its appointed membership, drawn largely from the ranks of the Hong Kong establishment, would have been unlikely proponents in the past of the virtues of democracy.

From 1991, when almost one third of legislators were directly elected for the first time, the relationship between the two councils became particularly strained. The Executive Council could not become a British-style cabinet, representing the majority in the legislature, without completely changing the nature of Hong Kong's constitution. Not least to the Chinese, it would have looked as though we were reversing the promise that Hong Kong would remain an executive-led government, replacing it with a legislature-led government. Nor could the Executive Council become an American-style cabinet, representing the executive branch to the legislative, since most of its members were not government officials and had no executive functions within government. I concluded that the right way forward was to retain the Executive Council as a genuinely advisory body and to separate its membership from that of the legislature. The council I had inherited from my predecessor included some legislators, but none of them belonged to the democratic group that had won most of the minority of directly elected seats in the elections the year before. It seemed to me quite impossible to have some legislators on my Executive Council but to exclude any democrats for whatever trumped-up constitutional excuse. Everyone would know that the real reason for their exclusion was Chinese hostility. Separation therefore seemed sensible, and I went about reconstructing the council with the active assistance of the senior unofficial member, whom I retained, Baroness Dunn. We put together a very able team that represented all shades of opinion in the community; several members became good and loyal friends. Exco's ranks included a shipowning businessman, C. H. Tung, who in due course became my successor, the Chief Executive of the Hong Kong government in 1997, and the future Chief Justice, Andrew Li. We kept most of the team together for my full five years, and while we had some strong arguments, we rarely (certainly during the last three years) had any really difficult discussions. Baroness Dunn, a businesswoman (with the Swire's hong) of legendarily adroit instincts, also gave advice as we put together our proposals for the electoral arrangements.

Little if any work had been done on these and expectations were high. When the Foreign Secretary, Douglas Hurd, visited the territory shortly after my arrival and confirmed (alas, correctly) that there could be no increase in the number of directly elected seats—the most visible mark of democracy—he was roundly denounced by the press and by many politicians. This was a reminder of how little political space there was for maneuver if we kept, as we must, to the agreements made on democracy with China. I mentioned earlier the bare bones of these electoral arrangements. The broad agreement between Britain and China was as follows: The elections in 1991 had allowed for eighteen directly elected legislators; twenty-one legislators came from so-called functional constituencies, which represented professional and business interests (bankers, the chamber of commerce, teachers, and so on). There were three official members, representing the government, and eighteen other legislators were appointed. In 1995, there were to be twenty directly elected legislators; thirty legislators from functional constituencies; and ten chosen by an election committee. It was hoped that this legislature would survive the transition, and then in the elections in 1999 and 2003, the number of directly elected legislators could increase steadily at the expense of those who were chosen by the election committee. Beyond this date, when there would be an equal balance between the geographically based directly elected legislators and those representing functional constituencies (with, under the Basic Law, a clear majority in both groups necessary for any major decisions), Hong Kong would be able to decide whether it wanted to increase the directly elected element in the legislature and whether it should elect its Chief Executive. This could not be described as a precipitate gallop to democracy.

The outlines of this process were plain, if pretty mind-boggling. But the details had not been filled in. First, how were the directly elected legislators to be chosen? Since 1991, they had been elected on a first-past-the-post basis in geographical constituencies as happens in Britain. Hardly surprisingly, since the democrats were by far the most popular politicians, by the time I arrived they dominated these elections. Communist politicians in Hong Kong, and the erroneously named Liberal party (which was in effect the "colonial" party for Britain and became the "colonial" party for China), did badly in simple plurality voting elections, and they therefore favored a move to some form of proportional system. This came up at one of my first Executive Council meetings, with the team of advisers inherited from my predecessor Lord Wilson. Exco member Allen Lee, leader of the Liberal party, a likable man given to frequent changes of mind, tried to rush me into accepting his party's proposals on proportionality; they wanted multimember constituencies with the voters allowed only one vote. I saw no reason for proportional voting when the legislature already included so many different elements to ensure that it represented the whole community and when directly elected legislators were to be in the minority for some time to come.

The functional constituencies were an abomination. Whoever had devised them must have had a good working knowledge of the worst abuses of British eighteenth-century parliamentary history, and had presumably concluded that such a system would appeal to the business barons of Hong Kong as it had to those of Britain two centuries before. The attractions to China were also obvious. Some constituencies—those representing large professional groups like lawyers, teachers, and nurses—were reasonably open and clean. On the whole, the larger the number of voters and the more open the voting process, the more defensible the functional constituency system became. Other constituencies were tiny, which led to corruption (the representative of 1991's smallest constituency, covering a handful of voters from the Regional Council, went to prison for his electioneering methods), or were closed and corporatist, which led to other forms of abuse. Some of the functional constituencies representing business groups allowed a vote to every company that was a member of it. This meant that a tycoon with twenty companies that were all members of a trade organization could cast twenty votes. In other constituencies, there was only ever one candidate, and the Chinese-controlled functional constituencies (like the Chinese Chamber of Commerce) disposed of candidates if they departed a fraction from the Communist line on anything. The functional constituencies were supposed to be broadly representative of community groups. But there was no agreement with China that said exactly what the functional constituencies should be or whom they should represent. Nor was there any plan for how to constitute the nine additional functional constituencies that would be needed in 1995.

The Election Committee also remained to be defined, and beyond this there was a further clutch of electoral issues: Who should run the elections? At what age should people vote? What should be done about our local government—the district boards and the two municipal councils—where some members were elected and some were appointed?

As soon as I arrived in Hong Kong in July 1992, I threw myself into a round of consultations with political groups, establishment worthies, and business leaders. My officials and I tried to make sense of what emerged. We found ourselves putting together a program that represented most people's second-best option yet which certainly gave us arrangements that were fair and would give Hong Kong a defensible set of unriggable elections. We planned to establish a Boundaries and Elections Commission to supervise the arrangements, to allow voting at the age of eighteen, to abolish appointed seats in local government to bring it into line with the legislature, and to ensure that democracy would start to develop naturally at the local level. We would use all the directly elected members of district boards (Hong Kong's local councils) to constitute the Election Committee, which would choose ten legislators, thus giving this committee a democratic base. We would retain geographical constituencies for the directly elected members, but where there had previously been double-member constituencies, with every elector having two votes, we would introduce single-member constituencies, with electors casting one vote. In the functional constituencies, we would scrap corporate voting where it existed and replace it with individual voting; for example, all the directors of companies that were members of the General Chamber of Commerce would be able to vote for its representative rather than the votes being allocated to each company. As for the nine new functional constituencies, this caused us the most headaches. There were twenty-one existing functional constituencies, which represented a fraction of Hong Kong's workforce. We labored to find nine new groups of workers to enfranchise. We eventually concluded that the most logical thing to do was to take each of the existing, internationally accepted classifications in the industrial and commercial sector as a new functional constituency. There happened, neatly, to be nine of them. This would mean that we could give the functional constituencies a reasonably defensible basis, saying that they would represent everyone at their place of work. The replacement of corporate voting by individual, and the creation of the new constituencies, considerably increased the number of electors in these curious democratic entities, though the precise increase would depend on the extremely complicated registration that would now prove necessary.

This whole package was deftly woven together by an outstanding team of officials under the Secretary for Constitutional Affairs, Michael Sze. Sze was a principled, outgoing, and highly competent official who was to come under heavy personal pressure as subsequent events unfolded. He eventually left the civil service to become the executive director of Hong Kong's Trade Development Council. Sze's behavior and values provided my first experience in Hong Kong of the absurdity of arguing that there is a fundamental difference between the personal standards and moral principles of Asians on the one hand and Europeans and Americans on the other. Decency is decency, East and West. Sze was followed in this job by another first-rate official, Nicholas Ng.

The system that we had devised did not increase the pace of democratization in Hong Kong, and we were understandably to be criticized for this, but it made what had been allowed for as fair as we could manage. Hong Kong would have a legislative system that was justifiable even if it was not perfect. The very moderation of our proposals gives the lie to those who claimed subsequently that we had set out recklessly to rock the boat mindless of the consequences. What we had sought was a set of arrangements that Hong Kong people should be able to accept and China should be prepared to tolerate. This was not the casting down of a gauntlet.

Before we announced the proposals, I needed to secure London's endorsement, which I duly did at a cabinet committee meeting that I flew back to attend in September. We then briefed those who we thought deserved some warning of what was intended. I spoke, for example, to former Prime Ministers Edward Heath and Margaret Thatcher, to former Foreign Secretary Geoffrey Howe, and to my predecessors Lord Maclehose and Lord Wilson. None offered any criticism, although Lord Maclehose clearly had the gravest reservations about any move toward democracy in Hong Kong and regarded democratic politicians and their supporters there, in his own later words, as "a noisy minority." Most were supportive. Only Margaret Thatcher was to remain so in public and private, stalwartly and vigorously insisting that the Joint Declaration signed in her name should mean what it said.

I had in the past enjoyed a checkered relationship with Margaret Thatcher. When she became leader of the Conservative party in 1975 she inherited me, along with the curtains. I had been appointed by her predecessor, Edward Heath, as director of the party's Research Department and was well known for my sympathies and friends on the left of the party. My friends were not, therefore, hers! But she kept me on and we enjoyed an always friendly if occasionally argumentative relationship, not least at the party conference each autumn, when I was regularly recruited to help draft her speech with the best of all speechwriters in recent years, the playwright Sir Ronald Millar. I think she later found my determination to express my own opinions slightly tiresome. I protested noisily to her about her decision in 1979 to scrap the independence of the Research Department, which I had led and loved, and became as a young MP a fairly prominent dissenter from some of the early enthusiasms of the government's monetary policy. But although some of her right-wing friends may have disapproved, she promoted me to a junior ministerial post in 1983 and then raised me steadily through the ranks to an eventual cabinet post in 1989. In 1990, I was one of those cabinet members who told her that she should stand down as Conservative Leader after failing to gain the requisite number of votes in the first ballot of that year's contest. So I had not been an acolyte or a die-hard personal loyalist. Yet I never had the feeling that she held any of our disagreements against me. She was never mean-minded in dealing with me. More than that, when I needed her help in Hong Kong, she gave it unstintingly. I do not agree with some of her views—for example, on Europe—and I do not believe she was fair to her successor. But I regard her as a great political leader—brave, principled, and honest even when wrong. She was a better and stouter friend to me than she will ever know.

I had said to Ambassador Ma at our dinner on my boat that we would give the Chinese some warning of what would be in my October Policy Speech (Hong Kong's equivalent of an American president's State of the Union address) before I gave it. There had been some doubts in London about how much we should reveal and how far in advance we should do this; previous experience suggested that the Chinese leaked what they were told, to their own advantage. But it was agreed that Douglas Hurd should give his opposite number, Chinese Foreign Minister Qian Qichen, a point-by-point summary of what I intended to say when they met in the margins of the UN General Assembly in New York in September two weeks before my speech, and that a full text should be sent to Lu Ping just before delivery. Qian took his briefing very calmly, raising hardly any questions and promising merely to pass on what he had been told. If the purport of Hurd's message was really so explosive, Qian's reaction suggests that he must have been badly briefed in the extreme to react so mildly. Perhaps, until he was advised to the contrary, he did not understand that China would strongly object to any elections that were aboveboard.

After the meeting, there were some days of silence. The general advice I had received was that the Chinese were likely to react strongly but that the decibel count would fall some way below the nuclear threshold. Feet would certainly be stamped, voices raised . . . and then we would see. The reaction, when it came over the weekend before my speech, was at the harder and noisier end of what had been expected. We were sent a private message through one of Lu Ping's Hong Kong "trusties," and more formally, our Ambassador in Peking, Sir Robin McLaren, was summoned to see Lu. Lu argued that we should announce nothing about political developments in Hong Kong until we had consulted Peking and gotten its approval. I should shut up until I had talked to Lu. He had been planning to give me a present when I went to Peking, progress on the airport, but now there would be no *bonnes bouches* until—such was the drift—I learned to behave.

On October 7, I spoke to the Legislative Council, set out my agenda for five years, and before talking about elections noted that discussions on this subject had already been opened by the Foreign Secretary in New York. I went on, using words drafted some weeks before: "Let us be clear why we are discussing with the Chinese government all these issues relating to the 1995 elections. The community wants more representative government. But I think it is equally plain that the majority want constitutional reform to be compatible, as far as possible, with the Basic Law, and, accordingly, to transcend 1997. I respect these views. At the same time, we have to take account of the opinions of both the present and the future sovereign powers. For this reason, the proposals I am putting forward this afternoon will require serious discussion with Peking." I went on to explain what my starting point— the proposals I have already outlined—would be in these discussions. It seemed to me quite impossible to embark on discussions without in some way showing one's hand. To have done so would have been to invite justified criticism in Hong Kong that people were once again being kept in the dark about their future; it would subject us once more to the usual debilitating Chinese tactics of delay and leak; and it would risk an even more calamitous reversal than we had recently received over the Court of Final Appeal, on which, it will be remembered, we had reached a secret deal with the Chinese that had then been rejected by the legislature (on the grounds that the proposed court would not contain enough foreign judges). A similar outcome over the electoral arrangements would be disastrous. I believed that it would be politically hazardous and morally indefensible to refuse to tell people our ideas on elections, though I recognized that I would likely be criticized later for any retreats that I had to make in negotiations. I preferred the idea of defending myself for making compromises to that of defending myself for trying to keep everything under wraps. At the end of the day, Hong Kong—through its Legislative Council—would have to decide what arrangements were acceptable. While the council was an imperfectly democratic institution, it was the only one we had. I was convinced that on an issue as fundamental as this to the 6 million people for whom Britain was responsible, the only acceptable basis for policy was to go no further than Hong Kongers themselves were prepared to go, but no less far, either. Hong Kong's Legislative Council was the body that would have to judge where this balance lay.

I have dealt with these matters in some detail because they were to form the *casus belli* of our subsequent relationship with China. I am even more amazed in retrospect than I was at the time by the amount of heat that could be generated by these intricate and cautious steps along the road to democracy. I do not intend to deal with the rest of my governorship in similar detail. I will draw on events and experiences to illustrate general arguments in later chapters. But an outline of what happened in the next four and a half years will put in context some of the overall questions and lessons that emerged.

Initial reactions to my speech were very positive from politicians, many businesspeople, and most of the media. I was praised for being imaginative and brave. Then, in the immediate run-up to my planned visit to Peking on October 19, the Communist press in Hong Kong got into its stride, attacking me noisily for allegedly breaking the Joint Declaration and the Basic Law. We pored again over these sacred texts, as did our lawyers, to see if the Chinese had a leg to stand on. We seemed to be totally in the clear, and indeed the Chinese were general rather than specific in their attacks, suggesting that they could not really identify a particular breach. We had sinned, but it was not entirely clear how. I had brought two excellent special advisers with me to Hong Kong—Martin Dinham, who had been my private secretary when I was Overseas Development Minister and had then run Britain's aid program in Asia, and Edward Llewellyn, who had briefed me on European affairs when I was party chairman and had then worked during the general election campaign for John Major. Dinham and Llewellyn were formidably good—the former, wise, very hardworking, and immensely popular in London and Hong Kong; the latter, ubiquitously well connected on every continent and politically smart. They worked as part of a Government House team led by my private secretary, Richard Hoare, an excellent civil servant succeeded in later years by two equally good Chinese officials, Bowen Leung and John Tsang. Dinham and Llewellyn were helping to coordinate my Peking briefing, and were determined to ensure that every angle was covered and that I was not caught out over anything unsuspected during my talks. Llewellyn in particular dug around for anything that Chinese officials could throw at me. Alas, he found it. At the end of the voluminous briefing for my trip, there was a reference section of background material. It included an exchange of correspondence between Douglas Hurd and Qian Qichen in 1990. It had never before been mentioned to me by anyone, let alone been brought to my attention.

The seven Hurd/Qian letters in telegram form principally concerned the number of directly elected seats in the legislature. China had agreed that the number should be twenty in 1995 and grow to thirty by 2003. Other matters affecting the electoral arrangements had been canvassed, but there was clearly no agreement between the two sides. Indeed, Lu Ping had been publicly suggesting electoral proposals different from those considered in the letters long after they had been exchanged. With the exception of the directly elected seats (and on those we were sticking to the letter of what had been agreed between Hurd and Qian), there was nothing else that constituted even a general Sino-British understanding. When later, in evidence to the Foreign Affairs Select Committee of the House of Commons, three different teams of international lawyers were asked to say whether our electoral proposals were a breach of the correspondence or of the Joint Declaration and the Basic Law, they answered in the negative, although they did think the lack of Chinese cooperation with Britain over the administration of Hong Kong in the run-up to the handover could be said to represent a breach of the Joint Declaration.

It was surprising that these letters had never been mentioned to me in London or when we worked up our ideas in Hong Kong, particularly since some of those who had actually played a hand in drafting the letters for the British Foreign Secretary were members of the team that was shaping my own plans. But I did not take too tragic a view of this. It would have been more comfortable to have known about the letters; I might have presented my proposals slightly differently, and the Chinese would have been denied their best propaganda point—that I had not taken account of the letters. Nevertheless, I could understand why the letters had not been shaken under my nose in previous months. After all, they did not constitute an agreement but only an exploration as to whether an overall agreement was possible. Had the letters been more significant than this, I suspect they would have been shown to me at my briefing meetings in London with those now-retired diplomats who had helped write them and who later became obsessive critics of my policies. The failure of Qian to say anything at his meeting with Hurd in New York about previous exchanges is also worth noting. We were sufficiently confident about the meaning and content of these letters to publish them shortly after my visit to Peking in response to constant Chinese attacks that we had somehow breached a "secret" understanding.

I think the Chinese made as much fuss about this as they did because they had no real criticism they could substantiate in relation to the Joint Declaration and the Basic Law. I suspect that Lu Ping had been sharply criticized by his superiors for the fact that the combination of the two documents did not seem to have lashed the British as firmly to the Chinese wagon as had probably been claimed was the case in Peking. Here we were, still able to behave decently. Certainly, Lu had little substantive to say during our discussions in Peking on anything other than the Foreign Ministers' letters, which he produced with a flourish toward the end of our meeting, only to discover to his surprise that I had read them.

The shape and drama of the visit corresponded very closely to what the great American public servant George Shultz, a former Secretary of State, had warned me to expect when we had breakfasted together the week before I went. In particular, there were three features that appeared to be pretty standard. The first related to the overall arrangements for the visit; the second, to the terms of our arguments; the third, to Chinese handling of public relations.

Hanging over the whole visit, as Shultz had forewarned, was an old Chinese political trick—the real or imagined snub. The whole press corps in Peking is accustomed to hunting for it and eventually spotting it. Lu had sent me a private message before I left Hong Kong, saying that he hoped I would behave properly in Peking and respect his "face." There was plainly no recognition that these things cut both ways. The snubs appeared with great frequency during my three days in Peking. The first sighting was on my arrival at the airport. My host for the talks, Lu Ping, was not there to greet me; he had sent his deputy. A frantic press conference ensued in an airport anteroom; journalists pressed in on me from all sides; microphones were pushed under my nose and almost up it. Had I been snubbed? I was asked. Then the questioning turned to the ways in which I intended to retreat from my "confrontational" stance. The next day's talks began with an even more noisy and uncontrolled encounter with the press. They were allowed into the meeting room where Lu Ping and I, with our teams of advisers, were to spend most of the day locked in fruitless exchanges. They filmed our opening pleasantries, scrambling for the best shots and the chance to shout questions. Two photographers came to blows in the ensuing chaos. But the best photo opportunities came later in the day, when the Daimler car in which I was traveling suffered a punctured tire. This heavy piece of symbolism almost fell into the snub category. Some thought it too good to be true that this had happened by accident.

The main snub sightings came on the second full day of my trip. There was much frenzied speculation about whether or not I would meet a senior leader. Eventually, we discovered that I would be allowed to meet someone at the bottom of the list; rather than the President or the Prime Minister, I would be seen by Qian, the Foreign Minister and a Vice-Premier. The meeting with Qian was a formal and stilted affair. He is a courteous and polished man; we sat together, our interpreters huddled between us, with lines of officials on either side. His message was that unless I backed down, the Chinese would simply ignore me and deal with the British government over my head. But the main message for the media was that Qian had not shaken my hand when we first met. To be honest, I had not noticed. This, nevertheless, was thought to constitute a commodious snub even by Chinese standards. When this was put to me by the press, I felt rather silly saying that I could not recall whether or not my hand had been grasped in a manly way by Qian; and we could hardly send the ambassador to the Ministry of Foreign Affairs to find out whether hands had indeed been shaken as custom and courtesy usually dictated. So the snub stood. Director Lu did not, of course, see me off at the airport.

My discussions, as George Shultz had again told me would be the case, had a Kafkaesque quality to them. One after another, Chinese officials—over the table or from the depths of their white antimacassared chairs—would accuse me of having broken the Joint Declaration and the Basic Law. "How have I done so?" I would respond. "Show me where." "You know you have done so," they would reply. "You must have done so, or else we wouldn't have said it." "But where?" "It is not for us to say; you must know that you have erred." "Give me a single instance," I would argue. "Well," they would usually claim somewhat lamely, "you have at least broken the spirit of the Joint Declaration and the Basic Law." "What do you mean by the 'spirit'? Do you just mean that you disagree with me? Why not then discuss what I have done? Put forward your own proposals." "We cannot put forward our own proposals until you return to the spirit of the text." The circles spun and looped; the arguments twisted and turned; the greased pig wriggled about the room, defying capture.

The other feature referred to by Shultz was "the post-visit blast." No sooner had the aircraft doors closed on my exhausted departure from the harangues, the antimacassars, and the carefully calibrated (or just unthinkingly ill-mannered) snubs than Lu Ping held a press conference at which I was denounced with the solemnity of bell, book, and candle. There would be no negotiations until I dropped my "triple violation" package—that is, proposals which allegedly breached the Joint Declaration, the Basic Law, and the "secret understanding." I was to be treated as a political leper. Sino-British relations would be plunged into the freezer with who knows what results for British exports to China. "We cannot be held responsible," as the Chinese like to say, assisted again by Kafka, "for the consequences of your actions."

On occasions like this, Lu was given to mild hysteria and to the use of language from the most extreme lexicon of the Cultural Revolution (he once said that I was a criminal who would be condemned for a thousand generations). On other occasions, I was denounced by Chinese officials or Communist newspapers as "the whore of the East," a "serpent," and (more exotically) "the tango dancer," a reference not to my slinky charms on the dance floor but to a comment I had made about whether or not there would be further talks with China—namely, that it took two to tango. Lu's occasionally graceless tone and behavior were surprising. He was a distinguished-looking and highly intelligent man, a lover of classical music (I added to his collection of CDs), and a speaker of beautiful English. He and his family had suffered appallingly during the Cultural Revolution. I could only guess at the political pressures he was under and the sharp-bladed bureaucratic skirmishing in which he had to indulge. He had a moderate reputation but tended to behave immoderately—partly, I suspect, because of a short temper that may have been exacerbated from time to time by illness. In other circumstances, I would have liked to get to know him, but the politics of China doomed us to an embrace of pantomime hostility.

The Chinese position during the talks and for the following months was simple: "We will not deal with you unless you drop your proposals." We replied: "We'll be happy to discuss them, but we are not just going to drop them." The manifestations of Chinese hostility immediately polarized the community, although the polls suggested that we continued to enjoy majority support. Some business leaders headed for the hills, anxious to avoid the shell-fire; others moved in quickly behind China's line, seeking to put pressure on the government in Hong Kong to back down, or on the government in London to make us back down. A former Hong Kong civil servant turned businessman put the most entertaining and revealing case for China's position. "Patten has got them completely wrong," he said. "They don't want to rig the elections, as he fears. They just want to know the result in advance." But one or two business leaders, to their credit, backed us privately and even publicly. When Jardine's (one of the greatest British hongs) did so—not least on the grounds of loyalty to its large Hong Kong workforce, who, they believed, deserved a say in their future—

their reward was to be attacked vitriolically and warned that they would get no more business in China. A project in which they had an interest, for building a further container terminal in Hong Kong's port, was hit by China's insistence that since it would straddle 1997, it could not go ahead without Chinese approval. Despite these assaults, Jardine's declined to cave in and distance themselves from our policy on elections. Their head man in Hong Kong, the taipan Nigel Rich, stoutly defended me. A senior director, Sir Charles Powell, an urbane former diplomat who had been one of Margaret Thatcher's private secretaries in Downing Street, gave me wise and steadfast support throughout the five years of my governorship. In those early days, the Chinese took every opportunity to apply pressure and other acts of economic terrorism, including further intransigence over the airport, which unsettled the markets.

The controlled and targeted nature of China's economic warfare came to be easily detectable; attacks would be preceded by heavy selling of shares by Chinese companies and investors and followed by repurchase at a lower price. The growing futures market was also covered with Chinese fingerprints. But it was noticeable that each Chinese bellow had a smaller and shorter-term effect on the Hang Seng Index; the market took Chinese antics in its stride, presumably reflecting the view that China's own economic and financial interests were so tied up with success in Hong Kong that there was a limit to how far the Chinese would be prepared to allow their political rage to take them. I myself believed that as long as the Chinese continued to put so much money into Hong Kong, and as long as Chinese leaders sent so many of their relatives and friends to Hong Kong to make their fortunes, we had little to fear.

Nevertheless, I cannot claim that the virulence and regularity of the attacks on me and on the government's policy during the autumn and winter of 1992–93 were other than unsettling. Day after day I went through a debilitating round, trying to convince important visitors from elsewhere that I had not taken leave of my senses and that Hong Kong was not about to collapse, patiently dealing with half-baked but detailed criticisms of our approach from Peking's fellow-traveling foot soldiers in Hong Kong, hiding (usually) my frustration about those who, while they should have known better, took China's side rather than ours, and holding my team together with as cheerful a demeanor as possible. The old black dog of despair did occasionally come and sit in the corner of my office, but I had an excellent team of officials in Government House who would shoo him out of the door. Whenever I felt really depressed, a public outing—a visit to a housing complex or rural district, a shopping expedition, or a meal at a local restaurant—would invariably cheer me up. People were friendly and supportive to an extent that regularly surprised any visitors to Hong Kong who accompanied me. In five years, I can think of only three or four occasions when anyone there was half as rude to me as would be standard and regular form in British politics. Hong Kong's enthusiasm more than made up for Peking's hostility. I counted my blessings that it was not the other way around.

Suddenly, a few days before Christmas, the Chinese barrage stopped. We could almost pinpoint the day—December 22, 1992. We had been led to expect that this would be the day of a blockbusting Chinese ultimatum, but the day came and the day went and the guns fell silent. It was as though a command had been passed along the line to stop firing. Maybe the Chinese had concluded that they had either to change tactics or else start firing live rounds rather than blanks, with the prospect of doing real damage to Hong Kong's economic interests and their own. Anyway having decided that they were not going to be able to bully us into backing down, the Chinese resorted to another stratagem, a longer-term sapping of our defenses, the painstaking and relentless attempt to isolate me from my civil service, from London, and from the community. But while the decibel count fell (and, apart from isolated incidents, it did not rise to the same sustained level again), life was never to be comfortable, though we established a degree of normalcy that cannot have been very different from the period before 1992. We confronted small-minded truculence rather than loud saber rattling. I knew which I preferred, and for the community, it was more or less business as usual.

On the two issues where the Chinese had hoped that economic necessity would force us to cave in, we had found a means of going our own way. The airport project and the development of the container terminal were economic issues that had the ill fortune to stand at the crossroads with politics. While it was never easy to carry on with the airport against a background of haggling over its costs, its funding, and its design, in November we beat back an attempt by China and its friends in the Legislative Council to deny us the funds to continue building, and we went ahead even though it was in a rather hand-to-mouth, month-by-month way. From then on, while completion of the project was delayed by a few months and was certainly made a bit more expensive, it never really caused us too many headaches. We eventually reached a comprehensive agreement on the airport with the Chinese in 1995. We had begun in the early nineties by wanting to make the most of Hong Kong's excellent credit rating and its ability to borrow cheap money; we ended by maximizing our equity investment in the project. As a result, Hong Kong's reserves were rather less than they would otherwise have been, the very reverse of China's original position. But politics can always make a nonsense of economics. As for the container terminal, we had been told by experts that unless we went ahead with it as a matter of urgency, movement in the port would simply coagulate. I had my doubts, which proved justified. Eventually, not long before the handover, an agreement on the terminal was reached that saved everyone's "face," especially China's, and allowed the development to go ahead while introducing more, very necessary competition into the port. In the meantime, increased productivity in the existing terminals largely dealt with the growth in through-trade.

The political story of 1993 was the drift into negotiations with China and the attempt to halt those negotiations when they were clearly going nowhere. While I had my doubts about the likelihood of successful negotiations—I simply did not believe that there was anyone on the Chinese side with the political clout and imagination to cut a deal—and would have liked to move on with the debate and legislation on the elections in Hong Kong so that we could get the issue out of the way, I realized that this was simply not an option. Majority opinion in the community understandably hoped for a negotiated settlement, and even most of our strongest democratic supporters recognized that we had to try talks in the distant hope that the Chinese might be persuaded to see something approximating to sense. But I embarked on the whole process with a pretty heavy heart, albeit with one made healthier by angioplasty following an angina attack suffered while playing tennis in January.

The talks were preceded by talks about talks, which provided a foretaste of the thin gruel that was to follow. We conceded most of the points of substance in order to get talks started—for example we accepted, inconvenient though it was, that all the talks about the elections should take place in Peking. But there were two points on which we would not concede. First, the main Chinese negotiator, a vice-minister of foreign affairs called Jiang Enzhu, insisted that the talks should be held in secret, by which he meant not that their content should be confidential but that the fact that they were being held at all should not be disclosed. The intention was, presumably, to spare China the embarrassment of explaining why talks were taking place despite our refusal to drop our proposals. The request was absurd and impossible to implement: We rejected it several times, and the Chinese backed down. But they clung insistently to their other demand—that there should be no Hong Kong members of our team. This took us right back to the "three-legged stool" rows. Hong Kong civil servants could appear only as third-class passengers, hewers of wood, and drawers of water. We stood our ground, much to Chinese surprise and outrage, and the talks about talks abruptly ended. This situation proved short-lived, since the Chinese were soon back in contact and substantive talks began in April 1993 on acceptable terms, with Hong Kong officials as full members of our negotiating team.

The talks dragged on and on, which was doubtless the Chinese intention. Seventeen rounds of negotiation saw no real Chinese movement on anything. The mulish opacity of the Chinese position was made all the more irksome by the personality of the chief Chinese negotiator, Jiang. Behind his sloppy smile lurked the personality of a bureaucratic speak-your-weight machine. He brought nothing to the table save the briefs that he unfailingly read out. All the skilled efforts of our own chief negotiator—the Ambassador in Peking, Sir Robin McLaren—to lure Jiang out of his redoubt into open country came to naught. I doubt whether McLaren, had he been in my shoes, would have taken the approach I had followed. We had talked it through together in Hong Kong in the summer of 1992, and he had made it clear then, as he did later, that all these things were matters of judgment. He was always studiously professional in warning about and reporting Chinese reactions, neither exaggerating nor telling us what it might have been more convenient to hear. McLaren clearly took the wholly correct view that it was for ministers to make policy on the best advice available to them and then for others to carry it out. In Hong Kong, we did not always agree with him, but we admired him and were genuinely fond of him, feeling considerable sympathy as the talks took a toll on his health. When McLaren retired from the embassy in 1994, we missed him greatly.

By the autumn of 1993, with the talks manifestly running into the sand, we were starting to get a little desperate. We had to put in place complicated arrangements for three sets of elections, starting in 1994. These would require several pieces of primary as well as subsidiary legislation, followed by a vast amount of difficult administrative work by the Boundaries and Election Commission. Time was starting to move against us. Our attempts to use the calendar to put a bit of pressure on the Chinese were negated when a senior, retired British diplomat told the Chinese what our real timing constraints were rather than the more foreshortened dates we had given them. As has been well said, in diplomacy your main problems come from your own side.

To the demands of the calendar were added a growing perception of two intractable problems. Most of the negotiation, such as it had been, had focused on the functional constituencies and the election committee. Our own compromise proposals (which, though not resiling from our principles, in my judgment sank dangerously close to politically hazardous levels) had been rejected by the Chinese side with contumely. But the two biggest obstacles still lay ahead. We had a view of China's position on both of them, and that view was deeply discouraging. First, it was evident that the Chinese would not accept any simple-majority voting system; this favored democratic candidates and must therefore go. Second, the Chinese gave us a glimpse of what they were proposing on the so-called through-train.

What was this vehicle, exactly? Like many metaphors seized on by the Chinese side in negotiation, it became a substitute for thought or for real exchanges of view. The notion was this: We should be working toward a set of constitutional arrangements that allowed legislators elected in 1995 to serve through to the end of the four-year term of their council in 1999. This would obviously mean that the Chinese would have to give their broad approval to the arrangements made for the 1995 elections. But the Chinese extended the concept to mean that they would need to approve the legislators as well as the method that produced them. There was already a through-train for civil servants and judges, and not unreasonably, senior civil servants and the judiciary would need to take a new oath to the future government of the

Special Administrative Region. We were wholly content that legislators should be obliged to take a similar oath, just as Members of Parliament in Britain take an oath between their election and assuming their seats in the House of Commons. This is an acceptable *objective* requirement. But the Chinese wanted us to sign up to a *subjective* requirement. They wanted us to agree to the establishment of a Selection Committee that would determine which of the legislators chosen in 1995 would be able to "ride the through-train" to 1999. In other words, they wanted to cherry-pick the legislature, to throw legislators they did not like off "the train" at the time of the transition. One did not need the gift of second sight to know who would have been sent packing.

Put aside for a moment every other argument; I do not know how any democratic politician in Britain or elsewhere could have accepted a proposal such as this. Could Edward Heath? Could Geoffrey Howe? Could any diplomat have advised acceptance? I tried to think through how one would set about trying to justify it to Hong Kong public opinion, the House of Commons, or the world community. The issue would have dominated our last years as the colonial government and would probably have led to constant harrying and political embarrassment. Had I been one of those chosen for vehicular defenestration, I would have known what to do. I would have resigned my seat, fought a by-election, and won by an embarrassingly large majority. Yet the Chinese were adamant, and it was clear why this was so. Their officials could not see how they could report a successful outcome to negotiations to their superiors that would still allow those leading democrats like Martin Lee, who had led the protests against the Tiananmen killings, to get elected to the Legislative Council. "The good news, Prime Minister Li, is that we've concluded a deal with the British that cuts their original proposals down to size. The slightly less good news is that some of the democrats are still going to be elected; indeed, they will probably win the majority of seats."

When I explained this—to me insuperable—problem to one of my predecessors, he responded that there would only be a few legislators thrown out on their ear. And the housemaid's baby was very small. Another critic, who also thought that we made too much of this point, was to argue later that by being so firm about it, we had created a situation in which the Chinese threw all the real democrats out of the legislature in 1997. But there always seemed to me to be a rather important distinction between us behaving badly and the Chinese behaving badly. I continued to see no good reason why we should do the dirty work for China.

In November 1993, with time pressing and the Chinese position still virtually immovable, we decided that we should ignore warnings of dire consequences and announce that we intended to start legislating on some of the priority issues (like the local elections) but would be happy to go on talking about other matters until legislation on them, too, became necessary. The Chinese went through the motions of a major fuss, refused to accept further talks if we legislated, and brought the whole dreary saga to a welcome end. No one in Hong Kong seemed very surprised. The Chinese themselves had probably concluded that we were not going to budge on any matters of principle and were still determined to hold fair elections. They had strung us along for almost a year while they tried but failed to isolate me and undermine support for our strategy. Now they would have to switch to other tactics, trying to weaken and constrain the government's authority by establishing rival power centers (the metaphor for this was the setting up of a "second stove") and preparing their own team for the handover.

The following summer, they reverted for a short time to trying to knock our proposals down. By then, we had already legislated successfully for the local elections and had sent the bill for the 1995 Legislative Council elections to the council for debate and decision. For a time it looked as though the bill would be killed by an alliance of the usual Peking party and of the pusillanimous, a group of centrist legislators who convinced themselves that what everyone really wanted was a much-watered-down bill. These people even persuaded themselves that I really wanted it too, despite the fact that I told them individually, severally, and noisily that this was not true. Quite apart from other considerations, I was wholly convinced in my own mind that if we lost the bill, or had it neutered, the impact on the government's authority and my own would be catastrophic. I told my wife that in these circumstances I would have no option but to resign straightaway.

Chinese officials smelled blood and, not surprisingly, tried to apply pressure to some of those legislators whose votes might still be up for grabs. Several legislators with beepers and cell phones found themselves called from Peking by Lu Ping and urged to think of the motherland. In the event, the mother city won and we carried the day, with a majority drawn from the most democratically elected legislators overcoming a minority drawn mainly from the appointed members and those from the smaller functional constituencies. Hong Kong had decided how far it wished to travel along the road to democracy at this late stage of the transition.

The day after this vote, the Chinese concluded an agreement with us on the future of the defense estate in Hong Kong. The discussions on this had lasted for seven years. They mattered to Hong Kong, which wanted to be able to develop land not needed anymore by the garrison, and also to the Chinese People's Liberation Army, which wished to protect its own future requirements. We hoped that those requirements did not include the PLA's taking a role in property development in Hong Kong as it did elsewhere in China. The fact that this agreement followed so closely after the Legislative Council's vote about elections rather confirmed our instinct that the Chinese had begun to behave in a more down-to-earth fashion, not allowing political hysterics to get in the way of essential business.

No one ever argued that the three sets of elections that followed our rows with China were other than fair. They attracted record numbers of candidates, record voter registration, and record numbers of voters. To those who suggested that the turnout should have been higher, it was reasonable to respond that Hong Kong was not voting for a government, that the turnout was higher than it had been in the last local elections in Britain in which I had campaigned as party chairman, and that Hong Kong was coming to democracy late but enthusiastically. At every election over a decade for local government and the Legislative Council, voter participation had risen sharply. And as for the results, the more democratic candidates did better in each round of elections, especially in those for the legislature. This may have had something to do with the fact that the "United Front" candidates (that is, the Communists and their allies) were able to make more of an impact at the very local level; it may also have been affected by the Chinese missile-threatening campaign over Taiwan that coincided with the run-up to the Legislative Council election in September 1995. United Front candidates accepted their defeats, on the whole, with good grace. Several of them, led by the leader of the most interesting and credible of the Front parties (the Democratic Alliance for the Betterment of Hong Kong), announced after their defeats that having failed to be elected to an elected legislature, they would certainly not accept places in an appointed one. They were later to change their mind, presumably under the sort of pressure many of us would find difficult to resist. But they had the decency to look embarrassed about the whole miserable business.

While this was undoubtedly our bloodiest engagement with China, it was far from the only one. Hardly a week went by without British and Hong Kong negotiators—led by the affable and polished diplomat Hugh Davies—heading for the trenches in Hong Kong's Kennedy Road, where the talks with China usually took place. The Front would move a few inches this way and a few inches that. None of our negotiators actually died on the barbed wire, but several must have come close to passing away from sheer boredom. On some rare occasions, we were surprised to achieve relatively painless success. This was certainly the case with difficult discussions in 1995 on the detailed implementation of the 1991 agreement on the Court of Final Appeal. Though this agreement had not been accepted by the legislature, there was no chance of renegotiating its overall thrust with the Chinese. We faced an unpleasant decision. We could not put forward legislation that went against our agreement with China. Any legislation dealing with detail as well as fundamentals would require Chinese approval. If we went ahead without a Chinese say-so, we risked being defeated by a combination of legislators, some of whom disliked the bill for the same reasons that they had in 1991 and others of whom would oppose us because we had gone ahead without China's acceptance. We were absolutely sure in our own minds that our commitment to the maintenance of the rule of law would oblige us to try to legislate before the summer's end. Yet defeat stared us in the face, an especially gloomy prospect since our every move was being second-guessed by some officials in London and Peking, who seemed to doubt our political judgment on the handling of this issue. They would be far too well mannered to crow if things went wrong, yet defeat would have weakened our hand in any future disagreements with them.

In the event, the Chinese negotiated sensibly and fast, pushed along, we thought, by their understanding of our determination to legislate on our own if necessary, and by the fact that they had been convinced by the business community that this was an extremely important matter. We cut a reasonable deal, at the price of an awkward argument with the democrats who disliked anything to do with the 1991 settlement. For once, I did not have much sympathy with their position.

The closer we got to 1997, the more we felt that the Chinese did not really have their heart in some of the quarrels they detonated. For example, after months of attempting fruitlessly to get their agreement to our major legislative proposals for bringing Hong Kong's civil-liberties legislation into line with the International Covenant and the Bill of Rights, we went ahead unilaterally with our bills. We had promised to do this, and I did not want Britain to be in the position after 1997 of having to stand by while old and unsatisfactory colonial legislation was used by the then government to restrict the civil liberties of Hong Kongers. Our moves were followed by some rather desultory fireworks displays by China, the odd Catherine wheel and a few damp thunder flashes. The handover date, June 30, 1997, was by now not far off. The Chinese could catch a distant glimpse of the tape; they could also see that the Hong Kong they were going to inherit was in remarkably good shape despite the colonial oppression of the Triple Violator. The Hang Seng Index soared; crime fell; the community was calm; tens of thousands commemorated the June 4 Tiananmen killings at a silent vigil, but it was all very orderly. No crash, no disorder, lots of money in the reserves—why make a fuss?

What the Chinese had tried to do over the years with little success, until near the end, was to establish their own shadow government and drain authority away from the real one. In 1993, they set up a Preliminary Working Committee (PWC) of their most-favored henchmen and -women—old-time Communist coelacanths; tycoons on the make; ambitious third-raters; Knights and Commanders of the Most Distinguished Order of the British Empire who had found another empire to serve; the earnestly ill advised. This body purported to be preparing the way for the post-'97 government. Despite the entreaties of some members of the business community, we had nothing to do with it, a decision that made life easier for the civil service, which could only serve one master at a time. The PWC was followed by a pukka Preparatory Committee, whose arrival had been long advertised in the Basic Law. It had the same aim as the PWC and much the same membership. Since it had legitimate credentials, we gave it such support as we thought it could reasonably request, mostly in the form of briefings on government policy. For the last few months, the Preparatory Committee coexisted with a Provisional Legislative Council, made up of those members of the existing legislature that Peking thought would do what they were told, and a topping-up of appointed United Front worthies, including a high proportion of defeated candidates from the 1995 polls. One of them claimed that she had not really been defeated but had just failed to get as many votes as her victorious opponent. The Provisional Legislative Council worked with my successor, a former member (until the early summer of 1996) of my Executive Council, C. H. Tung, who had been selected by a handpicked committee of those whom China could trust, in supposedly preparing legislation for the future governance of the Special Administrative Region of Hong Kong. They met rather furtively over the border on Saturday mornings, and we refused to have anything to do with them.

Inevitably, the closer we got to the handover, the more people looked elsewhere for policy and reassurance for the future. But thanks to the excellent and loyal Hong Kong civil service, whose loyalty transferred quite properly on July 1 to Mr. Tung, we kept the initiative and dominated the agenda until remarkably late in the day. Less than three months before the transition, we opened the bridges, tunnels, and roads connecting Hong Kong to its new airport; just over a week before I left, I opened a new town. It was a good and decisive administration, and we went on governing right until the end. Few would have predicted this five or ten years before. I had not spent my five years as governor pulling levers for Peking.

Was the consequence fatal for Hong Kong? That is what critics in 1992 and 1993 had warned would be the case. The condition of Hong Kong in 1997 answered that question better than I could ever have done. We had stood up for Hong Kong, belatedly honoring the promises made to it about freedom, democracy, and the rule of law. Where were the fatalities? Had the roof fallen in on us? For years the fundament of policy on Hong Kong had been that if one resisted China, if one stood up for one's own principles rather than surrendering to China's, then the dragon would breathe fire and burn Hong Kong to a cinder. It did not happen from 1992 to 1997, and if it did not happen then, is it not reasonable to ask whether it would have happened before? Had not policy on Hong Kong, at least throughout the 1980s and early 1990s, been based on a proposition that turned out to be demonstrably wrong? Here was Hong Kong in the summer of 1997, richer than we could ever have believed possible, with a good government that guaranteed its passage through the transition, with an independent judiciary enjoying the same guarantee, with a rich fabric of civil society, and with no disorder on the streets. The demonstrations, when they occurred, were politely directed against China, not Britain. Is this what those old China hands, who believed that the Chinese were thugs and would behave with incomparable thuggishness, would have predicted?

Hong Kong's collapse having conspicuously failed to materialize, some critics in Britain were thrown back on one other argument, as though they really cared about it. Because we had stood up to China, they said, Hong Kong would have less freedom and democracy after 1997 than would otherwise have been the case. This was a poor argument. It assumed, after all, that Hong Kong would have been better off in the long term if we had connived with China to give it less democracy and fewer civil liberties in the short term. At least Hong Kong had experienced a free and fair election, knew what it was like, had self-confidently enjoyed its liberties. The world would be watching closely to see whether Hong Kong's civil liberties were mangled; China had been put on its best behavior. We took every opportunity to interest local and foreign opinion in keeping a close eye on how the Chinese acted after the transition. For example, in my last major policy speech to the Legislative Council in October 1996, I set out benchmarks against which China's promises to protect Hong Kong's freedoms and autonomy could be measured, and I restated these regularly throughout the following months. China's subsequent handling of Hong Kong suggests that this may have had some effect. Nevertheless, it is true that on July 1, 1997, Hong Kong became the only example of decolonization deliberately accompanied by less democracy and a weaker protection of civil liberties. This was a cause for profound regret, especially for the departing colonial power. But it was China's doing and China's decision. I am pleased that Britain narrowly avoided complicity in the dishonorable act of denying the citizens of free Hong Kong what they had been promised in 1984.

3

Colonial Questions

Ordinary mortals know what's happening now,
  the Gods know what the future holds
because they alone are totally enlightened.
  Wise men are aware of future things
    just about to happen.

—C. P. Cavafy, from a poem based on lines by Philostratus

  The Master said: "To learn something and then to
put it in to practice at the right time: is this not a joy."

—*The Analects of Confucius,* 1.1

Within an hour of the handover ceremony in Hong Kong's magnificent new convention center, which looks like a mighty silver bird settling on the inky waters of the harbor, the royal yacht *Britannia* had slipped her moorings and, accompanied by five naval vessels and a flotilla of pleasure boats, had headed east for the open sea. There had been kilted pipers and massed bands, drenching rain, cheering crowds, a banquet for the mighty and the not so mighty, a goose-stepping Chinese honor guard, a president and a prince, speeches, flags, pride, and tears. Now we sailed down that ravine of high-rise buildings, the windows of each block of flats exploding with flashbulbs, the crowds gathered by the roadside at the Lei Yue Mun gap to wave us farewell. As we paused at the harbor's entrance to drop our pilot and Lance Brown, my aide-de-camp and friend, before steaming out into the choppy South China Sea, I looked back at Hong Kong dazzling across the night sky behind us. My experiences there during the previous five years had naturally taught me much about the views of China, the local and international business community, the British Foreign Office and British, American, and European politicians on Hong Kong, and the issues instigated by its history and its predicament. And those observations all raised more profound questions about politics and economics—questions that went well beyond the story of Hong Kong. To this substantial extent, I felt as I left that Hong Kong had marked and shaped me more than anything in my life before.

That night, we were leaving one of the greatest cities in the world, a Chinese city that was now a part of China, a colony now returned to its mighty motherland, in rather different shape from that in which it had become Britain's responsibility a century and a half before. Neither Britain nor any other colonial power had ever left a dependency so rich both in treasure and in the fabric of its civil society.

This was not what Chinese officials had said they expected. They had regularly, in public and in private, anticipated riot and ruin. As ever with a totalitarian system, it is a puzzle to know what was merely propaganda and what was actually believed. Understandably, the Chinese saw Britain's role in Hong Kong through the prism of humiliations heaped on the nineteenth-century Qing dynasty by the imperial powers. There must also have been real resentment at the fact that so many families who fled from Communism in China had made such a success of their lives under a foreign flag in a colonial citadel. Additionally, during China's more activist Maoist days in the third world, the Chinese Foreign Ministry had developed a version of postcolonial history that some of its diplomats applied to Hong Kong as well. Britain, it was argued, always left behind in its colonies delayed explosive devices designed in due course to wreck countries that it no longer governed. Insofar as the "explosive devices" were ever defined, they seemed to be concepts like multiparty democracy and the rule of law. This had doubtless been a comforting message for Chinese ambassadors to deliver to those African despots whose courts they attended in the 1970s.

Some Chinese may therefore have been surprised to find Hong Kong in such fine shape. Its huge reserves had not been shipped back to London in *Britannia*'s hold. Nor had Hong Kong's fiscal surpluses been dissipated on schemes that would prove popular in the short term but unaffordable in the longer term. They had certainly not been handed out in payments to British firms for contracts unfairly awarded. The charge that public-service contracts had in fact been allocated in this way had been frequently made—for example, when the contract for the largest of our new bridges went to a partly British consortium rather than to a cheaper Korean company. Little was heard of this criticism after a series of construction catastrophes hit Korea, including the tragic collapse of a new bridge. Truth to tell, British companies, like all others, operated on a level playing field, in which the award of contracts was overseen by both the Independent Commission Against Corruption and the Public Auditor. On one or two occasions, I found myself having to explain to British firms why it would be wrong for them to be shown any special favors by the Hong Kong government, and to defend figures for the award of major public contracts that would have seemed to suggest to anyone who believed that colonial administrations helped their own side that Hong Kong was a Japanese dependency. Hong Kong was run as any international city should be administered. It was open to all. I used occasionally to ask myself, taking one example at random, whether British companies would have been able to do as much business in a French colony as French companies were doing in a British one.

China inherited a success story, where the proceeds of success were still in the bank and where, if imaginary time bombs were somewhere ticking away, they were doing so very silently and for purposes that would appear to be decidedly counterproductive to those who were thought to have set them. Britain had a vast stake in Hong Kong's continuing success. There was almost £3 billion of direct British investment in Hong Kong; the capitalization of British companies on the Hong Kong stock market totaled about £70 billion; British exports to Hong Kong (some admittedly reexported) were about three and half times the size of those to China as a whole; there were over 50,000 Chinese families with British passports, whose future Britain would presumably prefer not to have to worry about. Hong Kong was Britain's main jumping-off point in the East, a source of quiet pride as well as handsome returns. Britain wanted Hong Kong to stay rich and stable, just as China did.

I like to think that the more sophisticated Chinese leaders understood those things and were not unduly surprised by what they found in the territory. Many of them would have had relations and friends there to tell them what it was really like. On the other hand, hardly any of them had ever been to Hong Kong; it was out of bounds to a whole generation of the Chinese leadership—a Chinese city languishing under the colonial yoke. And the Hong Kong experience actually gained by these leaders cannot always have been a very edifying one. They had encountered capitalist Chinese property tycoons, with expensive suits and a good deal of money in their pockets, who must have confirmed some of their northern prejudices about the gamy and glitzy boom-boom city of the south. They would not have witnessed at first hand all the other aspects of Hong Kong's life—cultural, intellectual, administrative, managerial, charitable—that gave the city such strength and depth. Hong Kong was a far better city even than its economic statistics suggested.

It was particularly difficult to believe that senior Chinese officials could have much comprehension of the relationship between Hong Kong's hardware, a capitalist economy, and its software, a pluralist society, and yet it was the latter that enabled the former to function so well. This relationship between economic progress—largely based on market forces rather than social ownership and control—and clean and open administration—the rule of law, public participation in government, a free press, and respect for civil liberties—is an issue at the center of debate in Asia and beyond in the post-Communist world. In the unlikely event of China's leaders understanding these issues, which inhabited an intellectual world in which they had never been allowed to dwell, no thanks would have been due to what they had been told about Hong Kong by the sort of local business leaders who talked to them and to whom they apparently listened. Hong Kong Chinese businessmen tended to tell Peking officials what they thought the latter wanted to hear: Hong Kong's development owed most to China's; there were no problems or anxieties about 1997; all would be well once Hong Kong was returned to the motherland, an event to which all looked forward with churning, yearning hearts. Sometimes, the flattering terms in which these messages were delivered surprised even China's supreme leaders. A Hong Kong businessman, who began his meeting with Li Peng by telling him that he was the greatest leader of the Chinese Communist party since Mao, was interrupted by the then Premier with the tart reminder that he was not in fact the leader of the Communist party. What the Cantonese call shoe-shining left many senior Chinese officials with sparkling toe caps after their meetings with Hong Kong business delegations.

It is difficult to know whether those who conveyed these messages—that capitalism would easily survive 1997 without much need to bother about those aspects of Hong Kong's life which really distinguished it politically and socially from China—genuinely took the view that these things did not matter, simply did not know that these things mattered, or were just saying the first thing that came into their heads that they thought would please their interlocutors. It was behavior that raised eyebrows around the world. I was often asked why so many of those who spoke in this way nevertheless went to so much trouble to acquire and to hold on to passports that would entitle them and their families to live in democratic countries should they wish to do so. If pluralism did not matter, why keep a pluralist option in the bottom drawer? Another point was occasionally put, most fiercely by a retired Commonwealth prime minister, who thought that some local business leaders had been prepared to do a sort of Faustian deal with China, in which they would give up the guarantees in the Joint Declaration about personal freedom and the rule of law in return for the promise that they could go on making a lot of money. "Hong Kong," he said, "is the only place I can think of where people are prepared to give up their freedom for money." While understandable, this was an unfair judgment—there were only "some" people in this category, and even they had also normally taken care to preserve their own avenues to freedom in case it proved necessary to use them. A few of them, too, if challenged on this point would have shrugged their shoulders and pointed to their own personal histories and those of their families in dealing with China in the past. To have been a refugee leaves its mark. Nevertheless, at the very least it is a sad fact that Peking's understanding of what made Hong Kong successful was not advanced by the messages delivered to the north by most local leaders of the business community.

Some visitors to Hong Kong were surprised by the disregard they heard expressed at the most prodigal dinner tables for the economic, as well as other, benefits of pluralism. (To other visitors, of course, the message came as a welcome confirmation of their prejudices.) This frequently made it more difficult to convince skeptics that Hong Kong's future success was assured. A few people convinced themselves that after 1997 Hong Kong was inevitably doomed to sink and slide rapidly into sleaze, corruption, cronyism, and civil disorder. It was relatively easy to dispose of these far-fetched anxieties. The more sophisticated pessimists posed more realistic questions about Hong Kong's prospects. They sometimes began from an analysis of the relationship between China and Hong Kong that chimed with the bleak insight offered by the American academic Perry Link in his brilliant book on China's intellectual community, *Evening Chats in Beijing:* "Even as some in Hong Kong badly underestimate the 'dragon' that resides in Beijing, many in Beijing overestimate, just as badly, the 'dragon slayers' they see in Hong Kong." Were this true, it would not be a recipe for a happy future. These doubters would go on to put their main worry about Hong Kong. They were usually prepared to accept that come July 1, 1997, the city would not be mortuary-bound right away. But was there not, they would contend, a real danger of Hong Kong ceasing to be a great international financial and business center—free, open, and cosmopolitan, the New York, London, or Frankfurt of East Asia? Might it not be irredeemably doomed to become merely the richest city in China—not the most dire of futures perhaps, but still a very different one from that normally advertised and predicted?

Why should this be so? The sophisticated pessimists usually hit most of the following buttons. They worried about cronyism and opacity distorting Hong Kong's economic management and paving the way for corruption. They were concerned that clean government and the rule of law would be inevitable casualties. They fretted over the consequences for civil liberties of a government that would be more concerned to explain Peking to Hong Kong than Hong Kong to Peking, that would think it more important to avoid challenging, however indirectly, China's system than to stand up for Hong Kong's. They feared the consequential closing of safety valves would mean that sooner or later Hong Kong would lose its seasoned and delicately balanced ability to cope peacefully and rationally with social and political pressures. They wondered just how agreeable a place Hong Kong would be for an educated international community if its tolerant and easygoing atmosphere were to change and its open and fair marketplace were to be compromised.

It was never easy to answer this skepticism. To a considerable extent, only time will provide the answers. I placed my faith in two things. First, I believed that the values Hong Kong represented, and was shaped by, were the values of the future in Asia as everywhere else, and that there was a momentum behind them which would be hard to stop. (That, in a way, is the argument of much of this book, an argument that has only been strengthened by Asia's financial crash in 1997.) Second, I also always strongly believed that China badly needed Hong Kong to be more than just its richest city. Hong Kong's continuance more or less as it was must surely be seen as a matter of supreme national interest to China's leaders.

That Hong Kong matters to China is a proposition so blindingly obvious as to advance the argument by only a fraction. What comparison can one make? It is like saying that modern New York would matter greatly to a United States whose different geographical parts were living in a scattering of periods from the two centuries since American independence. From Manchuria to Canton, from fertile coast to arid central Asian hinterland, China's present social and economic state contains examples of most of the centuries of the last millennium. It all encompasses, too, most known economic models from clapped-out public ownership to sweatshop capitalism, from peasant agriculture in village markets to trading in derivatives in futures markets. Its government is manned by Stalinist hacks and smart Stanford Business School graduates. Its prevailing political ethos—market Leninism, market socialism, capitalism with Chinese characteristics, Shanghai-style socialism, call it what you will—is intellectually incoherent but infused with an iron determination to hold on to power and a barely controlled nationalist rage. Add to this extraordinary mix in 1997 Hong Kong, the worldly-wise and modern capital of the overseas Chinese, with its regulated markets, common law, attractiveness for overseas investors, native managerial skills, competent administration, and experienced entrepreneurs—now, *that* produces a real spark of combustion. Hong Kong is at one and the same time China's window on the world, bridge to the world, shop front for the world, and paradigm for the world of what China as a whole could become.

The economic value of Hong Kong to China, therefore, tells only a part of the story, though a significant one. As China began to open up its economy in the late 1970s, Hong Kong acted as the main source of the money and the management skill to fuel and steer this process. Hong Kong has accounted for between 60 and 80 percent of foreign direct investment in China. As costs rose in the Colony, Hong Kong manufacturers were able to retain their competitiveness by shifting their factories north. Eight out of every ten Hong Kong manufacturers now have a plant in China. They employ 5 million workers on the mainland, which is greater than the entire Hong Kong labor force. This has not meant the end of manufacturing in Hong Kong but merely that the contributions to the manufacturing process there are at the higher value-added end of business—design, financing, marketing, quality control. Hong Kong entrepreneurs, at some of their 50,000 investment projects in China, have helped teach the Chinese to produce and design the articles that the rest of the world wants to buy. They have raised quality and reliability. While foreign investment may only be responsible for less than 5 percent of China's output, it covers two thirds of the value of the products that China exports. So, as Michael Yahuda has argued in his book *Hong Kong: China's Challenge*, Hong Kong is vital to the fastest-growing parts of the Chinese economy that underpin the rise in prosperity and in living standards that sustain the legitimacy of the Chinese leadership.

For the overseas Chinese as well as for so many foreign businesses, Hong Kong is the reassuring and safe commercial base for doing business in China. A contract signed in Hong Kong enjoys the security of a common-law system and independent courts. The city also provides the bridge to Taiwan, economic relations between Taiwan and China being largely conducted through Hong Kong. Taiwan will watch closely what happens farther down the coast: Can "one country, two systems" work in the former colony, and if it cannot do so there, the Taiwanese will ask, how could it possibly work for them?

For reasons, therefore, of the highest politics as well as of economics, it would be disastrous for the Chinese leadership if the bloom on Hong Kong were to fade, if Hong Kong were to become just China's most prosperous city. Hong Kong will be in every sense at the heart of the next stage of China's revolution as that vast country struggles with problems of political transition, with the enormous incubus of loss-making state-owned industry, with the requirement to begin establishing the framework of rules and regulations essential to a modern sophisticated economy, with environmental hazard, with institutional weakness, with the moral vacuum created by the intellectual and political decay of Marxism-Leninism. China's needs, as well as Hong Kong's vitality, should encourage optimism about the former colony's future. The way that the questions provoked by this relationship are answered will help shape not only China but the whole region in the next few years. It was this region that extravagantly raised and then dramatically dashed the hopes of the rest of the world in the 1990s.

Hong Kong had been a central part of the region's economic success story. Asian growth had begun in postwar Japan, sheltering under the American security umbrella, and then in the late 1950s and the following decades it had cascaded down, first lapping over the four tiger economies of Hong Kong, Taiwan, South Korea, and Singapore. Like Japan, they all enjoyed American (or British) protection against the conflicts among nationalism, communism, and colonialism that tore apart much of the rest of the continent. Later, in the years after the end of the Vietnam War, the tide of development moved on through East and Southeast Asia, sweeping up Malaysia, Indonesia, Thailand, the Philippines (after Marcos), China, and even Vietnam. Within two decades, we had moved from the Vietnamese invasion of Cambodia to the foreign investors' invasion of Vietnam.

Soaring growth rates throughout the region encouraged a search by Europeans and Americans for the secrets of success. Was there some Asian formula that could be taken, like ginseng, by jaded Westerners to transform their competitive performance? Some argued that Hong Kong showed the way and that unbridled capitalism was the answer to economic sclerosis. Yet capitalism was not wholly unbridled in Hong Kong, or in the other East Asian success stories, either. In trying myself, when Governor, to speak about some of the reasons for the growth rates that made Europeans and Americans envious, I would regularly add qualifications and caveats, ifs and buts, which made my remarks seem like a life insurance policy. Inconveniently, there was no simple, pat explanation, though there was a range of things that more or less accounted for Asia's relative success and provided some broad lessons upon which the rest of the world could probably draw. That there was still a lot more for Asia to learn from Europe and America was a sometimes unwelcome but relevant postscript.

One argument which became increasingly prevalent through the 1990s was that Asia's success was as much a cultural as an economic phenomenon. Asia had its own value system, rediscovered as the tides of Western exploitation and imperialism ebbed. The great architect of Singapore's success, Lee Kuan Yew, was the most intellectually rigorous of the exponents of this faith, its high priest if not its most obvious exemplar. There were adherents of this dogma at every level, and they included Europeans and Americans. There was, after all, a comprehensive convenience to the arguments about Asian values that made a particular mark on political debate in Hong Kong, especially since these values appeared to explain why Hong Kong required neither democracy nor any statutory defenses of its liberties.

The extent of the hostility to democracy, and the intellectual depths some people were prepared to plumb in order to justify that hostility, occasionally produced moments of comic sublimity. One Hong Kong broker and banker, called Philip Tose, whose investment bank, Peregrine, was taken by many (and certainly by him) to exemplify all that was most vigorous and self-confident in Asian business, was asked in April 1997 to address a meeting in Hong Kong of Harvard Business School alumni. During the course of his question-and-answer period, Tose was asked why it was that investors preferred China to India and why the latter's growth rate lagged behind China's. "In one word," he replied, "democracy." Now, there is, as it happens, an interesting discussion to be had about the relative merits of India's and China's approaches. It includes a comparison of positive developments in both: of human rights in India and health and education investment in China. It naturally covers which approach is likely to bring more stability and economic development in the longer term; it raises sharp questions about India's poor performance (despite, or because of, its socialist political settlement) in public health and basic education, and about China's culpably vicious record on human rights. But Mr. Tose did not pause to elaborate on these points. Advancing boldly, he told his increasingly restive audience that the United States too had begun to suffer economically from the moment when Americans were given "universal suffrage"—in other words, when laws were passed banning discrimination in voting registration. Desperate spin doctors subsequently tried to explain on the great banker's behalf that he had not had any racial group in mind, just the poor. "No representation without taxation" was the real burden of his argument. Democracy, Western-style, led to mobocracy. Government and politics should be left (he implied) to the rich, whose ranks probably still included Mr. Tose even after his much-vaunted bank collapsed spectacularly at the beginning of 1998, a casualty of one bit of cronyism too many.

What the *Asian Wall Street Journal* charitably called Mr. Tose's rather eighteenth-century way of looking at things clearly shocked Harvard's global alumni. But they could have heard much more of the same from Asians and Europeans alike if they had stayed around a little longer, when the message would be delivered with all the more vehemence, since it is the view Chinese officials want to have broadcast and acted upon.

Those members of the business community who took a different and more civilized view, and expressed it courageously and publicly, were made to suffer for their sins. Jimmy Lai, a refugee from mainland China who believed passionately in economic freedom (of an unbridled Hayek and Friedman sort) and political liberty, and who made fortunes in the retailing and publishing industries, was hammered in China (where the authorities closed down his clothes shops) and isolated commercially in Hong Kong. He cheerfully carried on, publishing a very popular and outspoken newspaper and magazine, believing that freedom would win in the end and that Hong Kong's people should in the meantime keep its flame burning in their hearts. Simon Murray, a highly successful British businessman who had once been Hong Kong mogul Li Kashing's right-hand man, had a similar brave and buccaneering commitment to the survival of democracy and pluralism. The New China News Agency, which operated as the Chinese Communist party's eyes and ears in Hong Kong, must have had a filing cabinet full of Murray's views on freedom and its foes.

Those views included strong support for Sir Jimmy McGregor, who was, when I arrived in Hong Kong, the representative for the General Chamber of Commerce functional constituency in the Legislative Council, having beaten off in 1991 a challenge from a Chinese businessman with quaintly Neanderthal views and an American passport. McGregor was a Scottish ex-serviceman who had worked for the government on the trade side before going into business. He had helped see Hong Kong through some of its toughest times (for instance, the Cultural Revolution riots in 1967) and had notched up a long and distinguished record of public service. He was a wise man who spoke his mind forcefully, and his opinions included a generosity of spirit about the poor and needy and an unshakable belief in democracy and the rule of law. The fact that he had been elected as the chamber's representative is a useful reminder that not all businessmen had reactionary views, though some inevitably were to stay quiet and keep their heads down as debate became more bitter and polarized in the run-up to the 1997 transition.

With Chinese officials pulling the strings, a campaign was mounted before the 1995 Legislative Council elections to unseat McGregor and to remove those who might sympathize with him from the chamber's governing body. With care and menace, the anti-McGregor faction collected proxy votes from obedient company chairmen, some of whom joined the chamber especially to do their patriotic duty. McGregor was duly defeated, and the chamber (in the reverse of what it claimed to want for the whole community) was duly politicized, becoming in effect a part of the United Front. It was wheeled out from time to time to deliver political messages, but no one took very much notice. Business was certainly vital to Hong Kong, and business interests needed to be heard—as I tried to ensure partly through the establishment of a Business Council of representative Hong Kong company bosses, who regularly discussed with me and my senior officials the major economic issues of the day. But business is about making profits, not about issuing political statements, and as long as Hong Kong's business went on making large quantities of the former, I did not have too many worries about the latter.

Public criticism by a handful of business leaders, and private criticism by rather more, never left us feeling beleaguered in Government House, for a number of reasons. First, there was the economic argument I have just adduced. Business in Hong Kong was enjoying a golden age. International confidence in our economy was high. Our currency was firm and our reserves were enormous. There was little or no labor unrest—the only major dispute in five years involved Cathay Pacific cabin staff in the winter of 1992–93. Second, the criticism and the prejudices were often too funny and too unashamedly two-faced to take seriously. Sitting next to a local and grand stockbroker at lunch one day, I was instructed to "tell that Martin Lee" (the leader of Hong Kong's democrats) "to go back to China where he belongs." As it happens, my apoplectic companion had "belonged" there more recently than Mr. Lee. On another occasion, an international financial newspaper ran a long and interesting interview with a local business magnate in which he advanced a sophisticated argument for confidence in the future and for the irrelevance of the survival of democracy to that optimism. To show how positive he was himself about the prospects, he was urging his son, who was studying at university in the United States, to return to settle and make his own future in Hong Kong. This was all very well said. For me, however, the effect was slightly spoiled by the knowledge that the father had lobbied every visiting British minister for British passports for his offspring.

I did not feel particularly resentful about local business bosses' occasional public hostility to my administration's policies, since I had some sympathy for their position. They were to some extent parroting not just what the future sovereign power wanted them to say but what the present sovereign power had been happy to hear them say in the past. "Hong Kong has done very nicely without politics [i.e., without democracy]. People in Hong Kong are not interested in political issues; they just want to get on with making money. No one here is too bothered about human rights provided the money keeps rolling in. That Martin Lee is a real menace, giving us such a bad reputation around the world." How much would these sentiments have been rejected and countered in the past? My arrival in Hong Kong led to some awkward intellectual confusion. The government's loudspeakers began to broadcast a rather different conventional wisdom.

Had it not been for the strong support that I received from the top of the British government, particularly from the Prime Minister, the Foreign Secretary, and the Chancellor of the Exchequer, the criticism from some parts of the British business establishment might have proved more awkward. Stirred up by one or two business leaders with a foot in both Hong Kong and London, and rattled by an energetic campaign of boardroom intimidation by Ambassador Ma (with a list in his hand of people to lobby, provided by a retired British diplomat), a handful of British chairmen and senior executives launched occasional sallies from the rear, muttering over City lunches, whispering in ministers' ears, roughing up civil servants. The burden of their argument was simple: "Patten is bad for business." To trade with China (or, presumably, with other tough authoritarian or totalitarian regimes) it was, they believed, essential to keep in those governments' good books. Political harmony was essential to business profits. Thanks to this fallacious argument (rarely challenged in any country and standing as a sort of fixed point in any discussion on China), I found myself in the middle of democratic and business crossfire. On the one hand, I was attacked for sacrificing Hong Kong to British trading interests; on the other, I was criticized for not sacrificing Hong Kong to British trading interests.

I was always incensed more by the behavior of British critics than by local ones; the British had less excuse. Particularly galling was their assumption of a sort of moral equivalence between China's attitude and our own. Trying to develop democratic institutions and defend civil liberties was seen, at best, as on a par with trying to tear those things down. They tended to accept China's side of every argument, believing that we were lying and playing crafty lawyers' tricks and that the Chinese were the plain dealers. For some it was a case of China, right or wrong. One former cabinet minister turned company chairman told the director of the New China News Agency that he would wholly understand it if the Chinese were to march in before 1997 and take back what was rightfully theirs. A bank chairman fawningly pointed out to Chinese officials how the United Kingdom's record highlighted some of the inadequacies of democracy. The chairman of another larger international bank, at an especially low point in the fortunes of the government back home, told me that unless I did a U-turn he would mobilize a group of like-minded business colleagues to line up before the British Prime Minister and say that the Conservative party would receive no more financial help or political support unless I was removed or forced to change my policies. Another very senior British businessman suggested that to stop all these arguments we should simply pull out of Hong Kong as soon as we could. When some people behave like this, it is not surprising that the Chinese go on bullying.

These attacks and these attitudes stung rather than hurt. They made some Foreign Office officials a little nervous (not surprisingly, since these were the civil servants who bore the brunt of the attacks in London) and some Department of Trade officials a touch aggressive. We had one or two awkward debates in the House of Lords, the nearest the British constitution gets to functional constituencies, with special-interests spokesmen for the China trade toeing the Peking line. But ministers stood firm, and so did most businesses and business leaders and executives. Some of the most successful British companies in the China market, when approached by Ambassador Ma and told that if they knew what was good for them they would lobby the British government against the Governor's policies, very politely but firmly said that they were not interested in politics, that they just wanted to invest and do business, and if that was not possible, it would be regrettable all around. Business went ahead. In particular, the Confederation of British Industry behaved very properly, concerned (who could not be?) to advance British exports to China and Asia as a whole while leaving politics to the politicians.

China's tactics in London and Hong Kong reflect those that it has employed with such success more widely, both before and more particularly after Tiananmen. In a sense they are a throwback to the approach regularly taken by the Middle Kingdom to those who wished to do business with it in past centuries. China is the most populous country in the world; its market is always potentially enormous; there are hundreds of millions of customers to satisfy. Access to this market appears to be closely guarded. Loan of the keys to the gate depends on good behavior. If company X behaves unacceptably, then there is always company Y waiting in line. And if the country where company X is based, where it employs workers and pays dividends to shareholders, crosses China's path, then the native land of company Y, whose government has not behaved so injudiciously, can be rewarded with the business. This, at least, is the theory.

The tactics are calibrated with brutal directness. Sophistication is not required. Europe is played off against America; one European country is played off against another. In the European Union and its single market, whatever the comradely rhetoric, national dog still eats national dog: "*Chien Frisst Perro.*" Chinese views of the venality of the Western world, and of the controlling influence there of business lobbyists, must be one of the few aspects of modern life that continues to give any relevance or vitality to Marxist and Maoist thought.

If there are ever any doubts in the West about going along with this crude and cynical strategy—tempering criticism of China's behavior at home or abroad in return for market access—they are usually doused in a shower of Asian values and in a particular Chinese variant of this downpour. Not only should we understand that things are done differently over there, it is argued, but we should sympathize with the scale of the problems faced by the Chinese government and recognize that eggs have to be broken in order to make omelettes. (No one ever volunteers to be one of the eggs.) The best way that we can help advance human rights in China is by investing and doing business there; this point is put forward as though it were an issue rarely far from the minds of its proponents.

Can we really blame businesses for putting these arguments forward when they often seem to be the stock-in-trade of governments and the foreign-policy establishment, too? A business executive presumably sees the business interest in terms of maximizing the chance for a company to make profits, increase dividends, secure the well-being of employees, and invest for the future. How does the executive define the conditions in which those things are most likely to happen? How does a business perspective relate to a government's view of what is in the national interest?

At its simplest, the relationship presumably looks like this: A government's foreign and trade policy should make it easier for a business from its own country to clinch a deal in another country. But things are rarely that straightforward, even if it were acceptable to restrict the meaning of national interest in that way, and even if one were to accept that doing whatever the government of a purchaser country wishes one to do is good for the immediate or longer-term pursuit of business in that country. Let us take an example. A company wishes to sell nuclear-energy technology to another country. That country has a reputation for selling more basic nuclear technology of its own to third countries that probably are attempting to manufacture nuclear weapons. In addition, the purchaser country has a record of stealing industrial secrets and using the information gained to set up its own import-beating industries. In circumstances like that, even if the company in your own country lands a large order, a government has to be clear that it is not going to see its national security threatened by the sale, or the prospects of its national company doing business next year and the year after that diminished. In other words, such matters are more complicated than they may immediately appear.

In relation to Hong Kong, the issues were often made to look blissfully straightforward. In May 1993, we were visited by former Labour Prime Minister Lord Callaghan, who was on his way for a meeting of the globally illustrious in Shanghai. It is the sort of trip all of us in politics hope will arrive at regular intervals during our years of retirement—the chance to exchange with our aging peers a few views from the summit about what is happening down on the plain before the obituary columns take us to their bosoms. Lord Callaghan is a man of courtesy and bluff charm, a retired premier who has behaved, since he left office, with faultless good political manners. He gave me his blunt advice: There was no point in trying to do much about democracy or the rule of law before 1997. I should not feel obliged to martyr myself for the future of Hong Kong. No one would thank me for it afterward. I would go down with the ship (Lord Callaghan is an ex-sailor) strapped to the wheel, and the waters would simply close over my head. We could not do anything to affect what the Chinese did after the handover. They would do whatever they wanted. The British interest was simple: to make sure our business-men could do a lot of trade with China.

This attitude had invariably played a part in British policy making on Hong Kong, though not always the decisive one. The mixture of influences and ingredients was always more complex than this. A cru-cial component was the "two ancient civilizations" theory. This was one of the particular contributions by some of the older sinologists to British foreign policy. Britain and China were two great nations. Our relationship went back centuries. We had both been custodians of magnificent cultural and scientific traditions. Sino-British relations were a precious entity, like a handsome Ming vase, which we could take out of the display cabinet, touch, walk around, and admire from time to time. Nothing so vulgar as the noise from Hong Kong, an un-fortunate relic of our respective nineteenth-century histories, should be allowed to get in the way of the broadening and deepening of Sino-British relations. Hong Kong, as one retired British ambassador fa-mously put it, was just a pimple on China's backside.

This rather grand view of geo-strategy and of Britain's role in world affairs (which I have barely exaggerated in the telling) overlooked two ingredients—one conceptual, the other factual. An international rela-tionship is not a freestanding object, isolated from the day-to-day traf-fic of governmental business, a museum piece to inspire and edify. The Sino-British relationship was the aggregate of all the different ways in which we got along together, although naturally it was infused by inter-ests of all kinds, including culture and scholarship. The main impact on that aggregate of issues came from Hong Kong. Britain has not in re-cent history had any other significant bilateral relationship containing an element as substantial as Hong Kong. The Colony's economy was equivalent to one fifth of China's GDP, and in earlier years, before

China's growth accelerated through the mid-1990s, the proportion had probably been higher still. Had London and the Home Counties been a Chinese colony, we would ourselves have been inclined to see our relationship with the Eastern colonial power through that speculum. Without Hong Kong, how much would Britain matter to China? We were admittedly the largest European investor in China; China ran a large trade surplus with us; and we were both members of the UN Security Council. But none of this was anywhere near as important as one fifth of China's GDP. Some pimple! British foreign policy could have been excused for looking at our relationship with China from Hong Kong up, not looking at Hong Kong from Peking down. The city was not an aggravation to the otherwise smooth passage of business between the two countries. It was a major responsibility, as great as Britain had anywhere, and it was morally and politically incumbent upon us to discharge it honorably and competently.

The slight sense that Hong Kong was an awkward intrusion into grand diplomacy was ever present in parts of the Foreign Office. Here were these colonial subjects, rich but ungrateful, always whining about something or other, not content to allow London to get on with deciding their future, suspicious about Britain's honorable intentions and its intuitive understanding of the country from which they had fled, failing to comprehend the most unpalatable truth of all—that (as Conor Cruise O'Brien once put it) if the Chinese wanted to send the tanks into Hong Kong after 1997, they would do so and no one could stop them. Ministers could be intellectually comforted by one or two senior Foreign Office mandarins that, in flirting with such views, they were taking an intelligent and tough-minded view of what was in everyone's best interest, and they could be politically tranquilized in later years particularly by the purring acquiescence of much of the Hong Kong establishment.

The one thing that always most puzzled me was this: How could democratic politicians in Britain find it more comfortable to deal with the aging bureaucrats of the Chinese Communist party than with other democratic politicians in Hong Kong? After all, Hong Kong's politicians had one characteristic that should have warmed the hearts of senior British ministers in the 1980s and early 1990s. They were elected themselves, or at least could provide a great deal of evidence that if they had the chance of a fair election, they would enjoy a democratic mandate. Even before there were elections, could it have surprised anyone in London to discover that those who advocated the same values in their colony as were practiced in Britain would enjoy majority support from their fellow citizens? These are the sort of things that politicians are supposed to bother about. If elected politicians do not inject these value judgments into the discussion of foreign policy and other public policies, then the justification for having elected ministers at all is somewhat reduced.

The best example for me of these personal and political puzzles was the relationship between Geoffrey Howe and Martin Lee. Geoffrey Howe is a fine public servant, an imaginative and thoughtful administrator with usually perfect manners. Like Martin Lee, he is a lawyer, with a passion for the law's fine points and an unshakable commitment to the rule of law. Geoffrey Howe deservedly regarded himself as one of the main designers, when Foreign Secretary, of the Joint Declaration and all that accompanied it. He stands jealous guard over his reputation as watchdog of Hong Kong's best interests.

Martin Lee is the only man to whom I have ever seen this quiet Welsh barrister behave rudely. Lee and his fellow democratic politicians riled Howe—they questioned his motives; they attacked his understanding of China; they believed in dark conspiracies where all was said to be daylight; they demanded the diplomatically impossible; they made, so he thought, one hell of a fuss. But what, I used to wonder, if the roles had been reversed? Would not Howe's admirable instincts have pushed him, like Lee, to behave occasionally tiresomely in pursuit of freedom, even to behave irrationally in pursuit of the wholly reasonable? Lee could be infuriating, but he was infuriating to me and infuriating to Howe in a far better cause than either of us represented in Hong Kong, and Lee and his colleagues, unlike us, were putting their lives, their livelihoods, and their families on the line for what they believed.

The most significant thing, however, about Martin Lee, Emily Lau, Szeto Wah, Yeung Sum, Fred Li, Lee Cheuk-yan, Lau Chin-shek, Christine Loh, Margaret Ng, Lee Wing-tat, and all the other democrats was how thoroughly reasonable and extraordinarily moderate they usually were. I sometimes used to feel guilty that their sheer decency and civilized restraint allowed us to get away with far too much. The best known of the democrats internationally after Martin

Lee, and certainly the best exponent of the incisive sound bite, was Emily Lau. She was a tough professional politician, handsome, well informed, and dashingly eloquent, who would have gotten to the top in any Western political system. Her starting point was that Britain had let Hong Kong down by denying its citizens passports, and having then agreed to turn a free city over to a Communist tyranny, Britain had an obligation to enhance democracy and the protection of freedom there. These always seemed to me to be pretty good points. Asked to choose between Ms. Lau's view of the world and that of some of Peking's local "shoe shiners," the exponents of Asian values and of the benign purposes of the Chinese Communist party, I had no doubt which side I was on.

Martin Lee led a party whose political philosophy would, I suppose, have been neatly accommodated between the views of Tony Blair on the one hand and Robin Cook on the other, or between those of President Bill Clinton and Representative Dick Gephardt. They were neither socialist nor radical; the extent of their Jacobinism was to favor higher spending and lower taxes at one and the same time, which is to say they behaved like most other politicians around the world (with the difference that in Hong Kong their aspirations were deliverable!). They did not fight with fire; they did not chain themselves to railings, though perhaps even they would have been driven to do so had they gone on being ignored and excluded throughout the 1990s.

Martin Lee used to be jeeringly referred to as Martyr Lee by some in the business community, who will doubtless privately have their fingers crossed that it never comes to that. Martyrdoms would be bad for business. There was a certain intensity about Lee. If El Greco had painted the Chinese, Lee would have been a natural candidate for portraiture, cowled and burning-eyed. A deceptively gentle manner marked great inner strength, fueled by religious faith and buttressed by an ascetic lifestyle. He was more fun than this makes him sound, but never (thank heavens) a naturally "touchy-feely" politician. In happier days, he would have gone from a lucrative practice at the bar to a seat on the judicial bench. Perhaps, if those happier days come, it will happen yet. In any event, Hong Kong was lucky to have him.

For a Governor, it did not always seem like that. It was a strategic difficulty for the democrats to have a Governor who sympathized with their ambitions. The Chinese propaganda machine could easily paint them as British stooges, the Government House party, if they were too supportive. So they rightly kept their distance, with the result that whatever the findings of the opinion polls, it sometimes looked as though the Governor was on his own.

Occasional leaks and briefings from London—winks and nudges— that the Governor was indeed on his own, that he was being sidelined by ministers in their dealings with China, that "normal service" as far as Hong Kong was concerned would be shortly resumed, did scant justice to my overall relationship with the Foreign Office as an institution and with those who worked for it. I had always wanted to work in the Foreign Office and with diplomats. I never believed that, coming from the left of the Conservative party, I would have much of a chance of leading it. But I had always hoped that one day I might become Foreign Secretary. Maybe it is unseemly to parade one's ambitions, but there it is. I was interested in foreign policy issues (an interest sharpened by my experience as Overseas Development Minister) and particularly interested in the relationship between political and strategic matters and international economics. Many of the best thinkers and most agreeable companions I had encountered as a minister were diplomats, both senior and much less than senior. Britain had one of the best foreign services in the world, underpaid and overstretched but still enabling us (as Douglas Hurd would put it) to punch above our weight. I was enthusiastic about the chance of working with members of the diplomatic service in Hong Kong.

I was right to be enthusiastic. I was superbly served there, not least by the two principal diplomatic advisers who worked for me for the majority of my governorship. My main Foreign Office aide, Bob Peirce, was tough, witty, and enviably clever. He commanded considerable respect in the Hong Kong government for his sheer decency and informed concern about Hong Kong's future. His number two, John Ashton, had a highly developed sense of what an ethical foreign policy should mean, long before ministers started expressing their enthusiasm for one. He added his own broad and liberal intelligence to what was by any standards a formidable partnership. The problems came elsewhere. Let me deal with them generically, to avoid personalizing the issues. First, while most of the younger diplomatic sinologists, after spending many character-forming years in the trenches negotiating with Peking, had become hardheaded about China and the best way to do business with it, there lingered elsewhere in the Foreign Office vestiges of the old and very different orthodoxy. Unless we kept our wits about us, we could still therefore find policy hijacked or the information providing the evidence for policy judgments by ministers carefully skewed. The traditional faith was on the whole practiced in secret, underground, but I had little doubt that at the earliest opportunity it would rapidly become once again the established church, with its episcopal princes returned triumphantly to their dioceses. And so, after July 1997, it largely proved.

Second, there are some officials who equate diplomacy with being nice to foreigners, with finding the middle point between the two extremes of an argument, with discovering verbal formulas for obfuscating points of substance and difference. I am sure that these qualities have their place, but not in dealing with anything important and certainly not in dealing with China. We did occasionally suffer from the fact that past agreements with China had been left vaguely capable of different interpretations by both sides. Beautiful drafting at the time had gotten around roadblocks only to ensure traffic accidents later on the journey. The best diplomats are not like this at all. But because of our desire for order and neatness, not least on the international stage, and because of our competence, the British do have a tendency to bring enthusiastic emollience rather than clearheaded angularity to every issue. It is a habit of mind and action that needs to be watched, as it was—to her credit—by Margaret Thatcher.

Third, there was what I call the Head Office Syndrome. I guess this is much the same in any large multinational company. I posed a particular problem for the Foreign Office: I was not one of them. I was, as it were, a minister sent out to take charge of Hong Kong, admittedly under the overall direction of the Foreign Secretary. The chain of command was not quite as it would have been had I been another member of the foreign service. I was a friend of the then Foreign Secretary, Douglas Hurd, and had helped run his bid for the leadership of the Conservative party in 1990. I also had a different cultural background from that of my predecessors. Yet some of my difficulties were inherent in the relationship with the management back home. Other organizations face similar situations. An executive is sent out to take charge of a sensitive overseas operation with full authority to sort things out and run the business on the ground. After a while, when one or two problems arise, the board starts to wonder whether its executive out there has it quite right. "I wonder whether this and that have been considered quite as fully as they might have been? Has everyone on the spot been properly consulted? Why didn't such and such get done?" Imperceptibly at first, and then more openly, Head Office succumbs to the temptation and starts to second-guess and micromanage from the center. Meanwhile, the people on the ground become extremely frustrated. Should they make a fuss? Doesn't it all look rather petty if they do? If they appeal to the chairman, won't the chairman regard that as a distraction from more important issues? I began in Hong Kong without any of these problems at all, but by the end of my tenure we were experiencing a raging dose of doubtless well-meant and certainly enthusiastic Head Office-itis, complete with every imaginable sort of *Yes, Minister* bureaucratic ploy.

I doubt whether ministers had much to do with this, at least until the change of government from Conservative to Labour in May 1997. Thereafter, for the weeks that remained of my governorship, I was treated, understandably enough, with wary courtesy rather than as a trusted adviser. For the overwhelming majority of my time in Hong Kong, ministers invariably backed my judgment whenever there was an argument. But I was reluctant to put this to the test every time I felt that institutional creep was cramping our position there.

If responsibility for the government of Hong Kong, our last colony, challenged Britain's definition of its national interest, the discharge of that responsibility gave us a pretty clear idea of how other people saw their own national interest. It also indicated who really mattered in Asia. It would be nice to think that the European Union, given its historic connections in the region and its substantial investment there, could have made a collective and imaginative impact. It was not to be, despite the establishment in the mid-1990s of a forum for regular discussion between the Asian and European nations. The European Commission tried hard to develop a coherent European position on Asia. Successive presidents, Monsieur Jacques Delors and Monsieur Jacques Santer, and the vice president responsible for world trade and for Asia, Sir Leon Brittan, worked hard and enthusiastically to articulate a European strategy and to incorporate within it a continuing concern for the well-being of Hong Kong. They appointed an excellent representative to Hong Kong and built up the bilateral relationship between the Brussels Commission and the Hong Kong administration. Sir Leon Brittan himself was prepared to warn the Chinese against any trade discrimination against British firms because of the U.K.'s policy over Hong Kong. The European Parliament also took a welcome interest in the survival of civil liberties and democracy in the Colony.

Elsewhere, the gap between the rhetoric about a common European foreign and security policy and the reality that we witnessed on the ground was oceans wide. European ministers and governments were concerned about being tainted by Hong Kong in their dealings with China. With one or two honorable exceptions, like the Luxembourg Prime Minister, they were reluctant to say much, if anything, about the European interest in the survival of Hong Kong's freedoms in their contacts with Chinese officials. They did not want to "spoil the atmosphere." China played one European country off against another over trade and human rights, leading to the debacle in 1997 when several members of the European Union failed to back the Geneva Human Rights Resolution on China that all member states had previously supported. Nor was Europe inclined to be helpful over the award of visa-free access to Hong Kong citizens, a largely cost-free gesture that was routinely refused.

While European governments defended their inertia over Hong Kong by saying (correctly) that in the past Britain had clearly regarded the Colony as very much its own turf, they conveniently ignored more recent attempts to excite their interest. For most of them, the overriding concern was to stay on the right side of China. Insofar as they thought about Hong Kong at all, it was as an excellent export market for their goods. As a Francophile, I was particularly concerned to strengthen the relationship between Hong Kong and France. Visiting France in 1996, I found myself in a meeting with the Foreign Minister, Monsieur Hervé de Charette, pressing the French government to understand that it would send the wrong message to Hong Kong if the major European countries were to walk away from the Geneva Human Rights Resolution just before the handover of the Colony. We went back and forth for a few moments, and then M. Charette said, "But now let's turn to something that really matters, the duty you levy on our wines and cognac." I hoped he was joking.

From Hong Kong's perspective, the countries that really mattered were Japan and, particularly, the United States. The Japanese had always taken a keen interest in Hong Kong and its well-being. They were large investors. We had a big trading relationship. They sent a succession of their highest fliers from the Foreign Ministry as consuls general. They regularly raised concerns about Hong Kong's future with Chinese interlocutors. I found the Japanese skeptical about Hong Kong's continuance as a free international city, just as they were nervous about China's regional behavior and doubtful about its ability to emerge from its Communist chrysalis a beautiful capitalist butterfly. Residual anti-Japanese nationalist hostility in Hong Kong probably fed their doubts and fears about the Colony. Those who claim that the next century belongs to Asia have first to tell us how China and Japan are going to work out their relationship and when Japan is going to accept the more assertive regional and global role that its economic weight makes sometime inevitable.

Other countries had walk-on parts in our affairs from time to time. Canada had been especially supportive during the Mulroney years, opening its doors to Hong Kong immigrants and putting out the welcome mat for them. Despite the continuing friendliness of the Chrétien government and its avowed interest in human rights, we got the distinct impression that concerns about trade with China inhibited outspokenness about political issues on which China appeared sensitive. The Australian government, too, shifted its ground. When Gareth Evans was Australia's Foreign Minister, we received outspoken support that did not survive the change of government, genial though his successor proved to be. The China lobby appeared to get the upper hand once again in the Australian Foreign Ministry. Evans had carried off with aplomb a policy that rightly assumed there was no contradiction between playing a more positive role in Asia and standing up for the universality of human rights. He is an attractive man, highly intelligent, and articulate to the point of political peril. His wit and demotic eloquence regularly carry him into the very center of minefields, but they usually see him through to the other side without too many prosthetic requirements. Not all the foreign ministers I met were delightful company. Evans was. He smoothed the way for me to meet his Prime Minister, Paul Keating, during a visit to Australia, trying to convince Keating that I was not the right-wing blimp he expected. In the event, I had a good meeting with the Prime Minister, who was a bit surprised to discover that, like him, I came from Irish immigrant stock. Evans telephoned Keating after the meeting. "So what do you think now of the Tory weasel?" he asked.

The brightest star in our firmament was the United States. America is still the only big kid on the block, prepared to accept a global leadership role despite the fact that those who most benefit from it will rarely if ever concede that they have cause for any gratitude. For China, as for Japan, incomparably the most important relationship is that with the United States. It was therefore immensely valuable for us in Hong Kong that the U.S. administration, Congress, and much of the business community (especially as represented by the outstanding American Chamber of Commerce in the Colony) were regularly and unequivocally supportive. They understood, it seemed instinctively, that Hong Kong was the sort of Asian city which it was in America's interest to see survive—open to goods and ideas, living under the rule of law, practicing and believing in the values of a free society. Chinese men and women in Hong Kong, as in California and Taiwan, enjoyed and thrived on their liberties. Despite the suggestions by some local members of our business community that the Americans should not take any notice of what happened in Hong Kong except to give us the maximum trade advantages, and despite the equally maladroit claims to Americans from the same quarter that Hong Kong Chinese did not really care about issues like human rights, the United States at every level—from Washington to city halls, from Supreme Court justices to the heads of local bar associations—continued to take an active interest in Hong Kong and to speak up for Hong Kong on the international stage. When I consider, at the end of this book, the role of the Pacific Rim countries as we move into the next millennium, I will come back to the hopes that reside in American leadership and American espousal of the values of pluralism. The largest of the questions that hovered over the last years of colonial government on the south China coast was the extent to which those values would come to shape the rest of the continent at whose heart Hong Kong glittered.

PART TWO
The View from Hong Kong

"Is there one single maxim that could ruin a country?"
   Confucius replied: "Mere words could not achieve this.
There is this saying, however: 'The only pleasure of being a
prince is never having to suffer contradiction.' If you are

right and no one contradicts you, that's fine; but if you are
wrong and no one contradicts you—is this not almost a case
of 'one single maxim that could ruin a country'?"

—*The Analects of Confucius,* 13.15

4

Tiger Talk

Why should that apple always descend perpendicularly to the ground, thought [Sir Isaac Newton] to himself? Why should it not go sideways or upwards, but constantly to the earth's centre?

—William Stukeley, from *Memoirs of Sir Isaac Newton's Life*, 1752

I am writing these words a few months after sailing away from Hong Kong. I left Asia when the world's airwaves were still humming with "tiger talk," excited hype about Asia's recent economic record and future prospects. On the desk in front of me is a small pile of books cautioning the West—"Watch out: Asia is coming." On top of the pile is a recent book whose prologue tells me that its author, who plans to spend his graying years after 2020 with a smart town house in Shanghai (by then one of the richest cities in the world) and a weekend place in Bali (like Carmel or Provence by that time), believes that Asia's currencies are going to rise against every rich world currency except the yen. I hope he did not put his money where his laptop was.

In a few weeks over the summer and autumn of 1997, the tiger talk lost its voice; the hype turned to ashes. Indeed, ashes played all too large a part in Asia's life. As currencies and stock markets crashed all across the continent, the heavens darkened with banks of smoke from raging forest fires in Indonesia. Cronyism and institutional weakness in Jakarta precipitated an environmental disaster for the whole region. It exposed another aspect of Asia's "miracle." The BBC World Service reported that Malaysia had forbidden academics at its universities to make any more comments about the effect on their own country of their neighbor's environmental catastrophe lest the bad news should damage the tourist industry. If you are not allowed to say it or repeat it, it cannot have happened, and now we see the results from Bangkok to Jakarta to Seoul to Tokyo.

Clichés jostle for a place in the line. Hubris is always followed by nemesis; pride regularly precedes a fall; what goes up just as surely comes down. All that is true, but it would be folly to exchange all the bulls for bears, to allow overstatement of the Asian success story to be followed by overlooking just how much Asia has achieved and just how important it is to the rest of the world that Asia pick itself up and deal sensibly with its problems and keep moving forward. Perhaps the greatest truth for all of us—and that includes Asian leaders—to grasp about Asia is that the same laws of political and economic gravity apply to everyone, everywhere. The apples and the lychees descend perpendicularly on every continent.

Fascination with Asia in general, and China in particular, is as old as Western exploration of the East. The Venetian Marco Polo is said to have returned home from China at the very end of the thirteenth century with stories of a civilization far richer and more technologically advanced than anything that medieval Europe could then comprehend. He was nicknamed Il Milione, the man who talked in millions. The centuries have not dimmed the allure; the millions are still registered and admired. But predictions of Asia's—and in particular China's—coming global dominance have an unhappy track record. In the middle of the last century, an American Secretary of State, William Seward (best known for his purchase of Alaska from Russia), predicted that this present one would be the Pacific Century, and others said much the same in the following years. But bloody as it was for Europe, for Asia much of the twentieth century was even worse. At the end of it, more than half the world's population lives in Asia. They have suffered for a hundred years more than half the world's misery, a lot more than half the world's poverty; their economic statistics have lagged well behind their demographic numbers. For over thirty years now, that has been changing, slowly at first and then with quickening pace. It is an exciting story and it is good news for everyone.

I have carried with me for some time two Asian photographs, which tell different parts of the tale. The first of them used to hang on my office wall in Hong Kong. It shows the narrow end of a cheap, crudely built public-sector housing block in the city. The landings are packed with people. It was taken in a working-class district, Wong Tai

Sin, in 1965 during the Chinese New Year celebrations. The people were all looking down toward the street as a parade of lion dancers went past. It is a striking photo, full of action and laughter and the evidence that social history draws on: the poor clothing, the rough, unfinished cement on the walls, the graffiti, the cheerful sense of community solidarity—working people and their families, most of them probably refugees, taken out of themselves for a moment by the happy spectacle below. The people in the photograph—of every age from babes in arms to grandparents—are not rich; that is for sure. They are city strivers. They would have needed to be street-smart to survive and prosper in the tough economic climate of the day.

What would have concerned them? I used to wonder. What would they have worried about? The answer was obvious—rice-bowl issues. Their welfare. Their food. The roof over their heads—was it now safe from fire and landslide? How could they fit an aged parent into their tiny one-room apartment? What chance would their children have of getting into secondary school? How could they best treat the hacking cough they had had for years? Would they get a wage raise this year for making more plastic flowers and toys? How long would water rationing last this year? Would it be possible to get a place on the bus for an outing to the beach on the weekend?

Most of the people in that photograph must be still alive. Not all of them will be in Hong Kong; some will have emigrated. But most will be there and still worrying even now about economic and social issues. That agenda will have changed a good deal. Can they afford to repay the mortgage on their apartment? How can they get an elderly parent into a specially built apartment or a nursing home? Should they buy a new car this year? Can they get on a retraining course so as to move from the factory floor into an office job? How much will they have to contribute to help their student children pay their way through college? Can they manage a vacation in Malaysia this year or a trip to visit relatives in the United States? That is what growth and progress mean in a successful Asian city: Problems do not go away. They are, however, no longer the basic problems of survival.

The other photograph reminds me that to think of Asia as though it were one is wrong. The photograph comes from Bangladesh and is now ten years old. I had gone there as Development Minister in the wake of devastating floods, an environmental disaster caused (unlike

Indonesia's recent one) less by cupidity than by grinding poverty. We flew one day to see an Oxfam project to which my ministry was contributing. Oxfam was reequipping a group of villages from which the floodwaters had recently ebbed with basic agricultural implements and seeds, and the local peasant farmers were picking themselves up out of the mud and trying to put together again their wretched, impoverished lives. As we were leaving, we noticed an old lady in the crowd carrying a baby wrapped in rags. The baby girl's face looked as old as her grandmother's. She was dying of malnutrition. We persuaded the old lady to let us take the baby back to the hospital in the nearest town. Six months later, the Oxfam field workers wrote to me and enclosed a photograph. It was of a plump, smiling child—the baby saved, by strange chance, from dehydration and death. Saved for what, precisely? She will not be enjoying for the foreseeable future the fruits of an "economic miracle." Things may have inched forward since I was there, but Bangladesh is no tiger. So Asia is not homogenous, and its surging growth has passed some by. The first thing we should do when we discuss Asia's progress is define our terms geographically.

Asia is a rather Western concept: "east" or "sunrise," it means in the original Assyrian. The sun rises in the east on some very different countries, cultures, and economic stories. The Asian Development Bank, in the most hardheaded and useful of the surveys of Asia's economic and social revolution ("Emerging Asia: Changes and Challenges," 1997), while leaving Japan out of the picture, usefully distinguishes among the countries of East Asia—the original four tiger economies of Taiwan, South Korea, Singapore, and Hong Kong—those of Southeast Asia—Indonesia, Malaysia, the Philippines, and Thailand—standing on its own the People's Republic of China, and the South Asian countries—Bangladesh, India, Pakistan, and Sri Lanka. The East Asian countries have seen the most spectacular advance; Southeast Asia has been climbing fast, as has China; South Asia has lagged far behind.

The first two groups have seen years of double-digit annual growth, or at least growth rates in high single figures. As growth has propelled economies up the league tables, it has tended to decelerate. There appears to be a built-in touch on the brakes in the process of economic development. Yet even the more constrained growth figures of recent years in East Asia still look pretty sensational by modern European and American standards. The longest period for which we can make accurate comparisons covers 1965–90. During those years, GDP per head in Asia as a whole grew by 3.8 percent a year; in East Asia the figure was 6.7 percent (by comparison, in the United States it was 1.9 percent; in the United Kingdom, 2.1 percent; and in the European Union countries, 2.7 percent). At the beginning of the period, Asia's average income per head was 13 percent of the level in the United States; the figure had doubled to 26 percent by 1990. The figures for East Asia are still more spectacular. GDP per person soared from 17 percent of the figure for the United States in 1965 to approaching 70 percent in 1990. The trends through the 1990s have been similar, with the poorer performers in South Asia starting to do better and laying the basis for more rapid growth in the years ahead.

There have been some stellar Asian performers in the last three decades, like Singapore, Malaysia, and Indonesia. China, which first opened its doors to the global economy in the late 1970s, grew by an annual average of 9.3 percent in the 1980s and has topped 10 percent in the current decade. Hong Kong and Singapore have overtaken the average GDP-per-head figures of many of the world's richest nations. The real incomes per head of Asia's newly industrialized economies have gone up sevenfold in the last thirty years, and these economies' share of world trade has quadrupled. Most of the superlatives about this performance have been earned. It has been literally unique, in that there has been nothing quite like it before. Economic history has been well recorded for nearly two centuries, and during that period several countries have achieved short bursts of fast growth, or even rather longer stretches. No other countries have matched the sustained period of fast growth of several Asian economies since the mid-1960s. They have moved at a sprinter's pace for a marathon runner's distance.

We should look behind the economic statistics. What do leaps in GDP per head mean for the heads in question? Well, they live longer and healthier lives, and as mortality rates fall, so too do birthrates. If your children are more likely to survive their early years, you tend to have fewer of them. The infant-mortality figures in Hong Kong, to take one example, are now better than those of the United States. With economic growth come better diet and less disease. Literacy rates rise, and more children go first to primary school, then to secondary school, and finally are able to enroll in a growing tertiary sector of education. People are better housed. They have roofs that do not leak and, if they are lucky, clean water on tap. The sewage no longer runs raw in the streets. More families are lifted out of poverty, partly as more leave their villages and go to find work in the booming cities that are growth's main motors. More women are educated, marry later, survive childbirth, are spared some of the drudgery that accompanies poverty, find their own jobs outside the home, make and save their own money. This is what economic growth means. The West should not feel threatened, as some protectionists there clearly do, by Asians enjoying what Winston Churchill called "better pastures and brighter days."

The gleaming new skyscrapers of Asia's cities, the traffic jams, the busy airports, the industrial smog, the smart and expensive beach resorts, the acres of marbled hotel lobbies, the golf courses and driving ranges, the shopping malls splashed with the neon-lit names of designer chic, the beep of pagers in restaurants—all these things should also remind us that surging growth has created a large and growing Asian middle class. Economists predicted in mid-decade that by the end of the nineties there would be 400 million Asians with incomes equivalent to the average in today's rich countries, a threefold increase in the size of Asia's middle class in ten years. It is a huge market for every item of prosperous modern lifestyles—televisions, personal computers, telephones, cars, clothes, sports equipment, holidays, air travel, insurance, pensions, books and magazines, wines and spirits. First-growth claret is swilled by the magnum in Hong Kong, China, and some other Asian countries, even if it is sometimes mixed with 7UP. Hong Kong may be a slightly special case, described as it has been as the epitome of "shop-till-you-drop" capitalism (a reflection of the nineteenth-century description of the inhabitants of Manchester as the "shopocracy"). But where Hong Kong's credit cards lead the way, other Asian cities will never be far behind.

So—unique, spectacular, exciting, brimful of promise, Asia's economic story is all these things. But is it miraculous? I take it that this loosely used word is meant to convey the sense that what has happened has been not only at the furthest extremes of the extraordinary but that in some sense it is beyond conventional explanation, and as such conveys some hint of menace to those who have not been transformed by it.

One school would have us believe that the Asian tale has not been extraordinary at all and that even before the 1997 crash, it was stuttering toward its end. These pessimists, such as the distinguished American economist Paul Krugman, argue that Asia's so-called miracle is the "result of perspiration, not inspiration." Krugman compares the Asian economies to the Soviet Union's, arguing that their growth was the result of massive investment and a big switch in the labor force from farms to factories. He suggests that there has been no significant productivity gain in Asia as a result either of advances in technology or of changes in corporate or public-sector management and organization. Economic momentum has been achieved by the sheer weight of cash and labor, a process that cannot be repeated.

Before the crash, Krugman's arguments were furiously refuted. Some economists claimed that the productivity gains in Asia had been much greater than he suggested. Others pointed to the effectiveness of investment in Asia, to the skill of Asians in acquiring technology from elsewhere, and to the successful mix of macroeconomic and labor market policies followed by Asian governments. They argued that East Asian and Southeast Asian economies still had a lot of catching up to do, which they would take in their stride as the gap between the capital supporting their own workers and the much larger figures in the "old rich" countries started to close.

The events of 1997 and 1998 may have tipped the scales in favor of Krugman's vision of economic history. But it seemed to me that anecdote added its unscientific weight to the case that something rather more special than he suggests happened in Asia. What you saw in Singapore or Hong Kong, Taipei or Seoul, looked like much more than perspiration; it often looked pretty smart to me. It was not just the rolling up of sleeves that enabled Hong Kong to make so smoothly and successfully the transition from being a low-technology manufacturing center of cheap goods to being a higher value-added economy with services and the more profitable sectors of manufacturing most prominent. Inspiration as well as sweat went into creating Asian products that have often driven Western competitors off the shelves and counters. Economic managers in Asia like John Cowperthwaite in Hong Kong and Lee Kuan Yew's team in Singapore looked inspired in comparison with some of their perspiring Western peers. What is more, as hundreds of millions of Asians discovered market forces for the first time, they seemed to take naturally to capitalist entrepreneurialism, like West Indians to cricket or Puerto Ricans to baseball.

Nevertheless, there are two essential truths in the arguments that surround Paul Krugman's thesis, and they are more important to a comprehension of Asia's future than any dispute about productivity figures. First of all, as the second half of 1997 demonstrated in the spectacular market collapses throughout the region, Asia has not found a way around all the usual economic rules. Second, what has been happening in Asia is not alien. It is not in the literal sense a miracle. You cannot explain miracles; you can, on the other hand, explain Asia's economic advance (and its recent pandemonium). Asia's advance is wholly explicable: What has happened there is very similar to what has lifted every economy in the past off its agrarian knees, but the process has dramatically speeded up as technology has advanced. So miracles may have happened in Fatima and Lourdes, but there has been no economic miracle either in Asia or anywhere else.

The successful Asian economies have implemented a mix of similar economic and social policies that has helped them expand as it helped others do in the past. At the same time, we have seen extraordinary technological progress and the victory of liberal economics throughout most of the world. Taken together, these two constitute the heart of what we call globalization. This again is not something new. Eight of my late stepfather's uncles emigrated from Ireland in the early years of the century to find work in North America. They were part of the massive contemporary migration across frontiers in search of work and economic opportunity. They would have been surprised to be told that globalization was something that would be discovered at the end of the century. Those Irish economic migrants were making their way in a remarkably well integrated world economy. It is true that today we benefit from more tightly meshed financial markets, lower communication and mobility costs (of people, goods, and information), and a safety net of multilateral agreements. But before the First World War, the world economy worked in practice with gold as its single currency, and overseas investment by the richest developed countries was huge. Britain's capital investment abroad in those days was not far short of double figures as a percentage of gross domestic product. Today (or at least in 1996), it stands at 3.8 percent; and the comparable figure for the United States is 1.2 percent.

Liberal economics have opened the world's markets to Asia's goods, and technology quickened the rate at which the Asian economies were able to take advantage of that opening. In the 1960s the Nobel Prize–winning economist Gunnar Myrdal dispiritingly wrote off Asia's economic prospects, partly on the ground that in his judgment the epoch of rapidly growing export markets had ended. That prediction represents the reverse of what has happened. World trade has been growing in the intervening years by about 7 percent a year, and is in total today about ten times what it was in 1960. A much higher proportion of the world's output is exported today than before, and Asia's boom has been based largely on an aggressive and successful exporting strategy. The doors to Europe's and America's markets have been opened through the commitment in recent years to freer trade, achieved through multilateral agreements and the elimination of exchange controls on the import of services and goods. The number of countries that have scrapped such controls jumped from thirty-five in 1970 to 137 by 1997.

The foundations for Asia's prosperity are to be found on the counters of the department stores of America and Europe and on the warehouse shelves of their factories. Exports from East Asia grew at a rate of 11.8 percent a year during the 1960s; 24.6 percent during the 1970s; 9.5 percent during the 1980s; and 11.8 percent in the first half of the current decade, a result of deliberate government planning and policy. The growth rates of exports from the big and older industrial countries were much lower. East Asia's total exports to the rest of the world went up from $143 billion in 1980 to about $855 billion in 1995. The large and open American market is vital to most of the Asian economies. Exports to the United States add up to a third of Singapore's GDP, a quarter of Hong Kong's, and 16 percent of Malaysia's. In the 1980s, Chinese exports to the United States amounted to less than 1 percent of its GDP. That figure has now grown to about 5 percent, and China's trade surplus with America has shot up. American purchasing power keeps the wheels spinning right across Asia.

It was not enough for Asian countries to have access to increasingly open markets and to enjoy the reduced costs of communication provided by technological progress. To take an obvious comparison, some African countries had similar opportunities, but no one has been writing newspaper articles or making television programs about the African economic miracle. In the 1950s, in the last years of their struggle for independence, several African countries had more or less the same income level as Asian countries like South Korea and, in a number of cases, such as Congo, were far richer than East Asia in natural resources. Before its 1997 troubles, South Korea had a per capita income almost seventy times the $150 of the Congo. It had become the world's eleventh-largest economy. Some African countries are trying to learn from the Asian experience, copying the policies that characterized Asia's advance.

Those policies have enabled Asian countries to take the maximum advantage of the benefits of globalization, which—largely because of technology—come more rapidly these days. It took Britain about sixty years to double its output from the beginning of its economic revolution in 1780. It took the United States about fifty years to double output after 1840. Japan took thirty-three years after 1880. More recently, the pace of change has picked up sharply. Indonesia doubled output in seventeen years after 1965, South Korea did it in eleven years after 1970, and China in ten years after 1978. The process is faster, but it is still fundamentally the same process, not a miracle bearing an original Asian patent.

It is inaccurate to see Asia's success as a triumph for pure laissez-faire economics. The closest to the classic free market in Asia has been Hong Kong, and even there government has invested substantially in support of the health, housing, and education of its people and in the infrastructure of the city. Generally, governments have intervened in the economy and supported industry in ways that contradict the textbooks of such economics. However, they have not sought to take over the job of private business, and on the whole, they have not so distorted their economies by subsidy and intervention as to blunt industry's competitive edge. In most countries, private-sector business has been allowed to dominate the economy.

Private business in East and Southeast Asia has been kept competitive because of the emphasis placed on export promotion. Openness to world market conditions has ensured that Asian firms in these countries have to be fast on their feet, and rapid export growth has enabled them to import increasingly sophisticated technology. They have also benefited from the very high levels of investment that are the results of impressive domestic savings. In the quarter century to the middle of this decade, private investment represented about a fifth of GDP each year in South Korea, Indonesia, Malaysia, and Thailand, almost twice the figure for all developing countries together.

High savings and investment are themselves the result of the conditions created by East and Southeast Asian governments. They have benefited from a demographic bulge as the very young populations of the 1950s and 1960s have moved into the economically active, wealth-creating workforce. But above all it has been the success of frugal governments in keeping tax and inflation low that has left people with money in their pockets and encouraged them to save it. In a later chapter, I shall consider whether there are lessons in this for the West. For the moment, it is sufficient to point out that by avoiding the creation of a costly welfare burden for their taxpayers, Asian governments have helped create the growth which ensures that fewer people need welfare support. On the center left in Europe and America there is a fascination with the levels of Asian savings and investment. Any talk of low tax levels or the small proportion of GDP taken by the state in these countries as reasons for high economic growth there is rebutted by references to savings and investment, as though the savings and investment were conjured by governments from thin air. To discuss those economic benefits without considering where they come from and why they arise, to ignore the importance of small governments with small appetites, is like discussing why people choose to vacation in Florida or the Mediterranean without ever mentioning the weather.

East and Southeast Asian governments have spent and invested in some areas crucial to overall economic performance—in transforming their agricultural production (important outside the city-states of Singapore and Hong Kong), in improving basic health care, and in significantly raising education levels. One of the reasons why South Asia has lagged behind the rest of the continent is that it has put far fewer resources into programs of this kind despite decades of socialist rhetoric there about equality and fairness. In the fastest-growing Asian economies, the average number of years of education for children more than doubled in three decades from just over three in 1960 to nearly seven in 1990. This is about twice the rate of progress achieved in Latin America. Women have benefited particularly from this improvement, learning enhanced skills to take into the workforce on leaving school. Secondary-school enrollment has risen, especially in

East Asia. Overall, almost half Asia's teenagers are attending school; nineteen out of twenty of them will have been at primary school. Ninety-six percent of East Asia's population, excluding China, is now literate; the figures for Southeast Asia and South Asia are 86 percent and 50 percent, respectively. When American or European firms set up plants in Malaysia or Taiwan, South Korea or the Philippines, they do not have much difficulty in finding people with the basic skills to work on the production lines.

The booming Asia of the precrash years, constantly raising its game, outwitting many of the West's manufacturers, filling our business schools with its smart-as-a-whip young graduates, self-confidently throwing some of its newly acquired weight around, bragging about its values, buying more military hardware, assuring us that "we ain't seen nothing yet"—was all this a threat, as some politicians in Europe and American argued, more than enough to have us shaking in our ("Made in China") shoes? I admit to some conceptual difficulty with this whole question, which I have perhaps already betrayed by admitting that other people's good luck has never much bothered me. In the boom-boom days, I did not feel under siege from Asia's improved fortunes. For people who had been recently poor, often hungry, rarely literate, and frequently prone to life-threatening epidemic disease to have in the 1990s credit cards, full stomachs, subscriptions to *Forbes*, *The Economist*, and the *Asian Wall Street Journal*, and a good chance of living longer than I will seemed to me to be cause for celebration rather than perturbation. Good news for others is, in the aggregate, good news for us, too. That is most apparent when we consider trade, which is patently not a zero-sum game. I will look later at the powerful arguments against protectionism and in favor of free trade. For now it is sufficient to note that the figures given earlier in this chapter for Asia's exports should be accompanied by import figures as well. The surge we noted in East Asia's exports in the decade and a half from 1980 helped to pay for the sixfold increase in the value of the goods and services it bought from the rest of the world. In the memorable words of the first head of the World Trade Organization, Peter Sutherland, "If they can't sell, they can't buy."

I can naturally see that as the economic muscle of Asian countries in general, and China in particular, comes nearer to matching their demographic weight, this could prove a threat to the national security of Western democracies and the economic security of their citizens. On the other hand, some of these Asian countries were not exactly easy to live with when they were poor. We thought then, probably rightly, that their poverty helped spawn and sustain a political ideology that really did threaten our well-being. Growing prosperity has been nudging one country in Asia after another in a more hopeful direction.

Western worries about Asia are the perhaps inevitable consequence of exaggerations about what has been achieved there and what is likely to happen next. Such exaggeration was commonplace before Asian financial and stock markets went over the cliff in 1997. Trying in those pre-calamity days to put Asia's performance into context, focusing attention on the many reasons why there is no inexorable reason for Asia's growth to be exponential, was regarded then as a bit of a spoil-sport activity. Cold splashes of reality may not now be quite so necessary. But they are still useful in order to diminish some of the hostility that Asia's success has aroused and to encourage the development of public and commercial policies on Asia on the basis of the real world rather than a Disneyfied version of it.

We might best begin to sober up the debate by noting that what has been really happening in Asia is the recovery of ground lost over the last century or two. Asia is not springing forward from a position of strength but clawing back what was painfully forfeited. In the early decades of the nineteenth century, with Britain still in the throes of its Industrial Revolution, which really defined the beginning of the modern age, and with the United States about to embark on its similar economic journey, Asia still accounted for about 58 percent of the world's GDP. By 1920 this figure had been more than halved. Over the following twenty years, Asia's share fell further to 19 percent, though it was home to 60 percent of the world's population. Recent growth has now (1992 figures) almost doubled that figure to 37 percent. The Asian Development Bank believes that on what it described as "plausible assumptions" (which I hope are indeed still "plausible"), Asia could get back to slightly less than its early-nineteenth-century share of the world's wealth by 2025. It will have been a long journey back to "Go." The figures for the share of the world's output tell a similar tale, with Asia working hard to recover its 1900 position (of just under a third) by the end of the first decade of the next century.

The wide gap between Asia and the rich Western democracies has encouraged some critics of "tigerism," perhaps with tongue in cheek, to compare what they call the minnows of the East with the economic giants of Europe and America. Excepting Japan, they have a point. GDP figures put the idea of Asia as a threat to the OECD nations, or as an early competitor for global economic hegemony, into a rigorous statistical context. Britain, France, and Italy all have GDPs larger than China's; Germany's is almost twice, and America's between seven and eight times, the size of China's. Add together the GDPs of Hong Kong, Malaysia, the Philippines, Singapore, Taiwan, Thailand, Vietnam, and Indonesia and you still do not equal the individual sizes of France, Britain, or Italy.

If you divide overall GDP figures by population, the catch-up distance for Asia looks even greater. Wealth figures per head are probably the most reliable measure of relative prosperity. Allowing for a rising Asian population, and slackening growth as the economic advance in maturing economies decelerates, the Western lead looks even more impressive than is shown by a simple comparison of the aggregate GDP figures. All this reminds us that the history of the last century demonstrates that rich countries tend to remain rich and to retain their lead over the rest of the field. None of this belittles the progress made in Asia or the potential of Asia's markets. It does not imply that what is happening in Asia does not really change anything for the West. It merely serves as a useful correction to the more menacing or hyperbolic analyses.

These would come into the frame if exponentialism were the most accurate predictive tool in Asia. All those lines on the Asian graph paper—growth, exports, real incomes per head—have been heading north at a spectacular rate, and if you simply assume that past compounds into future then—hey, presto—you can demonstrate mathematically how swiftly Asia will surge past the European and American laggards. The clever thing to do is to predict when the lines on the graph paper are going to turn down or when their ascent is going to flatten. Slowing down and flattening always happen sometime. Bankers and investors can get poor very quickly if they fail to understand this, but can earn, on the contrary, a decent return on their money and a reputation for being savvy if they do. When I made these points in speeches from 1994 to 1997, it tended to provoke a certain restiveness in the audience. Here was the Governor of Hong Kong, brought in to lecture about Asian wonders, and he sounded—as P. G.

Wodehouse might have put it—like a Scotsman with a grievance. I suspect that some regarded me as woefully deficient in house spirit.

Asia's exponential rise hit the skids in the summer and autumn of 1997 beginning with the devaluation of the currency in Thailand. It had been both predictable and predicted, for example by *The Economist* magazine. Warnings had been largely ignored as Asia fever got the better of informed judgment. The trouble, once it had started, spread quickly. Markets plummeted, currencies crashed, debts soared, projected growth rates were slashed, governments fell, reputations were ripped to shreds—from Pollyanna to Cassandra in the space of a few anxious weeks. The rest of the world watched, increasingly nervous about the prospects of the contagion spreading beyond the region. Where in the first half of 1997 some in the West had worried about the threat of Asia's success, by the year's end they were wringing their hands about the perils of Asia's failure.

The proximate cause of the smash-up was the steep rise in the cost of borrowing for heavily indebted Asian governments, and particularly Asian companies as the dollar strengthened against their national currencies. The strain snapped one illusion after another; fundamental financial economic and political weaknesses were exposed. Thailand, Malaysia, Indonesia, and South Korea were hit hard. The markets paid little attention to the fact that Singapore, Taiwan, and Hong Kong were fundamentally in healthier shape; they were affected as well, with Hong Kong under intense pressure as the crucial link between its currency and the U.S. dollar was put to the test. The dynamos seemed transformed into dominoes.

As always happens, the markets exaggerated. When the elevator of market approval is ascending, loaded with bankers, investors, and shysters, it usually travels several floors beyond the level at which the sensible should choose to alight; descending, it deposits its passengers in the basement before they can press the button for a higher floor. Finance ministers and central bankers have been considering what they can do to limit the damage when the tide of economic fortune suddenly ebbs and huge capital movements are triggered by shifts in market sentiment. They talk about putting in place a new international financial architecture to try to protect us all from the imperfections of market forces. The measures proposed include getting the private sector to take more of the strain of financial crises, tougher supervision of banking systems in developing countries, and greater transparency nationally and internationally over financial data, which would give us more and clearer warning about incipient problems and make it easier to take precautionary action before it is too late. None of this should do any harm, and some of it may even do a bit of good. But it is not going to prevent further financial breakdowns. Technology has added immeasurably to the speed and scale with which disaster can strike, and the foolishness that has characterized every business crash since the tulipomania of the seventeenth century cannot be legislated out of existence by well-intentioned global concordats. Change the architecture by all means, but do not let us delude ourselves that we have changed the nature of commerce. There have, for example, always been foolish bankers (who had in the Asian crisis, as in others, plenty of forewarning of pending trouble—bad debts, growing property speculation, asset bubbles, and so on). Barring selective divine intervention, foolish (and overpaid) bankers are here to stay.

The chances of a reasonably swift recovery in Asia, such as had picked up Latin America after the Mexican crash, do not look good. There, the United States and U.S. banks were able to help lead the recovery. Japan, which might have been expected to do the same for Asia, has been hampered by its own financial problems. The world's biggest creditor nation is mired in financial problems and scandals, with the "you scratch my back and I'll scratch yours" relationship between its ill-regulated banks and financial services and its corporate sector aborting every effort to recover from slump.

Consternation at the sudden discovery in the autumn of 1997 that they should not have believed their own propaganda brought howls of rage from some Asian government leaders. Western speculators were targeted as the malign external agents of an imperialist conspiracy to halt Asia's rise in its tracks. Dr. Mahathir Mohamad, Malaysia's populist Prime Minister, took the lead in laying the blame for the region's rendezvous with reality at the door of George Soros, or, perhaps, "the Jews," who can rarely have been more improbably scapegoated. As ever, markets found themselves the villains when "buy" turned into "sell," when "invest" turned into "withdraw." The French, true to a mercantilist tradition in which the mighty dollar has frequently been a favorite whipping post, rallied egregiously to Dr. Mahathir's side; others hoped that Mahathir's deputy, the respected Mr. Anwar Ibrahim, would rescue Malaysia from his folly, while the British remembered a little shamefacedly that it had not been all that long ago that their own late Prime Minister Harold Wilson had blamed sterling's problems on "the gnomes of Zurich." Trying to shift the blame for one's own mistakes onto others is a universal characteristic.

There were slightly different contributory causes to the debacle in each country, but two basic and common ones. The first was a failure to remember the importance of economic fundamentals. In several countries, weak regulation of banks had allowed them to become hopelessly overextended with huge burdens of nonperforming loans. The bad loans weighing down Southeast Asia's banks were thought to represent about 15 percent of the region's GDP, though the figure may well have been higher. Banks had gotten too close to politicians, and to governments too. In some cases they were open tills for politicians; in others they were part of a system in which the allocation of credit had been hopelessly politicized. Too much cash was being poured into speculative property developments; too much investment was being directed to inflated prestige projects—highways, dams, industrial parks, airports. Second, the development of Asia's economies and their increasing sophistication raised expectations about them, and placed demands on them, for greater openness and accountability, which their systems of government were unable to satisfy. These economies were in many cases somewhere en route between quantity-led and quality-led growth—that is, between the growth that comes from the massive exploitation of human and natural resources through large-scale investment and the growth that provides greater added value from knowledge-based industries and services. In this more complex stage of development, economic freedom on its own is not enough to unlock all the talent that a drive for quality demands; I shall return in a later chapter to this argument.

Put bluntly, a number of Asian economies had outgrown their political structures, a point made by many Asians themselves as they surveyed the economic messages in the winter of 1997–98. Anwar Ibrahim noted in a speech in February 1998 that Asian leaders had suppressed democracy, played favoritism, and condoned corruption for too long. He expressed himself "thrilled" that Asian countries would now have to undertake effective reforms, transform their societies, and make their governments more transparent and answerable.

Politics had not been rendered a nugatory activity by Asia's advance; more sophisticated political parameters and behavior were required to allow more sophisticated economies to thrive and prosper. In Thailand, events highlighted both the economic and the political reasons for the crisis. A Bangkok newspaper headline plaintively pleaded, FINANCE EXPERT URGENTLY NEEDED. At the same time, newspapers reported the growing public pressure for a new constitution that would increase the transparency of economic management and would also target corruption. In many Asian countries the "fundamentals" were defied by graft and nepotism; they distorted economies and perverted good economic management. To defeat them required more accountable government, not more authoritarianism. Asia's 1997 crisis demonstrated the limits of authoritarianism in promoting successful free economies.

It was in addition a salutary reminder that, however remarkable and rapid Asia's economic progress had been, it could not be counted on to continue indefinitely, free of problems, and blessed by a comprehensive Oriental good fortune. Asian countries face formidable short- and long-term problems. Solving them will require skilled and subtle political leadership, capable of mobilizing public consent for changes (sometimes painful) that are often themselves the result of past success or the necessary prelude to future progress.

Demography poses two sorts of problems for Asia, which will test political skills in different ways. Usually more people have lived in Asia than in the other continents. At present about 3 billion live in Asia, just over half the world's population. This represents an increase of 1 billion in only two decades, in comparison with the million-year period that it took the world's population to rise from zero to its first billion. Economic growth has been accompanied, as we noted earlier, by the change from high to low birth and death rates, and the profile of the population has changed too. In East Asia in particular, the high proportion of very young people in the population in the 1950s and the 1960s entered the workforce in the subsequent decade or so; and this sharp increase in the number of those who were economically active was one of the reasons for the high savings and investment rates in those countries. In the early years of the next century, there will inevitably be just as fast a rise in the number of the retired. Improved lifestyles and better health will ensure that this increase is further enhanced, and lower birthrates will give a further boost to the proportion of the total population who are retired. In China the share of the population over sixty will double from 9 percent to 18 percent in only thirty-three years; in Singapore that will happen in just seventeen years. These are dramatically abrupt changes.

Care of the elderly will put great pressure on the family and the state, especially as the number of the very elderly (kept alive by better medical care) goes up as well. The government in Singapore reacted by passing the Maintenance of Parents Act in 1995, compelling children to take care of their parents if they could not look after themselves. This suggested that the acceptance of traditional obligations in extended families was fraying at the edges. Most important, however, will be the financial impact of paying for large retired populations in Asia. Pension funds have not played much of a role in most Asian economies so far, and will presumably need to expand dramatically in the future. Unless Asian governments establish good and well-managed savings programs for retirement, their own savings and investment figures will nose-dive and there will be a worldwide shortage of capital for investment. The graying of Asia's population is also bound to increase pressure for establishing or expanding state-funded health and welfare programs. Politicians will be pushed to increase spending on such objectives at the same time that growth may well be moderating; the state's take from national wealth could therefore mushroom. It may not be only European and North American politics that are dominated in the future by debate about the relationship between economic vitality (with high savings and low tax) and social cohesion (with—so the argument goes—higher public spending and bigger welfare programs).

The other demographic problem is the rise in the population of the towns and cities of Asia. Cities are the main agents of growth, and will attract greater migration from rural areas as the disparity between urban and rural incomes widens, as increases in agricultural productivity reduce the need for rural labor, and as industry demands more labor in urban areas. The Asian Development Bank has calculated that 55 percent of Asia's population will be urbanized by the end of the first quarter of the next century, compared with 35 percent in 1995. Even by the turn of the century, twelve of the world's twenty-five largest cities are likely to be Asian.

This rapid urbanization is one reason for the huge need for Asian infrastructure investment on, for example, urban transportation, sewage treatment, and water supply. The infrastructure requirements of Asia are variously billed by the World Bank and others at $1.5 trillion over the next decade to $10 trillion over the next thirty years. Managing investment on this scale will test government competence. In Hong Kong we were able to manage a vast infrastructure program and to attract funds to it—because the civil service was both competent and clean, because there was little or no politicization of the award of contracts, and because private investors could be attracted by the prospect of a reasonable rate of return on their investment. These conditions are the exception rather than the rule in Asia. In Indonesia, the family of former President Suharto was heavily involved in the allocation of infrastructure franchises. In China and India, there is still a reluctance to allow private investors fair rates of return. Elsewhere in Asia, the stock market has not historically been used much to raise the cash for infrastructure development. Failure to address these problems will choke off growth, as well as choke the inhabitants of heavily polluted cities. Traffic jams congeal from Bangkok to Seoul; power failures and brownouts plunge cities into darkness and halt production lines; air pollution worsens; water quality deteriorates. Thirteen of the fifteen most polluted cities in the world are in Asia.

The coincidental environmental and financial crises in 1997 had similar causes. As we noted earlier, the smoke that rose from Indonesia's burning forests and darkened the heavens across neighboring countries was a direct result of government that is neither open nor accountable, and of relations between political leaders and businessmen that are too close for everyone else's comfort. Crashing financial markets and health-threatening environmental disasters may find their remedies in similar reforms. Without political change, Asians seem doomed to many more years of environmental calamity even as growth increases their incomes. Rivers and coastal waters will be as filthy as the air, cities will be clogged with traffic, forests will be slashed and burned, land will be degraded.

Nowhere is this more true than in China, whose very size and speed of industrialization pose horrific environmental problems. Environmental writers reckon that damage to land, air, and water is already consuming 15 percent of China's national product, a far higher figure than the total combined state budgets for education, health, science, and culture. Urban air pollution figures are ten to twenty times those for the United States. In the early years of this decade, only about a third of the Chinese population had easy access to unpolluted water, and the figure seems unlikely to improve much soon. Land is being lost to erosion, desertification, and industrial development at a worrying rate, and too high a proportion of the vegetables grown on it are contaminated by pesticides. Hong Kong's environmental record was nothing to brag about. But as one flew into the city from the West on a clear day and looking north to the Pearl River Delta saw the horizon apparently painted a greenish yellow by a giant brush, one realized how relatively fortunate one would shortly be to breathe Hong Kong's dirty air rather than Guandong's. The haze of particulate filth hangs low over China, an ominous sign of problems ahead.

China stands four-square and five-starred at the heart of the most significant of all the issues that will determine Asia's way ahead and the future success of the Asian economies. How will the region, and China above all, cope with political transition in the coming years? This does not mean just the problems of succession, one president or prime minister or party secretary replacing another; it means the adjustment of Asian politics to the social and economic change recently unleashed. There will be problems for both the more and the less democratic Asian governments; but as South Korea has demonstrated in 1998, more representative forms of government are invariably better at handling change relatively smoothly and peacefully. There is a system that can accommodate disruption constitutionally. What will be the constitutional means for organizing and channeling the arrival of a new political order in the wake of President Suharto's abrupt removal from office in Indonesia? Is there some way of changing gears in that country that does not have a military hand on the gear lever? And if these questions are difficult to answer in Indonesia, how on earth does one begin to address them in China?

It is self-evidently difficult to generalize about more than a billion people and their system of government in a vast country encompassing such a variety of social and economic experience, the inheritors of an astonishing culture and civilization, the subjects of the last of our century's terrible experiments in hope through tyranny. Yet living on their doorstep for years, observing their public and private behavior, negotiating with their leaders, listening to and reading the real and the self-styled experts on their history, politics, and way of life, I became increasingly convinced (as I shall argue at greater length later) that we tend to be so obsessed with the differences between China and other places and cultures that we overlook the many similarities. I do not believe that life has written different laws for the Chinese, that the customary interactions of politics, economics, and social change are somehow reordered when they apply to China. Decency is decent everywhere; honesty is true; courage is brave; wickedness is evil; the same ambitions, hopes, and fears crowd around and result from similar experiences in every society. Naturally, much that happens in China is opaque to outsiders, and even to the Chinese themselves; the day-to-day political struggle takes place behind the palace walls of Peking. So Chinese politics are difficult to fathom for the same reason that totalitarian politics are always mysterious and murky. Who really knows who is up and who is down? Who accurately predicted the surprising defenestration of the Communist party's intelligent number three, Qiao Shi, at the last Party congress? Observing Chinese politics is a little like a nonsailor watching a yachting regatta. One is aware that there is a race in progress, but one has no inkling of whether it has just started or is about to finish, of who is in the lead and who is the back marker. There is, plainly, a good deal of colorful maritime activity, but heaven knows what it all means.

While that is true of the prosaic struggles of Peking politics, I doubt whether the bigger and broader political canvas is so difficult to see and to understand. You do not have to be a Marxist to believe that economic development produces social transformation and leads to political change. The failure to adjust political structures to what is happening elsewhere in society means that governing authority becomes an increasingly brittle carapace. The leadership of government may be stable but—as in China—there is not much evidence of stability lower down.

These points were cogently made by Zhao Ziyang, the Communist party leader who was dragged down by his colleagues for taking too moderate a position on the Tiananmen students' demonstrations in 1989. Five years after the event, the respected *Hong Kong Economic Journal* published the authentic transcript of Zhao's speech (minus a section on democracy) in which he defended himself before his peers for his handling of the Tiananmen crisis and the events that preceded it. It is worth quoting extensively because it goes right to the heart of the predicament that Chinese leaders currently refuse to confront; on the quandary that threatens to wreck the system that sustains them, they are "in denial."

> *Reform includes the interaction between reform of the economic structure and reform of the political structure. As I now see it, in addition to reform of the economic system and economic development, socialism must also demonstrate its superiority in the political system and the problem of democracy. In the course of practice, in relation to reform of the economic system, I felt more and more keenly that reform of the political system should neither outstrip it nor fall behind, but rather that the two should, on the whole, proceed at the same pace. I used to think that—so long as we did well in reforming the economic structure, developing the economy, and people's living standards went up—then the people would be satisfied and society would be stable. But as I later discovered this is not the way things are.*
>
> *After living standards and cultural levels have been raised, the people's sense of democracy and sense of political participation will grow stronger. If ideological education fails to keep up, and if the building of democracy and the legal system fails to keep up, then society will not be stable. Last December, I said at a military conference that—as is clear from the conditions in many countries— economic development often cannot automatically bring about a people's contentment, satisfaction, or social stability. I feel this presents us with two problems: first, we must persist in grasping with both hands and not overlook work in the ideological-political spheres. Second, reform of the political system—the building of socialist democracy and the legal system—must catch up [with the reform of the economic system].*

Zhao's argument is surprising only because it was expressed by a Chinese Communist leader. In effect, he was stating what most observers assume to be the fatal flaw in the strategy of Peking's market Leninists. Just because China is the country in question, there is no reason to suppose that it is possible to open up the economy while keeping an iron grip on politics. As Margaret Thatcher argued in a speech in Peking in November 1996, "I do not believe that in the long term [China] will be immune from the same processes which have affected its neighbors." Rising living standards, to borrow from Mr. Zhao, will strengthen "the people's sense of democracy."

Chinese Communists embarked on capitalism because communism had so manifestly failed, and its failures threatened to topple the Party from power. With their governmental competence questioned and their moral authority in tatters, Deng and his supporters argued through the late 1970s and the 1980s that in order to retain its control of China, the Communist party would have to show that it could after all make people better off. The only way it could accomplish that was by modernizing China, introducing capitalism and throwing the country's doors and windows open to the outside world. Deng's opponents argued that, far from saving the Party and preserving its control over society, economic liberalization would destroy it. China's inescapable dilemma is that both sides in this argument are right.

Improvements in the living standards of parts of China, and parts of Chinese society, have bought time. To many Chinese, as Perry Link has argued, "Shut up and I'll let you get rich" seemed about as good an offer as the Chinese were likely to get from their government. They preferred the freedom to make money to the absence of any freedom whatsoever. But this does not seem a solid long-term foundation for Communist party rule. Problems crowd in on every side. There are tensions between the "get rich quick" regions, principally in the south and on the eastern seaboard, and the poorer Chinese hinterland. There are also tensions between those groups in society that have been touched by the "feel-good" factor and those who live impoverished on the fringes of society or who find themselves trapped in jobs that cannot benefit from capitalism with Chinese characteristics. The egalitarianism of rationed joy and shared hardship has been replaced by jungle-law capitalism; the egalitarian spirit of those who get left behind will have developed a sharper edge and a sourer taste. Social instability bubbles away. Corruption is pandemic, with imperceptible distinctions between graft, fraud, organized crime, and accepted business practice. Violent crime stalks town and countryside. Ask a Hong Kong businessman whether he would be happy to drive home through Guangdong at night. Despite being far and away the world's number one center for capital punishment, China is plagued by kidnappings, drug traffic, violent robberies, the sale of people (male children, for example), and the organization of illegal immigration to Europe and the United States. In the last few years, there has been a growing number of reports of unrest in the countryside and labor disputes in the cities, on whose outskirts dwells an army of migrant labor.

This touches the issue that more than any other encapsulates China's dilemma, and that will have a profound effect on the whole of Asia. China has moved with praiseworthy speed from North Korean economics to something resembling a capitalist economy. It has opened up to the world and encouraged investment in capitalist development on green-field sites, the raw and gouged earth of Guangdong, the industrial estates of the Pudong in Shanghai. The next stage of the economic journey is more difficult. It involves dismantling, slimming down, privatizing, making profitable the state-owned enterprises that are the legacy of Mao's China. This is the task that proved so difficult in the constituent parts of what was once the Soviet Union and in the countries of its European empire. Failure to tackle, for example, the problems of the "smokestack corridor" in Manchuria could thwart economic progress elsewhere.

Chinese economic statistics are notoriously unreliable. The most commonly used, and perhaps therefore credible, figures about the socialized industry crisis are these: There are probably about 110,000 medium- and large-size state-owned firms. At least half of them are losing money. They employ about 120 million people, of whom about 50 million are thought to have no useful work to do. Lending from the state banks to these firms is hollowing out China's banking system, which it would probably cost about 25 to 30 percent of China's GDP to recapitalize. This makes the quicksand of Japanese banks seem like pretty firm ground. China's high savings are in effect drained away each year to bail out the money-losing state enterprises, which swallow three quarters of the country's investment but deliver well under half its industrial production. This is why China is so crucially dependent on attracting foreign investment, which has clearly peaked and is now falling. That will intensify the pressure to sort out China's big industrial losers.

A channel recently used quite successfully for attracting outside investment into quasi-privatized state firms was the flotation of Chinese companies, reflecting various collections of assets from tourist access to the Great Wall to cell phone franchises, on the Hong Kong stock exchange as so-called red chip shares. Early enthusiasm about these shares bore little relationship to any proven managerial record in maximizing the return on the assets that were aggregated in each shop-window company. The market price appeared to reflect the assumption that Chinese assets would be in effect stripped—knocked down to bargain-basement prices for the benefit of Hong Kong shareholders (with some of the sugar sticking to the fingers of the original managers). You did not have to be an experienced China watcher to deduce as well that your red chip company would be given any number of inside tracks to further strippable assets. The Hang Seng's crash in the wake of the crisis in the rest of Asia both exposed the questionable financial judgments behind these investments and reflected the fact that many of the red chips were distinctly tatty offerings to shareholders. This experience will make it more difficult to attract investors' interest in future attempts to float Chinese companies on the Hong Kong stock market. Investors will be far choosier, and China's economic managers will need to be more careful about what exactly they bring to market.

So the ability to buy time or elbow room in sorting out the state-owned enterprises is draining away. The radical measures promised at the last Party congress will have to be taken. More plants will have to close; millions of jobs will have to go; more "iron rice bowls"—the comprehensive, if basic, social provision promised to China's workers—will have to be shattered. How much pain can a totalitarian government inflict? Can China take on this biggest problem of all in its economic liberalization without an accompanying dose of political pluralism, both to reestablish the moral authority that governments need in order to do unpopular things and to provide the safety valves for letting off the huge head of steam that will have built up in the loss-making state giants and the communities that they have served? As the Chinese dissident Wang Dan (released from prison and exiled to America in the spring of 1998) wrote in 1995, "The Chinese government could reduce the chances of [the reform of state industries] leading to social unrest by allowing political reforms that would give the public a chance to express its dissatisfaction through democratic channels." This is the greatest economic and political question facing Asia as a whole. Its solution will require the new Prime Minister of China, Mr. Zhu Rongji, to be even better than the adulatory foreign press coverage he has received (and to some extent deserved) has made him out to be. But whatever his formidable managerial skills, it seems unlikely that some uniquely Asian set of principles and characteristics will see China smoothly around this double chicane, on its untroubled way to becoming a sort of Singapore writ mighty large on the global stage. That, however, is what some people would have us believe.

5

Asian Values

Jieyu, the Madman of Chu, went past Confucius, singing:
    "Phoenix, oh Phoenix!
    The past cannot be retrieved,
    But the future still holds a chance.
        Give up, give up!
    The days of those in office are numbered!"
Confucius stopped his chariot, for he wanted to speak with him, but the other
hurried away and disappeared. Confucius did not succeed in speaking to him.
—*The Analects of Confucius*, 18.5

Well, then, a commonwealth is the property of a people. But a people
is not any collection of human beings brought together in any sort of
way, but an assemblage of people in large numbers associated in an
agreement with respect to justice and a partnership for the common good.
The first cause of such an association is not so much the weakness of the
individual as a certain social spirit which nature has implanted in man.
—Marcus Tullius Cicero, from *The Republic*

I first met Lee Kuan Yew, the Senior Minister and Sage of Singapore, in July 1992, when I was traveling to Hong Kong to assume the governorship. Since my predecessor in the 1970s, Lord Maclehose, had made the same stopover on his journey to take up the job, this call had been an almost mandatory part of the ritual for new Governors. It reflected an admiration for the many achievements of this Asian city-state, an acknowledgment of the similar problems faced by the two most prosperous largely Chinese cities in the East, and—I suspect—a sort of unspoken understanding that Singapore represented the soft authoritarianism that Hong Kong could expect, and should even conceivably wish for, as its future.

I had two long conversations with Mr. Lee, the first in his office and the second over dinner at the British High Commissioner's house; it was the first time he had visited there for many years. Mr. Lee has a broad and clear intellect, and he uses words with the precision that demonstrates how hard he has thought about what he is saying. He has views on everything. Whether he has, as the Asian-currency-touting author of the book referred to in the last chapter describes him, "probably the most lucid and powerful intellect of any English-speaking political leader of the second half of the century" is a matter of nice judgment. He is certainly impressive, and it was kind and courteous of him to give me so much of his time, both then and on subsequent occasions. Our relationship was, I fear, intellectually fractious. "At least," Henry Kissinger once growled to me, "he doesn't think you're stupid." Maybe not, but he thought I was wrong—wrong about Hong Kong, about China, about freedom and democracy in Asia (perhaps everywhere), and about their relationship to economic success and human decency and satisfaction. I think that what I did in Hong Kong and what I said there and elsewhere were regarded by Mr. Lee as an almost personal affront, an attack on the very foundations of his philosophy of government. Just as there were "old China hands" in London who were willing us to fail in Hong Kong lest success—or at least the absence of any dramatic crash—should raise questions about the policies they had previously crafted, so Mr. Lee may not have relished the sight of another Chinese city, free, democratic, stable, and successful. Hong Kong's vitality was a sign that social engineering and an iron fist were not essential to success in a city of Chinese migrants.

There are two incidents that give the flavor of my relationship with Senior Minister Lee and of my argument with him and others. Shortly after I had delivered my first policy address, Mr. Lee visited Hong Kong, where he was (by his standards) moderately complimentary about what I had said and noted on the record that my constitutional proposals appeared to have ingeniously filled the gaps in the Joint Declaration and the Basic Law. He very kindly added: "The last thing I need to do is make Mr. Patten's job any harder; it is hard enough as it is." By the time of his next visit, after some weeks of full-throttle propaganda from Peking and backstabbing from one or two retired diplomats in London, Mr. Lee had changed his tune. I was invited to chair a public lecture that he had been asked to give at Hong Kong University.

The lecture was a worthy, slightly prosaic account of the respective histories of Singapore and Hong Kong over recent years. Afterward, Mr. Lee returned from the podium to sit next to me and answer questions, the first of which concerned whether Hong Kong deserved democracy. He produced from an inside pocket the makings of a second lecture—notes, clippings, and quotations—and proceeded to deliver an answer almost as long as his only slightly more prepared earlier remarks. The burden of his argument, laced with quotations from my critics, was that my proposals were part of a much wider American plan to bring democracy to China, a game in which Hong Kong was a mere pawn. I was the mouthpiece, but the plot was scripted by the United States. I sat patiently and poker-faced by his side as he delivered himself eloquently of this rubbish, which was sufficiently drawn out for me to be able to reflect at length (as doubtless have others) on which particular aspect of Singaporean values covers being so regularly rude and unhelpful to your hosts around the world. I limited my response to the observation that I hoped one day to have the right of reply—in Singapore.

Mr. Lee's copious recourse to the freedom of speech guaranteed in Hong Kong, a city where critics of the government are not pursued by defamation suits through the courts, sent exactly the wrong message to Peking, whose conspiracy theorists doubtless took what this international statesman said as proof positive that their paranoia about my modest plans was well founded. If any further hardening in China's position was possible, the Senior Minister must have helped it along.

The second incident tells more about me and the nature of my disagreement with Mr. Lee and others than it does about him. At a dinner party in Hong Kong with a group of genial businessmen, Chinese and expatriate, I was trying to demonstrate that because of the rule of law in Hong Kong and the nature of the statutory protection given to people's liberties, there were some attitudes that I was properly obliged to eschew. I recalled a discussion with Mr. Lee about how Singapore had dealt with its triads. He had said that several hundred of them had been locked up under a colonial regulation that he had retained. "Several hundred?" I responded. "Were they really all triads?" "Probably," replied the Senior Minister. I noted that whether or not I could ever imagine myself giving this reply, I would not be able to do so in Hong Kong. A similar reply there would have placed me very firmly off-limits. I subsequently learned that one of the other guests, an

American-educated Chinese man, had concluded after I left that this just proved that I did not understand Asian values, while another, who was British, had argued that this was the sort of do-gooding, lily-livered approach which would ensure that Western society went to the dogs while Asia rose and rose again. In discussing "Asian values," it is as well to remember that East and West are to be found on both sides of the argument; there are proponents of something very like Asian values in Europe and North America, arguing that "things aren't what they used to be; what we need is a bit more discipline." There are aspects of this argument with which, as I shall argue, I have a modest sympathy, but that does not encourage me to subscribe to the arguments that "tigerism" has its own coherent value system and that economic success is enhanced by a modicum of political repression.

Were it not for the ubiquity of the argument about Asian values, its convenience as an excuse for Westerners to close their eyes to abuses of human rights in Asia, and the extent to which it raises legitimate questions for every society about how to retain individual and communal identity, and social stability and coherence, in a fast-changing consumerist global economy, the debate would hardly be worth the effort. The case put for the invented concept of Asian values is so intellectually shallow that I rather suspect that even Lee Kuan Yew is keen to distance himself from what many people regard as mainly his, or Singapore's, contribution to the discussion about Asia's future. Let us first consider what the case for Asian values appears to be, and why it began to be put so forcefully.

Speaking at the World Conference on Human Rights in Vienna in 1993, Singapore's Foreign Minister warned that "universal recognition of the ideal of human rights can be harmful if universalism is used to deny or mask the reality of diversity." To which Warren Christopher, the U.S. Secretary of State, responded crisply, "We cannot let cultural relativism become the last refuge of repression." These two statements neatly encapsulate the debate. The Asian-values proponents believe that people like Mr. Christopher are trying to foist Western standards and Western notions of governance on societies where they would be inappropriate or damaging. Asians benefit from a different culture with deep roots in Confucianism. They put more emphasis on order, stability, hierarchy, family, and self-discipline than Westerners do. The individual has to recognize that there are broader interests to which he or she must be subordinate. As the Chinese Foreign Minister said at the same Vienna Conference, "Individuals must put the state's rights before their own."

The West's post-Enlightenment emphasis on the individual, it is argued, has gone too far. It led over the last century to one-person, one-vote democratic government (a system of whose superiority over others Lee Kuan Yew has told us he is not convinced), which has produced all sorts of problems. Malaysian radio announced in 1993 that the Prime Minister, Dr. Mahathir Mohamad, had "asked Malaysians not to accept Western-style democracy as it could result in negative effects. The Prime Minister said such an extreme principle had caused moral decay, homosexual activities, single parents, and economic slowdown because of poor work ethics." This sense of the decay and disorder in Western society is an important thread running through much of the argument about Asian values.

The most interesting part of a recent article for the *Journal of Democracy* by a leading Singapore diplomat, trying to reposition Singapore in a rather more sophisticated relationship to the whole Asian values debate, was the footnote in which the author listed all the recent publications in America and Europe about the West's ills and the extent to which the balance between rights and duties has swung too far in the direction of the former. The footnote—almost exclusively an inventory of Western breast-beating and rending of garments—lasts for thirty-five densely packed lines.

The rise in violent crime in American and European cities; the ready availability of guns in America; murders in open daylight on American streets; crack, cocaine, and heroin eroding the foundations of moral and social order; political terrorism in Europe; broken families, disobedient children, feckless parents, divorce as common as successful marriage; pornography in videos and on bookstalls and television; growing disrespect for politicians of whom, paradoxically, more is asked even when less is expected; a political process that turns into a taxpayer-subsidized auction for votes; bad schools, homeless people on the streets, dirty and inefficient public transport—that's the West for you. Clapped-out. Cynical. Selfish. Obsessed with self and sex—and probably sodomy, at that. Patriotism, a dirty word. "Just take a look at yourselves, America. Glance in the mirror, Europe. Isn't that what you see?"

There are plenty of problems for us to sort out on our own turf—certainly enough of them to discourage Westerners from being patronizing or "holier than thou" in their relationship with Asia. And in any event, triumphalism, even in the wake of crashing Asian economies, is ill-judged and counterproductive. But it may just be worth recording that the Western jungle, grim though it may be, appears to attract a lot of Asian family interest. There can hardly be a rich Asian family without a home or homes on America's and Europe's violent streets, without children at the West's drug-infested, wildly liberal schools and universities. The language of Asian values, in this case as in some others, hardly echoes the lifestyle of well-off Asians.

There is a steely economic edge to the Asian-values argument. In the West, it is said, government has become too big as a result of the exaggerated ambitions of politicians and the demands made on them by voters. Citizens in a sense sell their votes to the highest bidders, not realizing—poor mutts—that they are being bribed with their own money. Government finds itself making decisions, assuming responsibilities, that properly belong to individuals, families, firms. Vitality and initiative are seen as matters for government. "The Westerner," argues Senior Minister Lee, "says I'll fix things at the top. One magic formula, one grand plan. I will wave a wand and everything will work out. It's an interesting theory but not a proven method."*

All this has demotivated people in the West, removing incentives and the stimulants to hard work. Welfarism, made possible by economic growth, is now slowing growth rates, leaving the West with the choice of cutting back welfare or further depressing growth, or perhaps with Western societies having to face both these outcomes. In the East, by contrast, small governments, of which less is expected, tax less, spend less on welfare safety nets, concentrate on the things that really matter like education, and do not have to engage in auction politics with contesting groups of disaffected voters. Asian cultural values sustain an economic model that keeps the GDP growth figures pounding away.

There is some truth in this, as I shall argue in a later chapter. But what have these largely economic values and judgments got to do with the central Asian-values thesis that it is attitudes to liberty and order,

* *Foreign Affairs*, March–April 1994.

to the individual and the corporate or community interest, that lie at the heart of the recipe for Asia's success and of the causes for the West's alleged relative decline? Why do you need to be authoritarian to deliver a sensible macroeconomic policy? Which economic modelers can demonstrate some sort of connection between political repression and GDP growth? If it is a set of values that has determined Asia's performance, why has that performance only recently been so exciting? Had the values previously been lost, buried under the marble slabs of colonial rule, temporarily forgotten for a century or two? What do torturing people, censoring what they can read or write, locking them up without due legal process, hunting opponents into silence or exile, dispersing crowds with bullets, fiddling electoral systems—what do these things have to do with sensible management of a developing economy, investment in literacy and primary health, encouragement of exporting industries, high savings and investment? Economic growth is surely the result more of business-friendly policies than of people-*un*friendly ones, has to do more with sensible dependence on markets than with brutal dependence on phone tappers and armed policemen. It is the Asia-acclaimed relationship between the invisible helping hand of the market and the boot in the face that is so difficult to fathom.

Maybe the argument is that only a government not constantly buffeted by the demands of democratic accountability and the pressures of the electoral cycle can be counted on to deliver what is in the overall national interest. This aspect of good government—its long-term orientation—is much cited by Singaporeans, for example. They have a point. Yet whether there is something inherent in democracy that eventually works against long-termism and in favor of short-termism seems doubtful. I will consider this in the next chapter. It is probably the best of the arguments that seek to connect the political illiberalism of some Asian governments with their economic success.

It was that very economic success which was one of the instigators of the Asian-values ballyhoo, though in fact the argument precedes the days of "tigerism" and miracles. It infused the cultural imperialism of old colonial days, going well beyond fascination with the mysterious East to a self-justificatory assumption that Asian attitudes and ideals somehow legitimized the European and American rule of distant lands. The "white man's burden" was made all the heavier by alleged Asian reluctance to get involved in the management of their own affairs. Asians were apparently not interested in things like politics, democracy, habeas corpus, or the humdrum tasks of good governance. As I have noted, some of this attitude colored official British attitudes to Hong Kong until quite late in the days of our sovereign responsibility there.

Asian values had also come in handy as a bit of propaganda against the Western colonial powers by their wartime adversary Japan as it sought to establish its own Asian empire. Partly as an attempt to rationalize after the event Japanese intervention in China and Manchuria, the Japanese launched in the late 1930s their concept of a stand-alone East Asian order, called the Greater East Asia Co-Prosperity Sphere. While China was the first guest invited to the party, other invitations were certainly in the post. The West—colonialist, alien, and corrupt—was to be excluded from this New Order. The description of what was planned has contemporary echoes, well described by a Japanese scholar, Akira Iriye: "Asian unity was the antithesis of nationalism, individualism, liberalism, materialism, selfishness, imperialism, and all the other traits that characterized the bankrupt Western tradition. Instead, pan-Asianists stressed themes such as regional cooperation, harmony, selflessness, and the subordination of the individual to the community."* Commenting on this, the historian of the end of empire in Asia, John Keay, writes: "These values now have a familiar ring. At the time Western observers saw them as a smokescreen for totalitarianism and militarism. Later, when evoked by Asian nationalists like Sukarno, they would be interpreted as a feeble pretext for autocratic and unrepresentative dictatorship. Only in the 1990s, as the Far East crawled with 'tigers' flexing their economic muscles, did they begin to be hailed as the enviable 'Asian values' responsible for the enviable 'Asian miracle' of double-digit growth."†

Economic success, the applause of international financiers, the headlines in business magazines, the soaring stock markets, the visiting dignitaries all encouraged a growing self-confidence in Asia and in some countries a feistiness, even a cockiness, about their commendable record of achievement. They had put up with being patronized and pushed around by Westerners for long enough. Now it was time for

---

* *Power and Culture: The Japanese-American War, 1941–45,* 1981.
† *Last Post,* 1997.

Americans and Europeans to shut up and listen. There was presumably some adroit populist calculation about much of this. One must charitably assume, for example, that there is a domestic political audience for the more exaggerated of Dr. Mahathir's pronouncements and that he needs from time to time to play to his gallery. The "in-your-face" exaggerations, the braggadocio, the claims to the leadership of whatever the future has in store may be wholly understandable, but anyone passingly familiar with the classics of Greek tragedy must have had the rising impression that as these boasts boomed below, those listening in the heavens were assembling and polishing their thunderbolts.

Asian values also were increasingly summoned in aid in recent years as a sort of all-purpose justification for whatever Asian governments were doing or wished to do. Old men who wanted to stay in power, old networks of corruption intent on survival, old regimes that feared the verdict of the ballot box all could pull down the curtain between East and West and claim that whatever they were doing was blessed by an ancient culture and legitimized by the inscrutable riddles of the East. "If you are from the West, mind your own business and keep off the grass." Sporadically active Western interest in other people's human rights, an interest pursued most aggressively by Americans and Europeans in small countries where there are small markets, was the most usual reason for Asian governments' summoning Asian values to the colors—hence the clubbing together of Asian authoritarians before the Vienna Conference on human rights. Western interest in freedom and democracy and the rule of law appeared to be regarded by some in Asia as a sufficient reason for resisting developments in these areas, as though the very fact that Westerners talked about them meant that they were un-Asian. This is a bizarre argument. If a Western government or nongovernmental organization talks about a human rights abuse in an Asian country, that does not vindicate the continuation of the abuse on the grounds that it has become more authentically Asian because it has been condemned by outsiders. The argument also conveniently overlooks the extent to which it is also Asians (not just Westerners) who are campaigning for freedom and democracy and being locked up for their pains.

The very diversity of Asia questions the concept of Asian values. Take, for example, the differences between the indisputable but very different success stories of Singapore and Hong Kong. Singapore is a relatively small city, with a population of 3 million, though with a much more significant economic punch than its size would suggest. It has a GDP two thirds of Austria's with just over a third of the population. Its GDP is almost a third greater than New Zealand's, though its population is smaller. In the words of the academic Christopher Lingle, "[Singapore is] a tiny country bathed in sweltering tropical torpor which has achieved in a few decades a Western per capita income, with a sophisticated labor force and little unemployment or poverty."

Mr. Lee Kuan Yew can take justified pride in what he, more than anyone else, has created. His is a record that would, I imagine, usually enjoy electoral endorsement. But has that record been achievable only because of Mr. Lee's personal style and stern philosophy of government? He is well known to be sensitive to criticism; Mr. Lingle, for example, was hounded out of Singapore because he questioned that city-state's proselytizing of Asian values. Mr. Lee's political opponents tend to spend a good deal of their time in court. Is all this necessary to success? Does it explain success, or detract from the unqualified credit that success should bring? And does this smack of government have an authentically Asian feel to it? Singapore is an extremely well run city, which feels more Western to me than any other in Asia.

The social engineering by the government in Singapore would have been impossible in Hong Kong. People would not have stood for it. Rex Warner wrote an excellent political novel in the early 1940s, called *The Aerodrome*. It uses allegory or metaphor on the grand scale in a comic celebration of freedom and a denunciation of authoritarianism. On the outskirts of a degenerate village, with drunks, sluts, and a senescent squire, stands a smart new aerodrome dedicated to efficiency and cleanliness. Its commanding officer, who hammers out a doctrine of freedom through self-discipline, gradually takes over the village, subjecting its chaotic liberties to the firm hand of strong government, carrying all before him for a time as he denounces the past record of "confusion, deception, rankling hatred, low aims, indecision." Others no longer needed to bother their heads about what is good for them. They will be told when and what they need to know. People in Hong Kong would not have chosen or cared to live in this sort of lobotomocracy. They would not have taken kindly to the aerodrome commandant. Neither he nor I—nor, I suspect, any Singaporean leader—could have made Hong Kong quieter, could have stopped Hong Kongers chewing gum or spitting, could have spruced up the prosperity-creating clutter of their city, what Jane Jacobs, a historian and economist of urban life, calls "the complicated jumble." And Hong Kong, for all its British colonial past, is a very Asian city. Mr. Lee had created a flourishing city, and I had the good luck to govern another, both in Asia, both mainly Chinese, but very different. Which twin was the Confucian?

Consider the sheer scale of Asia, the languages, the cultures, the religions, the political systems, the geographic reach. Ian Buruma has questioned whether the concept of Asian values itself would make sense translated into Chinese, Malay, or Hindi. Only in English does it have any real resonance. It is as though people spoke about Latin American values but could express the idea only in Mandarin.

Consider the religions of Asia. What do Catholic followers of Jaime Cardinal Sin in the Philippines—believing, some of them, that it was divine intervention, the miraculous appearance of the Blessed Virgin Mary, that prevented the tanks from crushing the opposition to President Ferdinand Marcos—have in common with Japan's Zen Buddhists? What do the gentle adherents of Hinduism in Bali—the hotel receptionists beginning their day with a little offering placed in a graceful ceremony on the counter in front of them—have in common with Malaysia's ardent Muslims? Sometimes one sees the different cultures and traditions so marvelously mixed that they produce a powerful impact that is all their own. I witnessed in Hong Kong the installation of two new Catholic Chinese bishops in the archdiocese. Their appointment before 1997 had forestalled any problems (which I hope would never have arisen) of Chinese ultra-Montanism. It is, after all, for popes to appoint bishops, not politburos. The celebration was held in Hong Kong's cathedral. It was an intensely Chinese, indeed Cantonese, occasion, the church packed with members of Hong Kong's largest Christian denomination. Much of the emotional force of the occasion came from the enthusiasm, joy, and even wit of the vernacular. At the heart of the life of this very Chinese city, the Catholic Church—missionaries and locals, with so many Chinese priests and nuns today—contributes to public life and social service out of all proportion to its numbers. Of course, Hong Kong's Catholics are Asian, just as the vigorous Catholic congregation that I joined by happy accident one Sunday to celebrate the beatification of a Haitian in New York's St. Patrick's Cathedral was

American. But there is nothing exclusively Asian about the one or American about the other.

What is the value system that links umbilically the commuter in Japan, the forest dweller in Irian Jaya, the mid-level resident in a high-rise on Hong Kong's Victoria Island, the peasant in Sichuan setting out to try to find a job and a fortune in Shanghai or Guangdong? What is it that, within China itself, holds to its capacious bosom the follower of traditional Confucianism, the classical Buddhist or Taoist, the disciple of Islam, the Maoist atheist, the agnostic consumerist, the evangelical Christian? How do you generalize so glibly about those who eat with chopsticks or with forks or with hands?

And what is the form of government and the vision of society that best expresses Asia's values? It is a curiosity that, speak as they may of consensual politics, none of the tiger philosophers has created a consensual style or form of government. There is no institutional expression of the celebrated values. More usually, Asians develop forms of parliamentary democracy, constitutions that separate powers and confer elected legitimacy in genuine or sham forms. These constitutions invariably guarantee the freedoms that many Asian leaders then try to justify restricting. So there are democratic Potemkin villages—like China, with its parliament and its pledges about civil liberties—but there are the real things, too. The variety of Asia's politics and of the views of Asia's politicians is another challenge to the notion of Asian values. There is a nasty military dictatorship in Burma, which has exchanged one Orwellian name for another in a process that itself owed much to the forms of totalitarianism that Orwell savagely satirized. The State Law and Order Restoration Council was transmogrified into the State Peace and Development Council. There was no "Law" before, and there will be little "Development," peaceful or otherwise, until history sweeps these unpleasant generals off the board. Burma is set geographically between India, where democracy has flourished for more than fifty years, and China, where Maoist Marxism-Leninism has dropped at least the first two thirds of its title. There is a boisterous democracy in the Philippines, and what Prime Minister Goh in Singapore calls "trustee democracy" there. In the former, there is a very free and noisy press; *The Straits Times* in Singapore would not be thus described. Some say that corruption is somehow naturally Asian.

But in Singapore and Hong Kong, which both have clean governments, it would be vigorously stamped on if it appeared. In Thailand, there is a monarch who is loved and revered by his people. In Indonesia, there was until recently an elderly president whose extended family thrived on its connections. In Malaysia there is a populist prime minister who mixes it with real and imagined international critics and a deputy prime minister whose sophisticated competence helps to deal with the consequences. In Taiwan there is an elected president who says, "I don't think there are distinctly Asian values; there are human values." In China there is a president who has not been elected and who disagrees on this subject, as on much else, with his democratic fellow Chinese leader from Taiwan.

It is not only today's Asian leaders who are on opposite sides of the debate. In the past and the present, Asians have argued about democracy and freedom. "What do you say," a *Newsweek* journalist asked Malaysia's Deputy Prime Minister, Anwar Ibrahim, "when leaders in Singapore, Burma, China, Indonesia and other countries say democracy is inappropriate for Asia because of Asian values?" "Does Sun Yatsen," Anwar replied, "represent Asian values? Of course he does. He was a democrat and he believed in freedom of the press. And the media played a role in Sun's revolutionary era. The Philippines, Indonesia, Malaysia, Vietnam, Thailand—they all had similar experiences. The founding fathers always subscribed to moral fervor and traditional values—very Asian at that—but certainly they were great democrats." In a speech in 1994, Anwar made the important point that "to say that freedom is Western or un-Asian is to offend our own traditions as well as our forefathers who gave their lives in the struggle against tyranny and injustices." He was talking mainly about the anticolonial struggles of the years either side of the last world war. Aung San Suu Kyi in Burma, Martin Lee and Emily Lau in Hong Kong, freely elected President Kim Dae-Jung in South Korea, dissidents Wang Dan and Wei Jingsheng from China, and countless others are all part of this Asian tradition, subscribing to Anwar's argument in the same 1994 speech that "it is altogether shameful, if ingenious, to cite Asian values as an excuse for autocratic practices and denial of basic rights and civil liberties." He could have added that this argument rests ultimately, in logic, on the notion that Asians are inferior as individuals, which is indefensible even when put by Asians.

The diversity of Asia can itself be very Asian. Thailand and Malaysia and South Korea are very different from Italy, France, and Germany. But then Thailand, Malaysia, and Korea are very different from one another, just as Italy, France, and Germany are. The rights that the citizens of those countries enjoy can all be incorporated in the laws of those individual countries. My own government can give me a right to do this or that as a citizen of my own country. But what it cannot do is to usurp or deny rightfully through the laws it passes the rights to which I am entitled as a human being. As Amartya Sen, the master of Trinity College, Cambridge, has argued, there are some rights we should all enjoy as part of our shared humanity. Some rights are universal, whether you live in Tibet or Tianjin or Texas or Turin. You are entitled as a human being not to be tortured or locked up without trial, for instance. Shortly before the Asian authoritarian conclave that preceded the 1993 Vienna Conference, representatives of more than one hundred Asian non-governmental organizations met in Bangkok to assert the universalism of human rights. "Universal human rights standards," they said, "are rooted in many cultures. We affirm the basis of universality of human rights which afford protection to all of humanity, including special groups such as women, children, minorities and indigenous peoples, workers, refugees and displaced persons, the disabled and the elderly. While advocating cultural pluralism, those cultural practices which derogate from universally accepted human rights, including women's rights, must not be tolerated."

It feels much the same if you are beaten up by a policeman in Britain or Indonesia. The consequences for you and your family are similar wherever you live if you are taken away in the middle of the night and incarcerated without proper legal process. The censorship of the press, openly or by stealth, has the same effects on the health of every society. Forbidding men and women to worship as they wish is an offense against conscience right around the globe. Denying the right to peaceful protest is everywhere unwarranted. No alleged national traditions or cultural standards can make right in one place what is wrong in every place.

The Asian denial of this proposition rests largely on the claim that order and harmony, which may sometimes be translated in practice as repression and intolerance of dissent, have deep roots in the religious, philosophical, and cultural traditions of Asia. (One might equally argue that there is a long tradition of authoritarianism in Europe, emanating from belief in the divine right of kings.) Professor Sen has argued that there is a tendency to extrapolate backward from the contemporary Western regard for democracy and freedom and to assume as a consequence that the Western intellectual tradition has always put a greater emphasis than the Eastern on liberty and tolerance.* He points out that there is just as much support for the basic ideas of freedom and individual rights in a tolerant society in early Indian philosophical writing and statecraft as there is in European. There is nothing un-Asian about championing liberty and pluralism.

It is usually Confucius who is taken as the fount of Asian distaste and disregard for liberal values. Confucius, it is said, emphasized order, hierarchy, self-discipline, and obedience. Asian societies do the same and as a result they grow and prosper. Prosperity is the result of societies following instinctively their Confucianist cultural inheritance. Therefore, Confucianism is good for your GDP.

Confucius (the great sixth- and fifth-century B.C. humanist) has been the victim of even more distortion and reinterpretation than Jesus of Nazareth. At least the New Testament and its story of Jesus' life and teachings have usually been cited on both sides of arguments— for example, that the Christian message is above and beyond politics, or that it infuses politics with the unparalleled radicalism of what is required of those who believe in the Resurrection. In some cases, Christians have even found neat practical ways of squaring those circles of rival interpretation of Jesus' message. The worrying implication, if it were literally true, that it would be easier for a camel to pass through the eye of a needle than for a rich man to enter the kingdom of God was dealt with by naming one of the gates into the city of Jerusalem "The Needle's Eye." (It might have been easier simply to note the similarity between the words *rope* and *camel* in Aramaic and leave it at that.) The rich humanism of Confucius has been treated with much less suaveness.

In the foreword to his brilliant translation of *The Analects of Confucius*, Simon Leys points out that the greatest writer in modern China, Lu Xun, who died in 1936, argued that the world customarily coped with geniuses by trying first to suppress them, and then, when that

* *The New Republic*, 1997.

failed, to exalt them. (Ironically, Lu Xun was treated in both ways by the Communist party.) Confucius was largely ignored in his lifetime, at least by those whom he would have liked to serve politically, and was then placed on a pedestal by Chinese emperors, who promoted his ideas as a convenient official cult. Leys notes that "imperial Confucianism only extolled those statements from the Master that prescribed submission to the established authorities, whereas more essential notions were conveniently ignored—such as the precepts of social justice, political dissent and the moral duty for intellectuals to criticise the ruler (even at the risk of their lives) when he was abusing his power, or when he oppressed the people."

Given how often one is told that Asians in general, and Chinese in particular, are not really concerned about politics, it is interesting to note that Confucius regarded his true vocation as politics and was disappointed (as was the very different Machiavelli) that he could not find anyone who would let him put his political ideas and sense of mission into practice. His views on politics have a universal appeal and force. When I read the *Analects* for the first time, I was especially struck by some of their modern echoes. For example, one of my favorite political essays is George Orwell's "Politics and the English Language." Orwell argues, "It is clear that the decline of a language must ultimately have political and economic causes: it is not due simply to the bad influences of this or that individual writer. But an effect can become a cause, reinforcing the original cause and producing the same effect in an intensified form, and so on indefinitely. A man may take to drink because he feels himself to be a failure, and then fail all the more completely because he drinks. It is rather the same thing that is happening to the English language. It becomes ugly and inaccurate because our thoughts are foolish, but the slovenliness of our language makes it easier for us to have foolish thoughts." Compare Orwell with Confucius, who was asked one day by a disciple, "If a king were to entrust you with a territory which you could govern according to your ideas, what would you do first?" Confucius replied: "My first task would certainly be to rectify the names." The puzzled disciple asked, "Rectify the names? And that would be your first priority? Is this a joke?" Confucius was required to explain what he meant: "If the names are not correct, if they do not match realities, language has no object. If language is without an object, action becomes impossible—and therefore, all human affairs disintegrate and their management becomes pointless and impossible. Hence, the very first task of a true statesman is to rectify the names."

The discovery of Confucius as the reason for Asia's economic success would have puzzled some of his most faithful followers as well as earlier European philosophers and historians. Humanism is rarely analyzed in terms of GDP per capita, and insofar as it has been in the past, the assumption used to be, as Weber argued, that it was Confucianism which was responsible for Asia's economic torpor, because it lacked the animating work ethic of Protestantism. "Better ask any old peasant," replied Confucius sensibly enough when asked a question about agronomy. As a result, he has been blamed for setting back the development of science and technology in China. Yet his claimed endorsement of authoritarianism has made him popular with its modern Asian disciples, and when the Chinese—keen to find some way of filling the vacuum left by the collapse of such moral case as there may have been for Marxism—held a great conference in Peking to celebrate the 2,545th anniversary of Confucius's birth, they invited as the principal speaker Lee Kuan Yew to tell them how Confucius would teach them the way to yoke political control to capitalist success.

In order to use Confucianism to justify unswerving obedience to the state, you have to turn a blind eye to many passages in the *Analects* that endorse personal liberty. In 9.26, "The Master said: 'One may rob an army of its commander-in-chief; one cannot deprive the humblest man of his free will.'" Later, in 12.7, Zigong (a disciple of Confucius) asked about government; what was required? "The Master said: 'Sufficient food, sufficient weapons, and the trust of the people.' Zigong said, 'If you have to do without one of these three, which would you give up?'—'Weapons.'—'If you had to do without one of the remaining two, which would you give up?'—'Food; after all, everyone has to die eventually. But without the trust of the people, no government can stand.'" I am not sure how the former Chinese foreign minister, who believed that the individual should subject his own interests to those of the state, would have responded to Confucius's passionate defense of the family against state power. When the Governor of She praised a son as a man of "unbending integrity" for denouncing his father to the government for stealing a sheep, Confucius replied, "Among my people, men of integrity do things differently; a father covers up for his son, a son covers up for his father—and there is integrity in what they do."*

Claims about Asianness and the Asian way, and about the contrasts between Asian and other societies, are customarily rhetorical or anecdotal; not very much has been done to try to establish with any modest degree of social science measurement exactly what the differences may be. Evidence has not been sought or demanded for what is generally seen as an essentially political set of propositions. One of the few exceptions is the work done on East Asian attitudes by David Hitchcock, published in 1995, for Washington's Center for Strategic and International Studies. During the summer of 1994, he interviewed about a hundred religious and cultural leaders, academics, think tank experts, officials, businessmen, and journalists from East Asia, and in addition compared their answers about the priority accorded to different qualities and values with those given by twenty-eight Americans drawn from various foreign affairs agencies in Washington and East Asia. It is dangerous to generalize too much from research both painstakingly thorough and extremely limited in its range. But I think it is fair to deduce the following. First, in Hitchcock's own words: "On no other point was there more unanimity among those interviewed than on the question of an 'Asian way' and Asian 'kinship' or affinity. Most respondents found little significant kinship between their own country and their neighbors in the region." There is not much of a market here for the forceful exposition of Asian values; many of the interviewees were particularly critical of what they saw as Singapore's self-serving use of these arguments. Second, economic success has been accompanied by a growing self-confidence (which recent economic turmoil may have somewhat dented), but there is a recognition of the problem of how best to protect national tradition and culture while becoming modern and prosperous. Third, Hitchcock notes that we "cannot conclude that East Asia has found a way to strike the perfect balance between the individual and society, or between tradition and modernization. But . . . the region is striving . . . to find that balance." Perhaps one can add that in the search, the Asian intellectuals interviewed by Hitchcock were more likely to put stress on order and harmony, in contrast to the Americans who were questioned, who placed more emphasis on individual and personal freedom.

* *Analects,* 13.18

This nudges the debate onto more interesting ground. If there is no Asian way, are there institutions in Asian societies—attributes and practices—that are more vibrant than their equivalents in the West, and will Asians find it easier to preserve them than the West has done during the change that accompanies rapid economic advance?

In considering these questions, I find myself driven to the conclusion that what we see when we compare West and East is more a consequence of time lags than profound cultural differences. Let me take three issues that are often said to lie near the heart of the Asian contrast and to explain Asian success—social order, the family, and education.

Hong Kong is a well-ordered society. It is pretty peaceful and crime is low. Singapore is the same, though the methods of law enforcement there are different. Do we deduce from these examples that Asia is less crime-ridden and more orderly than the West? What about the crime levels in the cities of South Korea or Japan? Are they much different from those in Europe? What of the violent lawlessness in Thailand? Travel across Hong Kong's frontier with the rest of China and you find that crime is rising steeply, as the social controls associated with Maoism disintegrate and as rough-and-tumble capitalism attracts a migrant army from the countryside to the cities. Hong Kong and Singapore start to look like exceptions rather than the rule. What they have managed to do is to reduce social friction to the minimum by spreading the benefits of economic success across the community. Some "haves" have a lot more than others, but the number of "have nots" has been minimized. Life has gotten better for most people most of the time. These cities also have been able to afford high and very conspicuous levels of policing. I doubt whether many other Asian cities will be able to do as well.

Organized crime and drug abuse will be particularly acute problems. Triad shoot-outs in Taiwan and Macau are the visible signs of a spreading malignance. China's pell-mell scoot for capitalism is going to produce both the pickings and the urban ferment to encourage triad crime. Proximity to the "golden triangle"'s drug fields threatens to increase urban drug abuse. So can we seriously argue that Asia as a whole is more orderly than Europe or America? You are more likely to be shot, robbed, or raped in Detroit or Los Angeles than in Singapore. You are more likely to be mugged in London, Paris, or Madrid than in Hong Kong. But how would you fancy your chances driving through rural China at night as opposed to Montana or New Hampshire or the countryside anywhere in Europe? How much safer would you be on vacation in Thailand than in Tuscany? And how are relatively well ordered and peaceful communities in Asia going to be affected by economic change and urbanization? Will higher crime result as it has in other societies? I doubt whether there is a permanent Asian safety premium.

Family solidarity may be stronger in Asia than in the West. The traditional family is still the linchpin of Asian societies. There is less divorce, and, since there are fewer single-parent families, there is less pressure for welfare support from the state. Maybe, too, children are more likely to do what their parents tell them, and the responsibilities of the extended family, especially toward the elderly, are perhaps taken more seriously. Some of these things may be true, and they may even be objectively demonstrable, although it would be far from easy to prove conclusively that Asian families are on the whole stronger institutions than those in southern European countries. But even if we concede the Asian case here, how durable are these social strengths?

First, no one can say that they will last because they are the result of a superior sexual morality. Confucius noted that he had "never seen a man who loved virtue as much as sex." Just in case one might have missed the point (with which I do not happen to agree), exactly the same sentence appears twice in the *Analects*. Confucius would presumably, and nonselectively, have applied the adage to all men, from North, South, East, and West. Lust carries no passport. What do we learn about family values from sex shows in Bangkok or massage parlors in Amsterdam?

Second, I often heard references in Hong Kong and elsewhere in Asia to the close bonds, fierce loyalties, and strong sense of duty associated with the patriarchal family, and I saw some evidence of this, too. But I also often noted that the greatest beneficiary of the patriarchal family was, not surprisingly, the patriarch. Patriarchal structures cannot always have been much fun for the women members of the family. Women have not invariably been the beneficiaries of family values in Asia; to take the most cruel example, there is still today far too much evidence for comfort of the abandonment of female babies, and even of female infanticide, in "one-child" China.

Third, it will be a welcome surprise if economic circumstance, urban living, mobility, and rootlessness do not all put pressure on the Asian family as they have on families everywhere else. There will doubtless be some societies which will manage these pressures better than others. That already happens in Europe and North America. While I was there, Hong Kong's economic development and particular geographical circumstances were starting to result in the sort of strains on family life we have already seen in the West and will see in Asia. Divorce was increasing in the 1990s. The number of cases coming before the family law courts was on the rise. There seemed to be more instances of child abuse, though this may just have reflected an increased awareness of the problem and a greater preparedness to talk about it. A large number of Hong Kong men had a wife and a family on either side of the border, leading eventually to the abandonment of one or the other. The size of family apartments meant that fewer of the elderly lived with their families and more went into specially provided accommodations. We were trying to develop a sophisticated network of friendships for the growing number of retired people who were living on their own. The growth in the number of families where both parents went out to work had resulted, despite the increase in the number of kindergartens, in the abandonment of many children on their own at home during the day and many older latchkey schoolchildren coming home every afternoon to an empty, parentless flat. None of this suggests that Hong Kong is worse than other places, just that it is subject to the same pressures as exist in other rich cities and that as a result, it is becoming very similar to them, with a similar range of social problems.

The commitment to education also sends a rather unclear message about the enduring nature of particular Asian values. As I argued in the last chapter, I have no doubt that the emphasis they have placed on education is one of the reasons for the success of some Asian countries. The differences in this emphasis across Asia as a whole are considerable and are duly reflected in economic performance. Basic literacy levels in South Asia are shamefully low, at bad African levels; they are much higher in China; higher still in Southeast Asia; and at their best in the original four tigers. There is a tradition of scholarship in China, though it may have been pushed to one side in recent years, first by the demands of ideology and then by the attractions of making money. There are enviable levels of basic mathematical attainment by South Korean and other East Asian children. There is the commitment of families to secure the best education for their children, and the determination of many children, who benefit from parental sacrifice and involvement, to return this parental investment with interest. The devaluation of currencies all around Asia will have made it much more expensive for middle-class families to send their children away to Western schools and universities, but they will still be making the effort. Again and again in Hong Kong, I saw examples of this determination by families to do whatever they could to secure the best education for their children. On my very first evening outing to a fish restaurant in a New Territories village, I was mobbed by a crowd as I made my choice from the exotic crustaceans on the quayside. I asked one father of a little girl pushed to the front of the crowd to shake my hand where she went to school, thinking he would mention somewhere local. "Wycombe Abbey," he replied, naming one of England's most famous private boarding schools. At a dinner my wife and I once gave for senior civil servants and members of the Legislative Council, we realized afterward that of the six couples at our table, we were the only ones with a child being educated in Hong Kong. We had drivers and cooks at Government House who were paying for their children's education abroad. The children, if the evidence of one's own eyes is worth anything, repay the investment handsomely. I have done more than my share of speech days at private schools in Britain, and Asian children regularly appear to be monopolizing the prizewinners' books and cups. American university administrators would surely confirm this impression.

This may or may not be telling us something profound. There may be a more general commitment to the importance of education in much of Asia than in Europe and North America and a greater individual commitment by Asian pupils. I wonder how much these things are the result of social circumstance and development. Hong Kong is a migrant community; the people who came there had only their wits to sustain them. Will not a community like this always see education as the ladder to climb to better days? Is that not likely to be more generally true of societies at a given point of economic development? My grandparents were head teachers in Manchester primary schools at the beginning of the century, teaching the poor children of Irish immigrants. I have little doubt that such an immigrant society gave education—the best way out of the inner-city slums—a very high priority, and you would have found the same in the Jewish immigrant communities in East London at the same time. None of this belittles the regard for education presently shown in some Asian countries; it teaches us lessons in the West. I just doubt whether it is an abiding cultural phenomenon rather than a more complex consequence of social and economic circumstances.

The more that I have looked at all these questions, the more it seems to me that we all face similar problems, face them to different degrees according (partly) to how we have developed, and will discover similar solutions rooted in the same respect for human decency and in the same regard for an economic philosophy that maximizes the opportunity for the individual to excel. Some of the challenges cast at Western societies by Asians are wholly fair. "Certain basics about human nature," argues Lee Kuan Yew, "do not change. Man needs a certain moral sense of right and wrong. There is such a thing called evil, and it is not the result of being a victim of society. You are just an evil man, prone to do evil things, and you have to be stopped from doing them. Westerners have abandoned an ethical basis of society, believing that all problems are solvable by a good government, which we in the East never believed possible." I agree with much of this, though I believe that the sweeping condemnation of the West and the commendation of the East are overdrawn. We do, however, need to ask ourselves in Europe and North America how often our attempts to compromise with and blur the distinctions between right and wrong have led us straight back to savagery and the jungle. We are often more preoccupied nonjudgmentally with helping people cope with the consequence of foolish or evil actions than with deterring those actions in the first place. When we consider how to retain the best of what has made our societies civilized and prosperous, while at the same time changing and modernizing, a stronger attachment on both the right and left of politics to an ethical foundation for statecraft should plainly be essential. An "ethical basis" might be thought to contain not just an awareness of the difference between right and wrong but an understanding of shared humanity, of the respect and dignity due to every individual, not least on the part of government. Mr. Lee might also consider whether that is sufficiently widespread in Asia.

Aung San Suu Kyi asks whether the failings of Western society pointed out by Asian authoritarians are really the result, as they argue, of democracy and try-to-do-everything governments. "Many of the worst ills of American society," she notes, "increasingly to be found in varying degrees in other developed countries, can be traced not to the democratic legacy but to all the demands of modern materialism. Gross individualism and cutthroat morality arise when political and intellectual freedoms are curbed on the one hand while on the other fierce economic competitiveness is encouraged by making material success the measure of prestige and progress. The result is a society where cultural and human values are set aside and money value reigns supreme."* Men and women are political animals and not just economic machines and commercial appetites. For Burma's dissident elected leader, it seems clear that development of Asia's political life would help to sustain its cultural traditions.

Those of us who believe in markets, in liberal economics, right around the globe, have to be careful not to become crude advocates of a mindless materialism and of a concentration on the individualism of human beings as economic agents that obfuscates their civic and social roles. We have to be aware of value as well as price. We have to demand responsibilities of citizens and not inflate the notion that citizenship is only about rights. In what some may regard as a paradox, one way (certainly in Europe) in which we can best do that is by ensuring that men and women make more of their own economic decisions and bear more of their own economic responsibilities. When the state does more, those whom it serves will very often feel that they are justified in doing less. Successful liberal democracies need smaller governments and bigger citizens—bigger citizens playing a larger role in partnership for the common good.

It is the final commonplace of the debate about the values of East and West that we in the West should learn a little more about order, harmony, partnership, and responsibility from the East. Perhaps there

---

* *Freedom from Fear,* 1995.

is some truth in it. We need to seek a new point of balance in our societies that draws on the experience of smaller governments in some Asian societies. For their part, they might learn from us about a point of balance which gives more respect to citizens and which recognizes that, while too much focus on rights can be debilitating, citizens do actually have rights—above all, the right to esteem. Men and women want justice and dignity as well as economic progress, and they are more likely to achieve the last if they enjoy the benefits of the first.

6

Freedom and the Market

. . . the end of all our exploring
will be to arrive where we started
And know the place for the first time.
—T. S. Eliot, from "Little Gidding" from *Four Quartets*

Zigong asked: "Is there any single word that could
guide one's entire life?" The Master said: "Should it not be
reciprocity? What you do not wish for yourself, do not do to others."
—*The Analects of Confucius*, 15.24

Let me own up right away. On the subject of good government I am deeply prejudiced, and my prejudices are the result more of personal experience than of profound study. I believe they have a rational basis, but they were not arrived at after a long process of reasoned thought. I did not build logically from carefully considered premises until my whole edifice of opinions was complete. I tumbled headlong into them; it all started by accident, and continued that way as well.

After taking my final university examinations, I went on a long scholarship trip, more pleasure than study, to the United States. Toward the end of my tour, I was asked if I would like to spend a few weeks working in John Lindsay's 1965 Republican campaign to become mayor of New York. There seemed to be several good reasons for doing this. It would enable me to stay in New York through the autumn; I would be able to take in a lot of theater, opera, ballet, and galleries in the margins of the political campaigning; the other people in the campaign with whom I would be working appeared very congenial—sparky, liberal, button-down shirts but not button-down views. John Lindsay and the politics came some way down the list. But the campaign itself turned out to be

great fun, a lively adventure, partly because I was given the job of re-
searching the opinions of the suave and intelligent Conservative candidate, William F. Buckley, Jr. Mr. Buckley made a habit of embracing the
politically incorrect long before the concept was so horribly well known.
As a result, he added greatly to the gaiety of nations. Asked what his first
action would be if elected mayor, he drawled, "Demand a recount." As
far as politics was concerned, I was smitten, head over heels infatuated.
And so it has (largely) continued.

First a party apparatchik in London, then Member of Parliament
for a marginal constituency, finally a minister, I pursued my career in
the shadow or under the gilded and dark-timbered ceilings of the
Palace of Westminster. I served in the Mother of Parliaments, as she
likes to be called, and would be there still were it not for the "sweet adversity" of democratic politics. So I am a politician, a democratic
politician through and through, and that has left its mark on me. I respect other democratic politicians, men and women who know intimately the joys and humiliations of this honorable adventure, who
have smelled the sweat of their own fear as they confront the dramatic
theater of political conflict, who have experienced one of the greatest
of all democratic satisfactions—persuading men and women to choose
freely to do something, which they do not believe is in their immediate
interest, for some broader or deeper purpose. I have enjoyed seeing
good politicians go through their paces—watching President Clinton
work a room or a crowd, hearing a speech by Iain Macleod or Michael
Heseltine or Jacques Chirac or Michael Foot, reading one by Adlai
Stevenson or General Charles de Gaulle, admiring the urbane sweep
of Roy Jenkins and the intellectual thuggishness of Denis Healey, listening to the perceptive insights of a supreme political manager like
Helmut Kohl or a brilliant public servant like George Shultz, watching Margaret Thatcher slaughter and pillage her way through a meeting teasing some curious half-baked statistic in a footnote to the official
paper under discussion into the rhetorical equivalent of Semtex. I was
sad that I could not really get the full measure of some of Hong Kong's
politicians, since I did not understand the Cantonese in which several of
them spoke with wit and verve. I am not obsessed with politics. But it
has been my life. Democratic politics. It raised me up and, as it invariably does, it cast me down.

My experience in Hong Kong, my main experience in Asia, exposed me to something different. The late Professor S. E. Finer, in his magisterial *History of Government*, notes that a state can be liberal but not democratic, and gives colonial Hong Kong as an example. I was Chief Executive of Hong Kong, but appointed by London, not elected in the Colony. The administration I led was accountable to a legislature that, when I arrived, was only partly elected. While it is true that it was wholly elected in 1995, more than half the seats emerged from constitutional channels that would have raised eyebrows in most democratic societies. Hong Kong was therefore only on the way to democracy, but even before it had begun this journey, it had been a liberal society. The individual was protected from coercion or arbitrary action by the state. Rights to property, to freedom from arrest, and to the liberty to speak one's mind were guaranteed by law, and the law adjudicated impartially between individual citizens and between individuals and their government. All were subject to the rule of law, including Hong Kong's unelected governor. It was the system, broadly speaking, that had so attracted Sun Yat-sen's approbation in the 1920s, when he noted that four thousand years of Chinese history had produced nothing like Hong Kong, a city where the rule of law provided that security and majestic neutrality within which bank balances, ideas, and values could all flourish.

Democracy and the rule of law together constitute a liberal democracy, which combines the best of what we learned, and was passed down to us, from Greece and Rome. In the nineteenth century, as ideas of government were reshaped in America and Europe in the wake of the Enlightenment, the French and American revolutions, and the onset of industrialization, constitutions were created in the West that were perhaps more liberal than democratic. The steady broadening of suffrage continued well into this century. Though buffeted by war and economic adversity, liberal democracy survived, broadly acknowledged as the best form of governance ever devised. Even those who did not practice it aped many of its forms: They pretended to have constitutions that protected liberty and they called themselves democratic. Invariably, those countries with the word *democratic* in their name were anything but, as citizens of the East German state well knew. Those countries that were real liberal democracies enjoyed the things which are customarily believed to be present in a well-governed society—stability, partnership, protection of individual rights, the absence (usually) of extreme outcomes. While the point can perhaps be exaggerated, liberal democracies are more likely to live at peace with their neighbors (especially if their neighbors are liberal democracies too), and, as Amartya Sen has argued, they are more likely than closed societies to escape avoidable calamity such as famine (a point to which I shall return in relation to Asia's democratic example).

One of my favorite series of frescoes is the political manifesto of the fourteenth-century municipal government of Siena. Decorating the walls of its Palazzo Pubblico, these frescoes by Ambrogio Lorenzetti give allegorical representations of good and bad government. Spectacles of atrocity and violence vie with those of well-being and concord. To drive home the message about benign government, Siena's councillors even allowed Lorenzetti to paint a scene that apparently would have been forbidden by the local bylaws of the day. In the well-governed city—and Siena was, naturally, the example that painter and patrons had in mind—beautiful maidens dance in the streets to the rhythm of the tambourine.

Dancing in the streets as a measure of public satisfaction with government is, these days, a figurative comment and not a practical aim. But my own experiences of liberal democracy in Britain, and of governing a liberal society in Asia (whose economic policies were certainly more liberal in the classical sense than Britain's), persuade me that if I were asked to portray a city where the cobblestones rang to the sound of skipping feet, it would have to contain two ingredients. First, there would need to be free and open commercial life; second, there would have to be public participation in the business of government within a framework of law that reflected the community's values and aspirations.

In other words, I believe passionately that good government is synonymous with market economics and political pluralism: The best argument for such a combination is not the strength of my prejudices on the subject but what it delivers in terms of outcome, the order, decency, peace, and happiness all human societies should ideally offer their people (for example, Adenauer's Germany rather than Hitler's). Let me be absolutely clear what I am saying at the risk of sounding evangelically rhetorical: On every continent, societies that combine political and economic liberty will more probably be successful, stable, and content than those that do not.

I concede intellectually that it may be possible to have, in a given place and at a particular time, good government with neither of the building blocks that I deem to be essential. (Perhaps in Mussolini's Fascist, corporatist Italy the trains really did run on time.) I doubt whether good government can last long with neither political nor economic liberty, and would assume the existence of benign and competent government in these circumstances to be largely a coincidental consequence of geography, history, and the personality of an individual or group of individuals. The early years of Mao's China would certainly have been regarded at the time as providing government that was an improvement on what had gone before, and it would be churlish not to recognize some of the social advances made in the first stages of the Communist dynasty, especially in rural areas. Authoritarian or totalitarian systems based on individuals rather than ideologies, benevolent despotism for example, may be warmhearted and successful for a time, but they have always depended, fatally, on benevolent competence being hereditary. I also accept that you can have good government, and have had it, with only one or the other of the two desiderata I have mentioned. But good government is far more likely with both, and the partial or complete absence of either will reduce the prospects of order, prosperity, and happiness. Under the apartheid system in South Africa, some people had economic freedom and a good deal of political freedom, too. Many of that minority thought the South African government was a good one. To feel that way you had, of course, to be white.

These arguments about liberty would have been familiar at the beginning of the century. The sun appeared then to be rising on a liberal horizon. I have the same instinct a fairly grim hundred years later. As more countries accept enthusiastically—or stumble perforce—into market economics, a political agenda starts to unfold. They discover that opening the door to the market ushers in political liberty. But we are far from "game, set, and match" as far as this argument goes. As I noted in the last chapter, in Asia in particular it is still suggested that you can have economic freedom without political. And the contrary assertion—my case, as it were—is challenged by what is said to have happened already in Asia and will be further tested in due course by the pace of change and the inexorable inconvenience of events. To unravel some of all this, and to suggest a response that does credit to both the values and interests of those societies that are already free, we should begin by defining a few terms.

Most of us presumably accept that there are ultimate ethical values—beauty, goodness, and honesty, for instance. Liberty, for which men and women have fought for centuries, is an ultimate political value. Defining political liberty distinguishes it from license. By liberty I mean simply that we can live our own lives, think our own thoughts, speak our own minds. If that is both "my" liberty and "your" liberty, it follows that my freedom is constrained by the degree to which it is necessary to protect yours.

Liberty begins with our person—a principle encapsulated in the legal concept of habeas corpus. No one, no representatives of the state or the law, can oppress us. We cannot be accused or locked up except for offenses set out in statute and according to legally prescribed procedures, and if accused, we cannot be kept in custody without being brought to trial. We can use the law to defend ourselves against anyone, however powerful. The law is made by those we elect to represent us in a legislature or parliament, and it can be changed if we can persuade enough of our fellow citizens that it should be. We are therefore both rulers and ruled. We may express our thoughts freely through the media, on the street, or on a platform. We can worship whatever God we please, how we please, or we can worship no God at all. These are the things that make up political liberty. Exercising them extends and develops our humanity.

In 1948, reacting to the wickedness and cruelties of Nazi Germany and the years of the Second World War, the General Assembly of the United Nations set out a Declaration of Human Rights and followed it up with two covenants. These statements assumed that our shared humanity was reflected in shared rights, such as those mentioned in the last chapter—the right not to be tortured, not to be locked up without a fair trial, and so on. Other organizations and groupings of nations have taken the same path—for example, the Council of Europe and the Helsinki Conference. What are all these sacred texts about? What have these conferences been trying to achieve? What do Geneva's panels of experts, examining countries on their compliance with the conventions they have signed, seek to secure? It is not very difficult to answer these questions. We are not required to offer too intellectual or sophisticated a response. The answers are pretty easy, and were delivered with admirable directness and simplicity by the late Isaiah Berlin. "If you ask why we believe in human rights," he once said, "I can say because that is the only decent, even tolerable way human beings can live with each other, and if you ask what is 'decent,' I can say that is the only kind of life which we think that human beings should follow, if they are not to destroy each other." One measure of decency, of what human beings will find tolerable, is what we would like to happen to ourselves: If we treat others the way we would wish ourselves to be treated, that is likely to be tolerable.

This is the sensible principle of reciprocity referred to by Confucius in the quotation from the *Analects* at the head of this chapter—similar, of course, to the teachings of Jesus. Confucius felt strongly enough about the point to return to it three times. The single thread of his doctrine is defined in one passage (4.15) as "loyalty and reciprocity." Elsewhere, defining "the good man," he says that "what he wishes to achieve for himself, he helps others to achieve; what he wishes to obtain for himself, he enables others to obtain—the ability simply to take one's own aspirations as a guide is the recipe for goodness." It is also the recipe for a decent society and a good government—giving others the ability to obtain what you yourself wish to obtain, when the rules apply equally to everyone, when everyone has the same security and opportunity to excel, and when there is parity of esteem.

What happens when these things are absent? What happens when decency is not readily available? What, for example, are the consequences for the prosperity of a community and for the maximization of its resources? Can the wheels still go around and will the commercial mills grind profitably away? Totalitarian political structures and market economics are poor bedfellows; the attempt to exercise absolute power cannot encompass the exercise of economic choice. Authoritarian structures and market economics, on the other hand, can find it easier to sleep together, though I doubt whether they can do so for very long or as soundly as they would like. Why not? Because markets depend on freedom—the freedom of the producer and the customer. In a market economy, decision making is devolved to the manufacturer, the trader, and the customer. Instructions do not bind from top to bottom. The price mechanism is the scale by which economic activity finds its balance.

Companies and individuals in a market economy are free to trade as they wish, both within their own community and beyond its borders. By and large, they do not need to get their government's permission to buy or sell, except in the cases of some military and security items. Consumer choice decides what is produced, and customers determine what price they are prepared to pay. The power of the consumer in the marketplace inevitably helps to determine the shape of society. When customers buy televisions, satellite dishes, personal computers, and access to the global exchange of information, they create greater openness and social flexibility. Free economies trading as fairly as possible together encourage the exchange not just of goods and capital but of ideas and people. They have free labor markets in which the employee can always seek a different job. They are not completely uncontrolled or anarchic. The market needs rules to operate as well as it can. Free economies therefore operate within a framework of law: enforcing contract, protecting private property, safeguarding the consumer, watching over health and safety. Markets, by their nature, nurture responsibility in citizens. By encouraging freedom of choice, by devolving economic power and decisions, they spread responsibility more widely. Choice implies freedom, including the freedom to make a poor choice—the freedom to make mistakes. But it is by making mistakes and taking responsibility for them that businesses and individuals learn to compete more successfully in the marketplace.

Some politicians are prepared to sign up, at least in theory, to this idea of the market while insisting that the responsibilities the market encourages people to shoulder and the choices they are obliged to make can be kept separate from any political agenda. The economic citizen can be distinguished from the political—a community can be an economic entity without having a political identity. This is a curious argument which depends on defining politics solely in terms of those issues that turn on the untrammeled powers of the state and of those who are for the time being in charge of its government. But the powers of the state and the choices made in the market regularly clash and intermingle. How can the state control thought and communication, snuff out criticism, and claim a monopoly of wisdom when its citizens are learning more for themselves through the exercise of their power as consumers? How can the state decide that its national economic interest is to buy only so much from this or that other state when its citizens are seeking the best and the cheapest products on offer? The citizen on whom great economic responsibilities are placed is unlikely to accept for long the foreshortening of those responsibilities at the whim of government. A responsible economic citizen is a responsible citizen who cannot be split down the middle indefinitely, one moment the audacious master of his or her own destiny, the next an obedient, unquestioning stooge. In a community where reciprocity reigns, I am captain of my own soul, and that is not just a matter of making my living and supporting my family. So you cannot compartmentalize freedom. You may build walls between economics and politics, but they are walls of sand.

The free-market economic model has not been everyone's choice for the greater part of the second half of this century; indeed, there have been times (for example, in much of Europe in the postwar years) when it has been struggling to retain intellectual support and popular favor. Though its merits and benefits are proven, there has been a sustained determination to second-guess it, prove it wrong, replace it. One of the few places where it survived and prospered, unquestioned and unshaken over the postwar years, was Hong Kong. But the failure, relative and absolute, of every effort to improve on it has (to borrow a phrase from its severest opponents) helped it capture the commanding heights in every continent in the last few years. It does work better than any known or tried alternative. Recalling Isaiah Berlin's remarks, it delivers more decency; and it certainly brings more prosperity.

The spreading triumph of market economics comes hard on the heels of the collapse, or at least the emaciation, of totalitarianism almost everywhere. Nineteenth-century capitalism, particularly its cruder manifestations, begat the Marxist response, rooted in a quasi-scientific view of history and class, and drawing its inspiration from the murderous delusion of the French Revolution that it was possible for man to create heaven on earth. At its most extreme, associated both with the growth of the Soviet empire and with the depravities of individual tyrants—more plain wicked than convinced Marxist, but able to find in Marxism a theory to justify their absolutism—it institutionalized evil in structures that combined corruption, absurdity, and incompetence.

There was a gentler, genuinely democratic form of socialism, which we called social democracy or laborism. It was usually benign in its methods and objectives, though far from successful in its results. It assumed a prescience and wisdom in the state to which few if any bureaucracies were able to rise. Nanny, it turned out, did not always know best. Social democracy and laborism placed state ownership and redistributive taxation at the heart of the drive for greater social equity and improved industrial efficiency. This approach to some extent reflected the egalitarian wish for a more harmonious and socially coherent community that prevailed after the years of 1930s slump and 1940s warfare. If it had worked, it would have stayed in business. It did not work and it has had to repackage itself, skillfully and with some success. These days, social democrats everywhere speak of prudent fiscal policy and free markets, just like their political opponents. No successful parties in Europe or North America campaign demanding increased spending, bigger deficits, higher taxes, and greater government intervention in the economy. The center-left promises fiscal rectitude and free markets—with a heart; Milton Friedman rewritten by Barbara Cartland. There may be justified skepticism about what all this may come to mean in practice, yet it is better to be fighting on this terrain than on the old battlefields of nationalization and of tax-and-spend.

These political developments, especially in Europe, owe much to the decline of class as a determinant of voting behavior, or of much else for that matter. Economic growth, rises in net disposable income, increases in ownership (especially of property), greater personal mobility, the spread of television and the mass popular culture associated with it, the assault on previously structured and segmented tastes by shopping mall traders common to all, the collapse of deference, the decline of authority, and the erosion of hierarchy—these social and economic developments have fractured the voting blocks that underpinned class, employment, and political interests. Political competition in Europe and North America now revolves around how best to deliver socially responsible market economics, with the debate largely focused on the extent to which the exercise of social responsibility may inhibit the benign workings of the market.

What has happened in the developed world has been echoed in the successfully and less successfully developing parts of the world. The dusk of Empire—the years of independence movements and decolo-

nization in Africa and Asia—coincided with the intellectual domina-
tion of socialist economics in much of the democratic world and the
hard-as-nails rigidity of totalitarianism in Central and Eastern Europe
and in China. The 1950s began with Hannah Arendt, who was a
refugee from Hitler's Europe, arguing in her book *The Origins of Totalitarianism* that the modern tyrannies of Eastern Europe were invincible, not subject to the customary dynamics of internal change, and able
to deploy effectively in their own implacable defense all the contemporary technology of oppression.

By the end of the 1950s, much affected by the Hungarian uprising,
Arendt had concluded that her argument about the intractability of totalitarianism was wrong. She decided that the voices of Eastern Europe, speaking so plainly about truth and freedom, showed that you
could not change human nature and that however much you tried to
indoctrinate people, their desire for that same truth and freedom
would always survive the harshest winters and blossom again. It still
took thirty years for the walls to fall in Europe, for the barbed wire to
rust away, and for the tyrants to be bundled off to the cells. Totalitarianism was not after all permanent, a clenched iron fist forever. But it
seemed to some people immutable, perhaps even invincible, almost to
the end. A friend of mine, on a ministerial visit to Berlin in 1989, was
strongly advised against making a protest against some appalling bru-
tality committed on the Wall by East German security guards during
his visit. It was unnecessary; it would cause trouble; it might set back
an improvement in our delicate relations with East Germany. Within
months there was no East Germany and no Wall. All gone and gone
peacefully, like the snow in a warm spring.

Why? Because class-based history ran out of chapters. Because the
expense of cold-war technology broke the back of wretchedly backward
economies. Because communist economics did not work. Because of
the inherent absurdities of dictatorships—whether of the proletariat or
of any other sort. Because very few of those political creeds based on
cheerfully no-nonsense arguments about the need to knock a few
heads together to make things work ever actually do much more than
leave a lot of people with very sore heads. Above all, totalitarianism fell
because of the human spirit—expressed in heroism in front of tanks,
expressed in the blazing words of dissident poets, expressed in the
small revolutions contained in a thousand private jokes. In Russia, they

went on telling one of those jokes until it became true. A census official questions a Leningrad pensioner: "Where were you born?" "St. Petersburg." "Where were you educated?" "Petrograd." "Where do you live?" "Leningrad." "Where will you die?" "St. Petersburg." The last laugh was on Lenin.

In much of Africa, in parts of Asia, and (in rather different circumstances) in Latin America too, well-meaning development economics had seemed to offer socialism as a springboard to modernity; the tyrannies had offered social control as a guarantee of power. Leaders who were usually voted into power amid all the trappings of decent and carefully constructed postcolonial constitutional settlements found in totalitarian methods the way to retain power, stifle criticism, and brutalize opponents into submission. Marxism was often used as a spurious historical justification for despotism, and socialist economics became a convenient methodology for those who identified the state's interests with their own and who were able therefore to turn public ownership into private plundering.

The spectacular democratic revolution that swept across Europe as tyranny crumbled there has reverberated elsewhere—in Africa, for example. A majority of the countries in sub-Saharan Africa are at various stages of political liberalization. There are several reasons for this. First, the collapse of the Soviet empire sent signals and cut off cash; the cash may have been less important. The Warsaw Pact countries (just like China) did have an impoverished group of pretty beastly client states, but their own economic problems constrained their generosity as aid donors except as purveyors of crude military equipment at bargain-basement prices. Second, change in South Africa was a beacon for the whole continent. When Nelson Mandela was released from prison, when the ban on the African National Congress was lifted, when South Africa made with remarkable success the arduous journey to one-person, one-vote democracy, it became difficult to argue elsewhere in the continent against the principles that were being advocated there. If pluralism was right for South Africa, why was it not right farther north? Third, the development of civil society in Africa—of all those mediating institutions between the individual and the state, like the professions, churches, nongovernmental organizations, and labor unions—has cracked the husk of closed and brutally incompetent regimes. Across the continent, the churches and the legal profession have bravely pressed for pluralism and democracy. Fourth, demography has been a servant of liberty. Younger, more urbanized, better-educated men and women have developed a growing consensus for the proposition that social justice and economic progress require political freedom and multiparty competition. Fifth, the nasty inadequacy of authoritarian regimes, and the policies required to salvage their economies, have opened the doors to more pluralism and democracy, as they always will with time.

Corruption, confiscation, the destruction of enterprise (not least in rural areas), high tax, excessive regulations, subsidies, the bureaucratization of commerce and industry, fiscal improvidence, excessive expenditure on weapons—all these things resulted at least as much from political imperatives as from economic choices. Take any old Joe Tyrant in Africa, or in Asia or Latin America for that matter—the political and economic journey was similar everywhere from the 1960s onward. Joe wanted to keep the urban masses quiet, so he subsidized their food and their electricity. That meant less money for their education and their health care, and less money for agriculture research stations and the proper maintenance of power plants, which therefore soon broke down. He raised taxes to meet the bill for subsidies and guns. Fewer people could afford to pay them, so he confiscated the assets of those who could. Subsidizing food was getting more expensive, so he held down the prices paid to his farmers. They then produced less, so he had to import more and was then obliged to try to get his farmers to grow more expensive crops for export to pay for the basic crops he was importing. Joe had already taken over the main industries and helped himself to what was in the till when the need arose, so he could not invest in new capital equipment. As he became more unpopular, he had to spend more on his armed forces, so they consumed an increasing share of his budget—far more than was allocated to development. He could not afford to stop paying the soldiers, so the teachers and the nurses had to go without. Joe printed more money, so its value plummeted and inflation soared. The economy and the political structure spiraled down through subsidy, regulation, imprisonment without trial, deficits, welching on debts, locking up opponents, closing down newspapers, persecution of ethnically different but successful traders, overproduction, underproduction, inflation, famine—all into the Noah's flood or the slash-and-burn forest fires or the dust bowl of ecological catastrophe. This was the case, for example, in Ethiopia, which I visited three times at the end of the famine years in the 1980s. The country was torn apart by civil war. People starved as the Marxist government's policies penalized farmers and lowered food production. As the Ethiopians became poorer, they stripped the mountainsides of their forest cover to heat themselves and feed themselves and their animals. The soil was gouged by rain from the treeless mountains, leaving a gaunt, rocky backdrop to Ethiopia's human tragedy, which the rest of the world watched with horror and to which it responded with desperate lunges of generosity. Ethiopia was a dreadful example of the fatal consequences of Marxist tyranny in a developing country. To be fair, totalitarian economics and politics were only a part—albeit the largest part—of the story there and elsewhere in the developing world. Add to all that a world trading system that was often wickedly unfair to the poor, and you start to fill out the plot. But at its heart has been that arbitrary and disastrous mix of despotic politics and statist economics.

Once you began to open up and reform these economies, to regenerate enterprise, to scrap regulations, to privatize industries, to curb inflation, to cut army bills, to fight corruption, to use prices to encourage farmers and food production, to welcome foreign investment, to invest in basic infrastructure and social development, it became rapidly apparent that a political agenda was appearing as well. A more open economy lets in more ideas as well as more goods. Devolving economic decisions leaves less power at the center. Fewer regulations and subsidies mean less jobbery and graft. Dismantle economic controls, and in most places political repression founders, too.

The development of market economics in countries where various forms of command corruption had previously impoverished the community is neither trouble-free nor necessarily fast-working. The amount of political difficulty encountered often appears to depend on the level from which a country begins the reform process, as well (of course) as the skill with which reforms are implemented. A low standard of living and low expectations may make it easier to bear the social inequity that often accompanies the early stages of the dismantling of subsidies and controls. Conspicuous consumption, where previously there had been little consumption at all, may make fewer or smaller political waves, at least for a time, than is the case where there are more people with a rather higher standard of living to protect against erosion by the dismantling of state benefits and subsidies. I doubt whether the cruder manifestations of robber-baron capitalism—once memorably described by Edward Heath in 1973 as capitalism's unacceptable face—can be tolerated in the longer term as a community sees some opening up of economic opportunity. Huge disparities of income and wealth, the apparently random distribution of economic blessings, have usually had political consequences, especially if too many people seem to be left far behind. But the rougher practices and grosser inequities of capitalism—factory lockouts, tough hiring and firing policies, big profits for some, sweatshop pay rates for others—can be endured as an early and inevitable part of the business of economic takeoff in countries that have been very poor, like China.

Eastern and Central Europe showed the problems of dismantling socialism and establishing private rights—for example, the right to own property—in countries where a rather higher standard of living, even if an unsustainable one, made the initial impact of capitalism immensely disruptive. The choice faced in countries like this is to press ahead with reform or to put the brakes on. But there is really no choice. The problems rain down on you whatever path you choose to adopt, and if you decide that you will opt for edging tortoiselike into the marketplace, you may find it too difficult to get there at all. Like swimming in the English Channel or off America's Atlantic coast, the best bet is almost certainly to take the plunge, hoping that you will soon travel through the pain barrier. The political results are unlikely to be mild or easy to control, especially since technology, the speed of communication, and the easier access to information themselves can have liberalizing and therefore destabilizing results for statist societies. Once political and economic controls break down, however, the only real option is to go with the wind and the tide.

The idea that there is everywhere a relationship between political liberty, economic freedom, and good government does not go undisputed. It is challenged by reference to particular countries where the transition from some form of authoritarianism to basic democracy has merely replaced one set of unsavory policies and policy outcomes with another, and it is under particular attack in Asia, where some claim that the experiences of countries there demonstrate that democracy is not essential to the good life—indeed, that it may make building that life in an initially poor country more rather than less difficult. The argument has been strongly associated with Asia for three reasons. First, there has not really been anywhere else in the world where so many authoritarian governments have been able to point to a record of success, sustained over a reasonably lengthy period. It has been a political convenience for these governments to be able to argue *"post hoc, ergo propter hoc."* Economic success is a result, they claim, of authoritarianism, and as we have already seen, they assert that this very authoritarianism has deep cultural roots. Second, the example of the two most populous nations on earth has been summoned to the witness stand. We are invited to compare the economic record of India with that of China and to conclude that Leninism is good for you. Third, the present size and potential growth of Asian markets has in the past given some authoritarian Asian leaders more credibility outside their own region, and a degree of self-confidence in expressing in democratic countries criticisms of liberal democracy. The wreckage of 1997 may mean that the volume will now be turned down in the West when Asian leaders in the future give lectures about the perils of pluralism.

The proposition that the introduction of democracy does not change everything overnight and that it sometimes produces its own undesirable results is unanswerable. The world is scattered with such examples. Inevitably, when the democratic and free world is confronted by a nasty tyranny, it says, "What you need is democracy." Some appear to believe that once an election has been held, everything must be better, that they can breathe a sigh of relief and move on. But democracy, an election, is no more than a means to an end. Elections can and do sometimes terminate one form of illiberal authoritarian government only to legitimize another. They also can appear to endorse extreme forms of populism—for example, ethnic hatred. Remove the authoritarian cork from the bottle and all sorts of ethnic bitterness can come bubbling poisonously out (for example, in what we used to call Yugoslavia). That does not mean that authoritarianism is the only answer to ethnic conflict within a society. What is most significant is that these murderous hatreds can survive, under the surface, many years of heavy-handed suppression by government. In the end, ethnic differences are likely to be solved, if they are soluble at all, only by people learning to live side by side in some form of tolerant pluralism. Relative freedom may unleash ethnic violence, but such divisions are in the long run (and it may be a very long run) likely to be healed only within a free society, where people are obliged to face up to their own duties toward one another as human beings. That is certainly the conclusion to which I came after working as a minister in Northern Ireland.

A democracy may not provide for a particularly free society, or it may give freedom only to the majority. In democracies that simply validate the position, power, and prejudices of a majority, some citizens are not free. "If a democracy," writes Fareed Zakaria, "does not preserve liberty and law, it is small consolation that it is a democracy."* So democracy is not enough. What is required is liberal democracy—a system in which people not only elect their own government and lawmakers but also have their individual rights protected by a system of rules that apply to everyone. A liberal democracy has traffic lights and a highway code as well as motorways; you cannot simply press the accelerator flat to the car floor and drive wildly for your destination. By definition, as Professor Finer has pointed out, liberal democracy is qualified democracy, since the ability of the majority to get its way always and on everything is confined and constrained.

It is not therefore enough for opponents of authoritarianism to say that they want to see it replaced by elective democracy. There is more to a free society than occasional recourse to the ballot box. But a society with ballot boxes is far more likely to provide freedom for all its citizens than one without them, and societies that have elections but choke off civil liberties rapidly cease to be democratic at all.

"So," one is sometimes asked, "are you really suggesting that these large and complex societies in Asia (or elsewhere) should introduce one-person, one-vote just like that? Are you seriously arguing that they should try the leap into multiparty democracy overnight? It would be chaotic. Surely you should let them proceed at their own pace and they will get there in the end." This is usually an argument for doing nothing at all, and I am not sure quite how it accommodates the example of those like the Burmese, who had elections and then saw the results overturned by a repressive and incompetent military dictatorship. Some Asian countries have, however, been proceeding at their own pace more successfully toward pluralist freedom—for example,

* *Foreign Affairs*, November–December 1997.

Taiwan, South Korea, the Philippines, and now Thailand. The important thing is that they have actually been making progress, sometimes admittedly with the encouragement of crowds on the street. Political change and development in a previously authoritarian structure do involve risk (the greatest risk being for those on whom authoritarianism has conferred a monopoly of power and, invariably, a monopoly of the pickings). That change can be directed and managed relatively smoothly from the top; it can be demanded and imposed through demonstrations, unrest, and social breakdown; or—which is usually the case—there can be a mixture of the two. The resistance to change is more likely to provoke violence and chaos than its acceptance.

A democracy that is merely the validator of government by the majority can preside over capitalism and the rough outlines of a market economy, but it can also exist without capitalism. You could have a democracy in which the will of the majority (at least for a time) denied free economic activity—the right to hold property, for instance. But I do not see, on the other hand, how you can have a real market economy without liberal democracy, because a market economy requires checks and balances, an infrastructure of generally applicable laws, and the transparency that authoritarianism always denies.

It is occasionally asserted that all these things—independent courts, parliaments that protect liberties, newspapers that report the crimes and follies of the powerful—are of interest only to the better-off and the better-educated. Liberal democracy is said to be a rich man's club. The poor and the struggling are more interested in a roof over their heads and a full stomach. Without contesting for the moment the erroneous suggestion that people are more likely to enjoy economic rights if they are denied political ones, it is surely sufficient to suggest that perhaps they should be asked to make this choice for themselves rather than have their decision presumed by those who customarily speak out for the political illiteracy of the poor at a considerable social distance from them. It is difficult to think of many examples in history where the acquisition of political rights by the poor has been regarded by them as a threat to their prospects of becoming less poor. My Chinese critics were scandalized when they discovered that a consequence of our electoral proposals in Hong Kong was that shop-floor factory workers, chauffeurs, and hotel bellboys would have exactly the same electoral entitlements as their bosses. In Communist China, the empowerment of working men and women had clearly taken a distant and horrified second place to the confident assumption that rich people knew what was best for their economic inferiors.

The Asian authoritarians say, as others have done in the past, that democracy and freedom are at best irrelevant and at worst an impediment in building a successful modern nation out of a backward, impoverished, sometimes feudal and peasant society. Democracy makes nation-building more difficult. It prevents a wise leader or cadre of leaders from concentrating on a few, simple objectives. It distracts them from the long-term interest and confuses them with transient political pressures. They have to listen to too many voices, appease too many lobbies and interest groups. They lack the unquestionable authority to impose the social and economic discipline that is a requirement for rapid and sustained development. Democracy may be a luxury that can be afforded when a nation has been built, but first things first.

Nation-building in postcolonial societies was the task of governments and leaders who had themselves been elected. Having been democratically endorsed, they sometimes found it easier not to go through the same process in quite such a fair and open way again. Criticism can be a diversion. Making accommodations with political opponents can dilute the effectiveness of carefully considered and coherent policies. Electorates may even unwisely vote for politicians who are inept and dishonest and for policies that are wrong. All those things are true. But there is no inherent reason why policies that are in the long-term interest should be undeliverable in the fledgling democracy of a developing country. There must be some other reason for rejecting elections, and it is unlikely to be more sophisticated than the fear of losing them.

Why should investment in literacy and primary health care be politically unsellable? Why should agricultural reform? Why should concentration on competitive exporting industries? They should not, of course, but is there not a rather greater problem when it comes to small government, fiscal stringency, and low taxes? Will not electoral politics inevitably lead to fiscal incontinence, redistributive taxation, mounting public debt, high inflation, capital flight, low savings, and the discouragement of domestic and foreign investment? Well, this *could* certainly happen; yet it is not an inevitable consequence of pluralism, any more than economic virtue is an inevitable result of authoritarianism. I have already presented a litany of the economic woes of most authoritarian and totalitarian states. All that the attack on democratic profligacy and irresponsibility does is demonstrate that democracies can be economically illiterate, not that authoritarian systems are always more effective, always more likely to build a prosperous and stable nation. Indeed, those authoritarian governments that have made some progress toward the creation of well-off societies could be said to be the exceptions to the general rule that freedom works much better, and as I shall shortly argue, even these exceptions sooner or later arrive at a stage of development where the lack of civil liberties threatens further economic advance.

I admire the efforts of those who attempt regularly to make a calculus of economic and political freedoms around the world. It is a useful way of informing a debate in which otherwise value judgments and opinions bang heads unproductively. Yet I doubt whether the precision of league tables and percentage points is always a wholly accurate reflection of comparative lifestyles in different countries. These exercises do, however, sustain with some degree of measurable factual evidence three broad propositions: first, the countries most successful economically are, overwhelmingly, those that are free politically; second, countries economically free are invariably politically free; third, those countries that enjoy little economic freedom are usually denied political freedom as well. There is certainly no general evidence to sustain the proposition that political freedom is bad for economic performance, indeed quite the reverse. After the World Survey of Economic Freedom carried out in 1995 by Freedom House, the coordinator of the project, Richard E. Messick, concluded that its results showed unambiguously that "democracy, prosperity and economic freedom are all part of the same bundle. To treat one as less important than the others is to make the achievement of all three that much more difficult to realize."

Naturally, in a free and democratic society economic illiteracy is openly paraded, which is not to say that it is absent from closed societies. I saw manifestations of the sort of economics with which I strongly disagree among both the democratic and the antidemocratic camps in Hong Kong. Politicians seeking election, for example, would press for higher spending than the community could wisely afford, even lower taxes than the community was already paying, and unhelpful governmental intervention in open markets for sectional political purposes. I thought this merely confirmed that Asian values or not, Hong Kong's Chinese politicians were much like politicians everywhere else. But the whole process was manageable, and through managing it, the community became stronger, more stable and self-confident, and more economically vibrant, since the main capitalist ingredients of that vitality enjoyed public approval and support. You could win the argument for market economics in the public arena, and the act of engaging in the argument strengthened commitment to it. Such fragmentary evidence as Hong Kong provides does not suggest that the onset of democracy ends economic prudence. Hong Kong saw the beginnings of real democracy in 1991 and a wholly elected legislature in 1995. When I left Hong Kong, public spending as a proportion of GDP was lower than it had been in the early 1980s, when there had been an appointed legislature. So you could not deduce from the limited example of Hong Kong that when democracy comes in through the door, fiscal responsibility flies out the window.

How economically literate or sensible were the pressures that came from the antidemocratic camp in Hong Kong? A number of the most prominent business spokesmen and lobbyists (though, to be fair, not by any means all) gave every appearance of wanting to audition for walk-on parts as those businessmen who Adam Smith, in *The Wealth of Nations*, memorably described as seldom being able to meet together "even for merriment and diversion" without getting involved in a conspiracy against the public "or in some contrivance to raise prices." They were against competition, found monopolies extremely cozy, disliked open tendering (or open anything, for that matter), and believed that any regulation of markets or of corporate governance was thinly disguised socialism. In my experience, it would be as unwise to brand all democratic politicians as economic dumbbells as to equate all business prominence and success with economic wisdom and understanding.

I referred briefly in an earlier chapter to Hong Kong's housing problems and to the extent that they reflected Hong Kong's undemocratic "community-if-not-nation-building" past. In many respects the provision of so much public rented housing for so many people who had previously lived in wretched conditions in a relatively short time represented a considerable feat of public administration. It was municipal socialism writ large—a colonial version of Herbert Morrison's London County Council or Lee Kuan Yew's Singapore. Conservative ministers in the early 1970s sent the Hong Kong Governor, Lord Maclehose, to Singapore to see how socialism of a sort could meet housing needs. It was a fairly bizarre policy in what was otherwise the cradle of market economics, and with the best of intentions it produced all the usual distortions and inequalities that are associated with socialism. Rents became the most politicized aspect of government policy in Hong Kong, kept at such low levels in relation to household income that in many cases it would have been economically irrational for people to leave public apartments as they became better-off. More than 12 percent of households in the public subsidized sector (while staying put themselves) bought private accommodations to rent out to others. Better-off families paid lower rents for better accommodations than poorer families were paying for often rotten private-sector homes. Public housing went up at the rate of at least a hundred completed homes a day, but the waiting lists stretched into the next century. As usually happens, a combination of socialism and bureaucratic control misallocated resources, denied help to those who most needed it, and produced a political class of clients. With skillful leadership and competent administration, the Housing Authority kept the worst problems at bay and nudged things at the margins an inch or two in the right direction. Anything more radical would have involved more political pain than an unelected government could manage. I remain totally convinced that the best way of dealing with really tough political issues is by sharing responsibility for them with those affected. If people are responsible for sorting out their own problems, they are more likely to see the point of the measures required. Hong Kong will continue to face substantial housing problems, to distort its housing market, as long as the provision of housing disavows market forces and public participation in management. At least democratic control would ensure that those who are not housed by public authorities had a say in overall housing policy. I cite this as an example of the bureaucratic incapacity to make unpopular decisions. Elected politicians may be bad at doing necessary though unpopular things; unelected bureaucracies are even worse.

There are two other aspects of the nation-building argument to consider. The first is the history of Asia's greatest democracy, India, and the comparison between its economic performance and that of many countries to the east. The second is the consequence of one aspect of alleged nation-building—the corporatism, cronyism, and politicization of market operations in closed authoritarian economies. This is the part of the so-called Asian model that has, more than any other, driven the vehicle off the road and into the ditch.

India's story over the half century since Independence is in many respects a political triumph and an economic disaster. Democracy has prevailed despite almost every imaginable adversity, but economic development has been suffocated in a "license raj" that wrote socialism into its very constitution. A consequence of Indian socialism is that the resources required for basic education and health care have not been available or have been frittered away. Low literacy levels have acted as a constraint on full political democracy in India because many people cannot in practice participate in the democratic process. China, by comparison, has a better record in raising literacy and health standards, though this, paradoxically, does not stem from China's conversion to its own sort of capitalism but from the days of Maoism. There is much evidence of the return in the last decade in China of endemic diseases that were gotten rid of in the 1950s. More than 400 million Chinese live in areas where there is a problem of iodine deficiency. About 300 million people in the Chinese countryside are today directly exposed to snail fever or schistosomiasis, a deadly parasitic infection. China's assumed advantage over India in the provision of basic social investment may not be quite as great as it was when communism was pursued with however ill judged passion throughout the country.

On the other hand, China's growth figures continue to outstrip India's. China attracts much more outside investment, and can boast of increases in wealth per head way beyond India's performance. Has Indian democracy failed, therefore? Does India show conclusively that democracy is bad for your economy and bad for your ability to meet your population's basic requirements?

The real point about India is not that it has had too much freedom but that it has had too little. It has had political freedom but not economic. It was right in the 1940s to choose democracy, wrong to choose socialism and to stick to it against all the evidence of failure for so long. It has taken a very long time for the worm to turn. On the fiftieth anniversary of his country's independence, the Indian journalist Shekhar

Gupta argued, "If the choice of socialism is to be mourned . . . the choice of democracy should be celebrated. Contrary to what India's socioeconomic indicators show, in fact, democracy has been very good for India. Most of all, it has been the fundamental reason the country has held together as a reasonably strong union despite decades of internal discord, insurgencies and divisions of caste, religion, language and ethnicity. A secular, federal constitution, however imperfect, has been essential in giving this ethno-linguistic salad bowl of sixteen official languages a stake in a common identity. This explanation is not one that those coming from ethnically homogenous societies, such as the ones in most of East Asia, easily understand."

It is rare in politics to get the credit for the things that might well have happened but were skillfully avoided. India could have flown apart at the seams; it did not do so. It could have suffered some of the calamities that have befallen China; it has not done so. We should note again Amartya Sen's argument that "in the terrible history of famines round the world, no substantial famine has ever occurred in a democracy . . . in a country that is independent, has systematic multi-party elections, permits criticism of the government, and allows press freedoms. . . . In fact India continued to have famines right up to the time of independence in 1947 (in India, the last famine—the Bengal famine of 1943—killed between 2 million and 3 million people), and then famines stopped quite abruptly with the installation of a multi-party democratic system. No democratic government can afford to go to the polls after a big social calamity, nor can it, while in office, easily survive criticism from the media and opposition parties. The incentive effects of political and civil rights can be very powerful indeed."[*] Professor Sen draws the obvious comparisons with the Chinese famine from late 1959 to 1962, in which more than 30 million people died of famine-related illness. One of the most revealing observations in the account of those years by Mao's doctor, Li Zhisui, is his comment that the Chinese leader did not like hearing bad news about death and disease in the Chinese countryside; he called it "the dark side of things."[†] Dictators never do like being told bad news; democratic leaders have no choice in the matter—unless they respond to "the dark side of things," they perish.

[*] *Prospect*, October 1995.
[†] *The Private Life of Chairman Mao*, Li Zhisui, 1994.

If nation-building in India and China over the past fifty years takes into account the entire histories of those countries and not just recent growth rates, then it is worth saying in defense of Indian democracy that there has been no famine in India, no Cultural Revolution, no bamboo gulag. And India today has considerable strengths that will serve it well as it continues the process of economic liberalization that it has now begun and which commands much cross-party support. It has a legal system that will protect foreign investors and companies and a political system capable of accommodating and channeling social and economic change. Democracy and market forces in India will prove a potent combination, as the fund managers of New York, London, Tokyo, and Frankfurt will sooner or later recognize.

The Asian authoritarian model is often described as though the country concerned were a public company and its economic statistics a traded stock: Indonesia Co., Singapore, Inc.; Malaysia, Ltd. This sort of description contains an important truth. There is a confusion or agglomeration of roles that can make different parts of society seem just like related departments in a mega-company—quality control and design, accounts and personnel, and so on. The presidential palace, the relatives and cronies of the man and his wife at the top, the banks and financial services, the brokers, the big companies, the civil service in key departments, the governing party are all "company men"—part of the same clan, with a loyalty and commitment to its success that surpasses any notion of the rule of law or of the basic disciplines of a market economy. It is the mess that results from this that the Asians are now having to clean up. In South Korea, for example, the model created by a military dictatorship lumbered through the first years of South Korean democracy, showing increasing signs of strain, and finally crashed in the winter of 1997. The politicization of credit there—government departments directing who should get loans regardless of company balance sheets—covered up the simple fact that commercial enterprises, however vast, do at some time have to make a profit; losses cannot be hidden forever. South Korea has strength in depth; it has after all lifted itself in four decades from poverty to being one of the biggest economies in the world. Now it will need all its wits and brave political leadership to cope with the inheritance of the "nation builders." For example, in return for exceptionally hard work and low pay in the early years, South Korean workers were given job guarantees that cannot survive today's demands for more flexible labor markets. Was that an example of authoritarians taking the long view, or does it demonstrate that they are no less subject to unwise economic pressures than democratic leaders? In any event, it is now democratically elected leaders who have to deal with the results.

Clannishness and collusion beget cronyism and nepotism, which beget corruption and collapse. One spawns the others just as stagnant water breeds mosquitoes. Economies are distorted; losses are made and then hidden; bad debts and lies accumulate. Sooner or later, the markets read the writing on the wall. But it is not the market that is to blame for the subsequent collapse, any more than it is the bringer of bad news who deserves to be shot.

Policies will have to change and it will not be easy, because it will demand the opening up of systems, greater transparency and accountability, more pluralism, fewer of the practices of authoritarianism. Malaysians have to liberalize their closed system for awarding public-sector contracts. Indonesian banking and industrial policy can no longer be built around the interests of the President's extended family, as happened under Suharto. The Thais need to regulate their financial markets properly. Sensibly, they have recognized that economic liberalization requires political change; the financial crisis in Thailand was accompanied by successful pressures for a new constitution that should make corruption more difficult. Opening up closed economies will not be easy, and while the process creaks and squeals on its way, there will be a good deal of skepticism about the outcome. As always happens, having overlooked the bad when it was taking place, the international markets are likely to ignore or belittle improvements for some time to come.

The 1997 Asian crash is to some extent that continent's side of the same globalization argument that has raged in Europe and North America. Open and closet protectionists in the rich countries have worried about the effect on our markets and job opportunities of Asian standards (rates of pay, health and safety at work, and environmental regulations). The application of Western standards of financial regulation and transparency to Asian markets is regarded by some Asians as the cause of their own difficulties. This distorts a fair point. In a more open world market, the same conditions start to apply to everyone. You cannot expect investors to put money forever into projects where they face growing if hidden risks; and whatever the state of the global market, in every country sooner or later a bubble is seen as a bubble and a loss as a loss.

As economies grow up and become part of the global economy, they will be subject to pressures that push them, therefore, in the direction of greater pluralism. Technology, as I have argued, has the same effect, a point memorably made by Rupert Murdoch in a speech in which he argued that enterprises like his own (he had in mind principally satellite television) represented "an unambiguous threat to totalitarian regimes"; subsequently, he reacted unambiguously to objections from Peking by booting the BBC from his satellite channels. Open world markets, information technology, and modern communications—*pace* Mr. Murdoch—reinforce a process that occurs as economies mature and develop, shifting (as I have described) from quantity to quality growth.

Quantity-based growth, fueled by applying increasing amounts of capital and labor, eventually results in rapidly diminishing returns. You can cut down and sell your hardwood forests, putting more and more capital and labor into the process, but where will the growth come from when the forests are gone? Quality growth is essentially a matter of efficiency—the use of technology to devise new products, increase output, and reduce costs. This sort of growth puts a premium on inventiveness, creativity, and technological flexibility. The communities in Asia, as in other continents, best able to unleash these qualities will be those that provide their citizens with political liberty as well as economic, those communities that nurture their citizens' talents through pluralism. It is hard to see how a community can compete effectively for quality growth if the financial and business press operate under the threat of government sanctions, if scientists and academics are restricted in the books they can buy, the journals they can read, and the views they can advance, or if governments try to regulate matters that are better left to individuals, to families, and to businesses. Toleration of dissent, genuinely representative government, the rule of law, and the free press bestow real comparative advantages in the race for quality growth. As Alexis de Tocqueville argued in *Democracy in America*, even if in a democratic state the leaders turn out to be "less honest or less capable, the governed are more enlightened and more alert." A more open and accountable government, monitored by a genuinely representative legislature and uncensored media, is more likely to be a clean government, and more likely to preside over a fair business environment.

This is the "modernization" that much of Asia still requires and deserves, an argument put in China by the brave exiled dissident Wei Jingsheng to the consternation of the Communist leadership. For expressing this view Mr. Wei spent over seventeen years in prison, from which he was released into exile at the end of 1997. His main argument is clear:

> *What is true democracy? It means the right of the people to choose their own representatives to work according to their will and in their interests. Only this can be called democracy. Furthermore, the people must also have the power to replace their representatives any time so that these representatives cannot go on deceiving others in the name of the people. . . .*
>
> *Will there be great disorder across the land and defiance of laws human and divine once people enjoy democracy? Do not recent periodicals show that just because of the absence of democracy, dictators, big and small, were defying laws human and divine? How to maintain democratic order is the domestic problem requiring solution by the people themselves, and there is no need for the privileged overlords to worry about it.*
>
> *Therefore, judging from past history a democratic social system is the major premise or the prerequisite for all developments—or modernization. Without this major premise or prerequisite, it would be impossible not only to continue further development but also to preserve the fruits of the present stage of development. . . .*

The worst intellectual treason for political and business leaders in free societies to commit is to deny the arguments put by Asians like Mr. Wei and to give credibility to those who assert that economic success requires the suppression of political liberty, requires that men like Mr. Wei be locked up in a cell for their views. There are legitimate arguments about how far free societies should go in proselytizing their values (a point to which I will come later). But there is no case for moral relativism, for giving any credence to arguments that are intellectually shoddy, historically unfounded, and morally bankrupt.

Before I went to Hong Kong as Governor, I had never really thought very much about why I was a democrat; it had never occurred to me that I needed to think the question through. I had in similar fashion accepted the case for market economics rather loosely, never doing much more than to articulate a general preference for markets largely free from government interference and control. I shall always be grateful that the passions I encountered and to some extent engendered in Hong Kong and the arguments in which I became embroiled there, and in London and China, made me think more carefully about political and economic freedom than I would otherwise have done and made me concentrate on what I believe and why I believe it. In Hong Kong, rough-and-tumble though my experiences sometimes were, I arrived, as T. S. Eliot wrote, where I had started and perhaps "knew the place for the first time."

PART THREE
Looking to the Future

Engulfed by fear and suspicion . . .
We try desperately to invent ways out,
Plan how to avoid
The obvious danger that threatens us so terribly.
Yet we're mistaken, that's not the danger ahead . . .
Another disaster, one we never imagined,

suddenly, violently, descends upon us,
and finding us unprepared—there's no time now—
sweeps us away.

—from "Things Ended," by C. P. Cavafy

Preceding page: Student protesters in Tiananmen Square, May 16, 1989.

7

New World—Old Lessons

The Master said: "Put me in the company of any two people at random—they will invariably have something to teach me. I can take their qualities as a model and their defects as a warning."

—The Analects of Confucius, 7.22

Zizhang said: "How can one be generous without having to spend?" The Master said: "If you let the people pursue what is beneficial for them, aren't you being generous without having to spend?"

—The Analects of Confucius, 20.2

When I was asked to speak in Europe or America as Governor of Hong Kong, the subject requested would be as like as not the lessons that the West could learn from what was happening in Asia. Those were the high days and holidays of tigerism and "miracle" talk. I would be encouraged to speak about Asian approaches to economic policy, taxation, spending, savings and investment, to education and welfare provision, to the relationship between government and enterprise. But I was unable to offer my audiences a simple set of prescriptions, a password to prosperity that they could all cheer and try to remember on the way home. Increasingly, it seemed to me that while there were some things that by and large most East Asian governments had done pretty well—things that in Europe and America we could observe and sometimes learn from—the main points to draw from the Asian experience were not specifically Asian at all. The opening of markets and the dispersion through technology of market successes and failures—what we call today globalization—meant that there were lessons for all of us to learn, East and West: Some of us performed more successfully in one area; others did better elsewhere. More important still, the allegedly new phenomenon of globalization required us all to reacquaint ourselves with some old lessons.

In recent years, globalization has become the five-syllable terror of political economy. No clove of garlic can keep it at bay; there are no stakes to impale it at the crossroads. We are led to believe that it stalks lands and continents, sucks the lifeblood from economies, sacks industries, destroys jobs, impertinently challenges the sovereign authority of governments. It distributes its rewards and exacts its tribute with random terminality. The butterfly's wings flutter on one side of our planet, and economic chaos shortly reigns on the other.

Globalization may be a relatively recent (and unattractively clumsy) addition to the political lexicon, but as we have already seen, the notion that what it represents is new is laughable. Mass migration and integrated capital markets in the late nineteenth century provided the substance of globalization, even if the word itself did not trip from Victorian tongues. But the idea that we have somehow whistled up this economic El Niño ourselves dies hard. A little more historical memory would remind us also that it was the collapse of our earlier essay at globalization, the nineteenth-century liberal economic world order, that had such disastrous consequences. That breakdown, which began a hundred years ago, reached its calamitous conclusion in the protectionism of the interwar years. It spawned war and tyranny in Europe and beyond.

While the disciplines and opportunities of the world market may not be new, technology (the ability to transport people, goods, money, and information more rapidly and more cheaply than ever before) has certainly speeded and enhanced their advent and impact. Information and money move at lightning pace, their wonders to perform, their depredations to execute. On the whole, the latter have received more attention in the last few years, with people in the rich West warned that their standard of living was threatened by economic success in Asia, followed by people in Asia being told that their newly minted prosperity was jeopardized by a collapse of Western confidence in their currencies and stock markets. Whatever else was said about globalization, it appeared to be an equal-opportunity dispenser of misery.

One of the most spectacular casualties of globalization has been the delusion that governments are all-powerful. This does not mean that they have no power at all; indeed, their power to do sensible things remains unchanged. What they have lost is their ability to get away with doing the most damn-fool things—for example, in the West, extending their ambition to manage their citizens' affairs in areas barely contemplated in democratic societies before the second half of this century. In an understandable response to the results of the breakdown of liberalism—depression, war, hardship—Western governments, especially in Europe, from the 1940s onward had attempted to take on responsibility for most aspects of economic and social life. This was the heyday of bureaucratic triumphalism, thought necessary to salvage the fundamentals of capitalism and the moral legitimacy of the postwar state. The political ambition of those years takes the breath away. Governments offered womb-to-tomb welfare. They ran industries. They set prices and fixed wages—from the salaries of judges to the paychecks of grave diggers. They even thought they had virtually abolished economics: For the guru of modern British social democracy, Anthony Crosland, the dismal science was an irrelevance. Velázquez was thought by Picasso to have solved all the problems of painting; social democrats and welfare capitalists thought they had achieved similar success in solving the problems of governance. Political will and bureaucratic wisdom ruled and conquered.

For a time. The failure of aspiringly omniscient government preceded and instigated the return of those liberal orthodoxies that stand at the center of globalization. Barriers to trade were dismantled; industries "owned," or at least paid for, by taxpayers were returned to the marketplace; spending programs were snipped and trimmed to pacify overburdened and truculent taxpayers. The renaissance of liberal economic values opened new markets, encouraged greater trade, and laid the foundations for sustainable increases in prosperity for more people in the world than had ever enjoyed its fruits before.

There are other ill-judged things that governments can still do for which markets will eventually punish them. They can themselves borrow too much money or allow their banks, property developers, and industries to do so. They can turn a blind eye to corruption and cronyism. They can encourage opacity and collusion in financial transactions rather than transparency and openness. They can insist that credit continue to flow to commercial enterprises regardless of whether they make profits or losses. They can assume that the laws of economics do not apply to them, that they have invented some new economic order. Then suddenly the bottom will fall out of their world as reality catches up with them. All that is more or less what has recently happened in Asia.

At the heart of the international economic ferment of globalization are three elements—people, money, and technology. People can and do move their houses, families, and employment, though the scale of migration is lower today than a century ago, when, for instance, perhaps a million people were leaving Europe each year and many others were moving within it. But even where people are mobile, they are not as mobile as money or technology, and this is where the grumbles of rich and developing countries intersect. The Western grumble is that investment that should be creating jobs and sustaining communities in Europe and North America seeks lower labor costs in developing countries. Globalization thus pauperizes the unskilled in the developed world, and even threatens the well-being of skilled workers, too. In the developing countries, it is the ability of investors to take their money away, as well as to put it in, that poses the problem. The development needs of poorer countries are seen to be tossed like corks on the stormy waters of Western-dominated financial markets. On both sides, there is a dangerous and growing tendency to see money—investors, shareholders, and so on—as the villain of the piece. The interests of ordinary men and women are trampled underfoot; interventionist solutions are sought to protect them from the ravages of a casually cruel marketplace. These are not new charges. We have been here before, as far back as the enclosures of land in the Middle Ages in England or the Highland clearances in eighteenth-century Scotland. Denouncing the operations of the market two centuries ago, the English poet Oliver Goldsmith wrote: "Ill fares the land, to hast'ning ills a prey, Where wealth accumulates, and men decay."

It is in this debate about globalization and its ethics that I see the main present lessons to be absorbed from the Asian experience. The idea that there is some off-the-shelf Asian model which can be bought as it stands by growth-minded Western governments was always absurd, and now that the model, such as it was, appears to have fallen off the shelf and onto the floor, the argument is even more preposterous. What I take from the Asian experience, and from the changes in the developed world that helped to make Asian growth possible, is the importance of three fundamental issues, the first two of which in particular are central to any discussion about globalization.

The first of these issues is free trade, a main reason for Asia's recent success, but a principle that has been contested lately and is likely to come under fierce challenge in Asia and the West in the next few years. The second issue, which raises moral as well as political questions, is the role of government at the end of this century and the beginning of the next. What should government these days be expected to do, and what should taxpayers be asked to pay for? To what extent has overweight government led to underperforming economies, and has governments' eagerness to help their citizens sometimes exacerbated rather than alleviated these citizens' problems? The third question is how we can best give individuals the ability and the enthusiasm to do more for themselves and hence for the communities they comprise. I will begin with free trade and open markets, whose presence allows cities and countries to grow and prosper and whose absence sees them stagnate and decay.

Populism is not new. It is as old as quack medicine—as immemorial as snake oil salesmen and charlatan cures. It has been a recurring feature of democratic political life in Europe and America, and it is no stranger to Asia. Populism comes in waves, let loose by insecurity, by fear of change, by xenophobia, by blindness to sometimes uncomfortable reality, and by yearnings for a golden age.

It has sometimes focused on a single issue, like the concentration of Poujadistes on overtaxation in France in the 1950s. (This revolt of the grocers saw Jean-Marie Le Pen, now the xenophobic leader of France's extreme-right-wing National Front party, first elected to the National Assembly in 1956.) At other times, populism has been concentrated on minority ethnic groups—for example, the hostility toward Asian and Afro-Caribbean immigrants in Britain in the 1960s, or toward North African Arabs in France and Middle Eastern and Eastern European immigrants in Germany and Austria in recent years. Populism has also used one issue or panacea as the key to the padlocks on other prejudices, resentments, and dreams, and protectionism—the hostility to free trade, the raising rather than the lowering of barriers to the free exchange of goods and services—has regularly found itself in such a position whenever the right conditions have existed for this bacillus to thrive. In Britain, the fight between protectionism and free trade has spasmodically dominated our political history. We fought a war against Napoleon in part for free trade. We named a concert hall in one of our greatest industrial cities after it. On the other side, protectionism was sold for decades as the way to hold together Britain's fragmenting empire and to save jobs and preserve industries from decline. In the event, it proved more successful in shattering political parties and making and breaking political fortunes than in any of these other goals.

A populist cause like protectionism may be easier to pump up in Europe and America in an age when the moorings of politics seem to have come adrift. As I have already argued, class and ownership are no longer such substantial determinants of voting behavior, though there appears still to be some correlation between political affiliation and employment in the public or the private sectors. The intellectual divide between right and left is fuzzier as the primacy of markets is more generally acknowledged. For Western democracies as a whole, there is no longer an enemy at the gate, no simple and readily available Manichaean worldview, no tyrannical empire with rockets and secret police to confront. Certainties, both frightening and somehow comfortable because of their very familiarity, have been cast to the wind. As far back as President Carter's appointment of Zbigniew Brzezinski as his National Security Adviser, a cartoon character, Maudie Littlehampton, asked in a British newspaper "Brzezinski? Is he on our side or theirs?"

Similar questions furrow many more brows these days. Who is friend and who foe? What are we for and what against? Technological advance and the information revolution have further broken down political models by atomizing society. Political argument, once a three-hour oration in a drafty hall to an audience of thousands, is now reduced to a CNN or BBC sound bite beamed into the living room. Cut off from ideological stereotypes, if not entirely from ideology itself, political rhetoric searches for a home, a home for which the majority can be persuaded to vote. Where once presidents and prime ministers led opinion, now too often they seek to find out what it is so that it can lead them successfully to the polling booth.

With politics and politicians footless and—in so many cases—ideology-free, some of the conditions for populist protectionism in the developed world are primed; however, the motivations for it in America and Europe differ. First, the United States will remain for the foreseeable future the strongest economic power and the only superpower. The United States continues to act as both the world's policeman and its largest open marketplace. But gratitude is scarce. This inevitably puts a strain on the patience of American voters. I recall giving a series of speeches on the West Coast of the United States in 1994, just after the midterm elections had witnessed the (temporary) eclipse of Clintonism. The whiff of middle-class insurrection hung heavy in the air. Voters were fed up with the escalating costs of trying to be middle-class—taxes on income and property, the bill for education and health care, the expense of domestic security arrangements. They understandably were disinclined, after some years of pinched living standards, to contemplate acting generously at home or abroad. From Orange County to Seattle (which more or less covers the political as well as the geographical waterfront), my peroration that the world needed American leadership, even if it did not always say so very politely, was greeted with surprise and occasional mild resentment by people who appeared to feel that too much of the rest of the world was freeloading on them. Any political turmoil in Asia, particularly if it threatens regional stability, will lead to calls for the United States to get involved, just as the U.S. Navy steamed to the Taiwan Strait during the missile crisis of 1995. As like as not, plans for help will be accompanied by denunciations of modern imperialism, by DAMN YANKEE posters in Asia and the sneers of the intellectual left in Europe. "Screw them all" isolationism in Middle America will in that situation raise its head again.

With or without political unrest, trade imbalances with Asian countries will focus renewed interest on the slogans of the protectionists. Devaluations will give many of Asia's exported products a further competitive advantage, and China's overloaded inventories and flat domestic consumption may lead to dumping and heavy price cutting in her main markets. The absolute size of the U.S. deficit in dollars, rather than its relative size at probably no more than 1 percent of GDP, will grab the headlines. As we start the long run-up to the next presidential elections, all this may seem to provide politically profitable terrain for candidates looking to protectionist unions for financial support and using spurious environmental and moral arguments about the conditions in developing countries for the justification of their positions.

In Europe, I suspect that the appeal of protectionism may have similar though not identical roots. First, there is the "yellow perilism" threat to the postwar welfare settlement. There are those in Europe today who seek to justify protectionist policies directed against emerging nations in Asia or Africa or South America on the grounds that as these emerging nations do not have the same level of welfare and social protection as the rich countries of Europe, their competition is somehow unfair. This amounts to the absurd and callous proposition that to be poor is somehow to have an unfair trade advantage; it seeks to make our own economic lead unassailably permanent.

The safeguarding of Europe's welfare provision is clearly related to the defense of Europe's industrial base, old-fashioned Euromercantilism. Europeans are told by protectionists on the right and the left that they must safeguard the identity of European industry—the makers of cars and tractors, sewing machines and refrigerators, power stations and airplanes. Once it was American know-how and ownership that Europeans railed against; today, it is more likely to be Asian—as though slamming the doors to Asian products could preserve technological leads. The more uncomfortable Europe's continuing restructuring—with greater labor market flexibility, reforms in welfare provision, the slimming of older industries, and fiscal probity—the greater the likelihood of the sort of hunt for external dupes that still characterizes, for example, some of the political debate in France and—of late—Germany. This tendency will be exacerbated if, in the early years of economic and monetary union, Europe's new Central Bank feels obliged to keep monetary policy tight, with a consequent slowing down of growth rates and a rise in the jobless figures in some countries, in order to give the European Union's currency, the euro, credibility in financial markets.

What is it that protectionism claims to protect? The list is much the same everywhere. It is said to protect "our" living standards, "our" jobs, "our" firms, "our" welfare, "our" social programs, "our" stability, even "our" culture, "our" values, and "our" ability to make independently "our" own decisions and shape "our" own future.

Our living standards depend to a great extent on how productively we use the resources we have and on what we are able to sell to the rest of the world. On the whole, if other countries become better-off, we are likely to get better-off ourselves, provided we do not become less efficient or productive. To sell to the rest of the world, we need customers to buy our goods, and the more customers there are with money to spend, the more we can sell to them. During the recession of the early 1990s in Europe and North America, we sold more and more to the markets of Asia and Latin America. If those countries had not been growing, they would not have been able to purchase from us and our own recession would have been prolonged. When trade grows, most gain.

Countries that become big exporters invariably soon become big importers. Developing countries will probably account for the majority of the increase in world imports in the next couple of decades, provided they continue to have the money to pay for what they want to buy. If higher exports allow the output of poorer countries to rise, the likelihood is that output in the richer countries will increase, too. China is a good example of the relationship between exporting and importing. In Hong Kong, whose crowded port is China's main commercial artery to the rest of the world, we used to see the result every day as the containers moved in both directions. We counted them out, and we counted them in. At the beginning of the 1980s, China was the twenty-ninth-largest exporter in the world and the twenty-first-largest importer. By the early 1990s, it had moved into the top dozen in both lists.

What happens to living standards, especially in developed countries, if you shut out the goods from poorer countries? First, prices go up, hitting hardest the less well-off, who spend a larger part of their budgets on the sort of products, like footwear and clothes, targeted by protectionist tariffs. Second, the productivity growth that raises standards all around, as well as increasing growth rates, is slowed down, because the spur of competition is removed from less efficient industries. Faced by competition, they have to invest and improve their performance or else they suffer and decline. A protected economy uses its resources inefficiently; they go to support the losers, not to increase the number of winners.

Protectionism is always loser-driven, however it is dressed up. When Joseph Chamberlain, champion of protectionism as the way of binding together Britain's colonies and dominions, argued a century ago (in a classical protectionist text), "You cannot go on watching with indifference the disappearance of your principal industries," he was pitching hard for the losers. What if he had managed to prolong (at a cost) some of Britain's mid–Industrial Revolution technology—some of the country's textile capacity, for example. How long could it possibly have survived? What would have been the price, in the delayed introduction of new technology, new processes, and new skills? Protectionism tries to stop the clock. You may be able to stop your own timepiece, but you cannot stop other countries'. The clocks tick on. Technology passes you by until, painfully, you make the inevitable and essential adjustments that would have been easier at an earlier time.

Watching the disappearance in Europe and North America of what were once our principal industries is a distressing business, from Indiana to Lancashire to the valley of the upper Loire to the Franco-German border to Silesia to the Slovakian plain. The rust eats away at the metal. The landscape is blotted by the detritus of wrecked heavy-industry plants. In the middle of the day, the men loiter in sullen groups at street corners. Their wives seek low-paid work in new shopping malls or factories a long bus journey's distance away. Their children's motivation ebbs away as the prospect of a full-time job with a future dwindles. We have all seen that. It is a sad and bitter condemnation of our inability sometimes to extend the notion of community to the whole of our community. But things can be and are transformed over time as new industries and new economic opportunities develop, and the process is more rapid where labor is more mobile, as in the United States. In Europe as a whole, and even within European countries—for example, Germany—labor is less mobile and change takes longer.

It is easier to denounce this painful working out of market solutions than to find any other means of changing economic and industrial gears. Naturally, it is sometimes managed more competently and more sensitively, sometimes less so. In Britain in the 1980s, as the country's industrial heartlands were blitzed by change, some Conservative ministers and financial officials gave the impression that none of this was of any great consequence, since manufacturing did not matter anymore. They were right to argue that manufacturing was not the only eternal, virtuous commercial enterprise. There are other ways of doing a productive and honest day's toil than working up a sweat and getting oil and dirt on your hands. But facing up to reality requires sympathetic explanation, not blunt dressing-down. One of Britain's most successful Treasury ministers of the century, Rab Butler, once said that people who talked about creating pools of unemployment should be thrown into them and told to swim.

To what extent can protectionism save jobs from the scrap heap, save communities from decay, save rural landscapes from depopulation? Protectionist policies probably can save some jobs for a time, the length of which will inevitably vary. But the salvation comes with a high price tag, and it is time-limited—it cannot go on forever. It is estimated that protecting a job by shutting out foreign competition costs a protectionist economy between three and eight times the annual wage of that job. How does paying that price make an economy better off? And how are individual workers helped in the long run? Recent U.S. statistics, which are unlikely to be very much out of line with the situation in Europe, show that jobs in the export sector pay on average about 17 percent more than those in the import sector. So if you pay to preserve jobs against foreign competition, what you do in fact is to pin workers down in low-paid, low-skilled jobs instead of helping them move to higher-paid, higher-skilled jobs. Where do the sense and fairness lie in that?

What else do you preserve? For a time, maybe, you can keep declining industries going at the exhausted heart of declining communities. It is easy to regard that as an act of benevolence, an act of cultural solidarity, provided you yourself do not have to go on living in a community rotting away at the center, with no future save trying to defy markets and consumers for just a little longer. The bigger and more positive challenge is to help those communities acquire new vitality.

In Europe, we have used protectionist policies to try to prevent a further drift of people from the countryside. The expense has been enormous; the effects, bizarre. European consumers have paid more as the prices on supermarket shelves have risen. Developing-country producers have been driven out of markets where they should have been able to sell their goods. Landscapes have been transformed as subsidies encourage new crops and cycles of agricultural production. Big landowners in some areas have gained. Smaller farmers have continued to contribute to what Thomas Gray called "the short and simple annals of the poor." Anyone who believes that Europe's Common Agriculture Policy has swelled every farmer's income and featherbedded farming communities should visit the region of France where I have a house. It is beautiful but poor. "I cannot understand you," said one of my neighbors, a pig farmer. "Why do you want to come and live here? All our children leave, and we want to follow in their footsteps."

He and countless others like him have not been much helped by a protectionist, high-food-price policy. It has not begun to tackle the problems of job creation, low income levels, bad services, and inadequate housing and transport in rural areas.

As I noted earlier, the mobility of capital has encouraged a fear that money, earmarked in an earlier age for investment in new factories and job creation in developed countries, will be put instead into countries where labor costs are lower, health and safety at work and environmental standards laxer, and returns on investment greater. Ross Perot invited American television audiences to listen for the giant sucking sound as jobs were vacuumed out of the United States and into Mexico. A first cousin of this argument is that we are being obliged in developed countries, in the name of flexible labor markets, to strip down the social services previously available to workers, to limit their entitlements and benefits and worsen their conditions at work, in order to persuade employers to stay in Europe (the argument applies less to the United States) rather than move elsewhere.

When I was an Overseas Development Minister in the 1980s, I often had to deal with the criticism by aid lobbyists that there was no net investment by the rich North of the globe in the poor South. The position in the 1990s changed significantly. As official aid programs were cut, private investment (especially in Asia) soared, peaking at $260 billion in 1996, according to American Treasury secretary Robert Rubin. But even a figure as high as this almost certainly lagged proportionately well behind the figures of investment by rich countries in poorer ones in the years before the First World War. Moreover, Paul Krugman has pointed out (for example, in the *Harvard Business Review*, July–August 1994) that the high external investment figures of the first half of the 1990s cannot possibly be regarded as a devastating diversion of resources from the developed world when compared with the combined GNPs of North America, Western Europe, and Japan (over $20 trillion in the mid-1990s), their combined investment (over $3.5 trillion) and capital stocks (over $60 trillion). And where do the returns from these investments go? Partly, no doubt, they build up the pension funds of Western workers and help sustain other forms of investments, job creation, and job preservation in the developed countries, where the multinational companies concerned are still based.

Nevertheless, I find one argument about today's capital flows quite persuasive. It has long been a cliché of those who believe that growth solves every problem to argue that when the economic tide comes in all the boats rise. In other words, when a country gets richer—its productivity rising and its competitiveness increasing—all improve their standard of living. Is this still true today? Critics of this view believe that, at least to some extent, in a global economy, where capital and some forms of technology can be readily transferred, goods can be made quite easily—making some allowance for infrastructure, transportation, and education levels—wherever the cost of manufacturing is lowest. When Asian currencies were tumbling in the autumn of 1997, some Western companies (for example, the Swedish-Swiss engineering giant ABB) announced that they were cutting jobs in Europe and North America and increasing production in Asia, to take advantage of the more competitive exchange rates there. So as more manufacturing (especially in lower technologies) is sourced in poor countries, the supply of unskilled workers expands enormously. This results in falling wages or rising unemployment for the unskilled in richer countries; there has been a fall in many individual wages in the United States even while per capita GDP there has grown. According to this argument, those who are described as socially excluded—the jobless, urban poor—become permanently excluded by the ready availability of still poorer workers elsewhere able to do repetitive, unskilled jobs at a fraction of the cost.

But the answer to this problem—occasionally exaggerated but real enough to be worrying—is not to try to protect low-paid and low-skilled jobs in developed countries by shutting out competition from developing ones. What we have to do is to raise the skill level of the urban poor in rich countries. Their best hope lies with better teachers and trainers, not with protectionist trade officials. They also deserve a benefit system that does not discourage them from returning to the disciplines and routines of the workplace.

Even without the spur of competition from poorer countries, the richer ones—especially in Europe—would need to look hard at the cost of labor, both direct wages and social overheads, and at its flexibility. How easy is it to hire and fire, train and retrain, move people from one job to another? The greater the cost of employing labor, the greater the disincentive to do so, regardless of developing-country competition. That is one major reason why unemployment is at least twice as high in France and Germany as in Britain. If we had totally protected markets in the rich North, would that mean that we could guarantee permanent jobs, increase vacations, raise wage rates, and reduce working hours without any worries? In the absence of foreign competition, measures that reduced the productive efficiency of wealth-creating operations and increased their costs would still not be supportable for long. The arguments for greater flexibility in labor markets are persuasive even without Asian competition, though that certainly gives them a sharper edge.

There is a further argument about the damage done by free trade and free capital flows that has been heard more in Europe than in North America. It enjoyed its prime in the days when tiger success was exaggerated and feared, and it was much associated with the late Sir James Goldsmith and his supporters, especially in France. It is at once cozy and discomfiting. Asian success—or that of any developing country—threatens Europe's very identity: our farms and our cottage industries, our factories and our city streets. Where Japanese videos and third-world oil seeds lead the way, hordes of North Africans and Slavs will surely follow. The traditional values of a cohesive society—low unemployment, prosperity for all, a proper balance between urban and rural living, cultural homogeneity—are all under attack.

On what grounds, the argument continues, do we justify slavish adherence to market forces? We claim that they bring us economic growth, but that is not the only measure of success. Look at the United States. Its economy grows and so do its social problems, from drugs and violence to marital breakdown and racial tension. We should not be dazzled by economic indicators; other simple things matter more in life. Who, sensibly, would not sympathize with that last point? It is not the fault of the billionaire protectionists of recent years (like Ross Perot and Sir James) that the super-rich, blameless and generous to a fault though they may be, are never the most convincing exponents of homely, austere virtues. St. Francis, perhaps foreseeing the likely criticism, gave away his cloak and his father's legacy before taking his own demotic denunciation of GDP to the highways, the byways, and the pulpits of medieval Umbria.

Economic growth can wreck the stability of communities just as it can imperil the balance of nature. But no growth at all is usually, today, much more dangerous. In richer countries, it thwarts ambitions for future progress and foments bitter debate about difficult choices of priorities. In poor countries, it pins down the population in misery. I never thought there was all that much to be said for romanticizing the nobility of the savage; I see none at all for romanticizing poverty. Growth may not guarantee improvement for the poor in developing countries, but it is more likely than stagnation to bring some amelioration of their conditions. Poverty is also one of the main environmental menaces—not because of any fault of the poor, but because of the consequences of the poor's struggle to eke out a miserably low standard of living from a harsh environment. What we require, whether on the bare mountain slopes of Eritrea, the flooded plains of Bangladesh, or the crumbling streets of Watts or Hackney, is economic development—sustainable development, of course, as though anyone could seriously countenance any other sort.

Attacks by open and closet protectionists on free trade principles and on the opening of markets were in the past linked with Asian success. They will not much diminish even with Asia temporarily in the dumps. Sharp devaluations right across the region are likely, as I have suggested, to increase Asian exports even as the contraction in Asia's own markets damps down the amount they import. Asian trade surpluses in the future may soar. At the same time, within Asia itself, financial catastrophe will from time to time provoke nationalist outrage. Bankruptcies, the squeeze on middle-class standards of living, mounting personal and corporate debt, cuts in spending programs and subsidies, rising taxes and prices, job losses, failing banks, political tension, national humiliation seeming to follow so improbably hard on the heels of vaulting success—all these things will be associated by some with Western money, Western global interests, Western racism, Western values, and Western solutions. As migrant workers are sent home from better-off developing countries to poorer ones, as political and business leaders count the costs of their mistakes, as the hunt for fall guys gathers pace, as the public (which will have to bear much of the pain of reform programs) is encouraged to believe that it is paying the price to bail out foreign bankers and investors, a nasty bout of nationalist foot-stamping is possible. The failures, as it were, of Suharto's regime in Indonesia may provoke a clamor for reversion to the nationalist protectionism of the years of his predecessor, Sukarno. It will be important in Asia and beyond to reassert constantly that it was free trade and open markets that propelled Asia up the league tables of growth and prosperity, and it is those same policies that eventually will help Asia to recover and revive, on the road to more soundly based growth in a more pluralist political framework. We now know (as if we did not already) that the sun also sets. But it rises again, too.

The second big issue raised by growing competition in a more open world market revolves around government—namely, its size and role. In the days when any traveler from the vibrant, booming East was regularly asked by interested if distant observers in Europe and America to spill the beans and divulge the secrets of Oriental success, the reply invariably homed in on either side of the same point. There might be some preliminary description of the close relations among government, banks, and industry (previously admired by corporatists on the left and the right), and then after that celebration of now disgraced collusion, those to the left of center would applaud the high levels of savings and investment and those to the right the low levels of public spending and tax. I have already noted the relationship between the one and the other, like pollen and honey or sunshine and ripe tomatoes. The relevance of this point to our condition in the richer developed countries remains high, despite the Asian crash. It is manifestly not enough to be sensible about spending and tax, but it is a good start to successful economic management.

The electorates in developed countries, especially in Europe, want faster economic growth than they have known in the last few years. Nothing gets much better without growth, and since ties of community are strained by its absence, it is at least worth challenging the assumption that any more radical efforts to revitalize our economies would inevitably require policies that tear communities apart. They are tearing apart anyway. The radicalism that we should consider is to take a hard look at what governments do, at the taxes they raise, and at their relationship with the citizens they serve and represent. The appetite of states, the proportion of the community's income taken in taxes and public spending, has grown in the West, and while recently curbed, it remains high. Does this make people happy, moderate, and more consensual? We seem, at least in Europe, to have the worst of every world: ambitious, large, and bossy governments and disaffected citizens, with larger numbers in some countries like France and Germany drifting to the political extremes or even beyond them into a world of random violence.

Let us begin with the size of government in Asia, measured by its appetite. When I left Hong Kong, where health and education standards were on a par with those for the OECD countries as a whole, we were committing just over 16 percent of our GDP to public spending; we took under 12 percent in tax. The figures elsewhere in Asia were similar. The Koreans took about 18 percent of GDP in public spending. In Taiwan the figure was almost 16 percent; in Thailand, about 15 percent; in Singapore, about 20 percent; in Malaysia, a whopping 25 percent. I do not wish to overdo the point. There are problems of definition (substantial ones, for example, in Singapore), and it is hard to make strict comparisons of like with like. Yet it is broadly true to say that lower levels of public spending as a proportion of GDP have been a hallmark of the recently booming Asian economies. There are other qualifications that one should properly make. Lower proportions of public spending may be in part a consequence of less advanced stages of economic development. The Japanese figures, for example, are closer to those in Europe and North America. Moreover, the figures in Asia may edge up in response to growing demands for public services and as once giddy rates of growth fall to more sustainable levels. So these are arguments and comparisons that come complete with health warnings.

Having begun the list of cautions, let me add one or two more before I switch on the ignition of an argument that can all too easily crash on the first bend. First, in advocating a steady reduction in the role and size of the state, I am not advocating a slash-and-burn approach to public spending or underestimating the political difficulties of the enterprise. I have not sat in the sun so long or been so distanced from the daily pressures and vulgarities of democratic public office as to underestimate the size of the task in reforming public spending and public attitudes. Reform and retrenchment in the public sector, which is a long-term project, will naturally stand an incomparably greater chance of lasting success if it is pursued with as broad a base of public and political support as possible; it should not be something that opposition parties denounce and then come to halfheartedly in government. The pity of it is that Western governments these days invariably win elections promising that public spending is safe (that is, too high) in their hands, before being forced by the logic and pressure of events to take the shears rather timidly to its outer edges. Sooner or later politicians will try rather harder to develop a cross-party, cross-community consensus for what needs to be done, challenging the assumption that there is an umbilical connection between public morality and public spending, and being obliged to recognize in doing so the validity of G. K. Chesterton's observation that "it is only the last and wildest kind of courage that can stand on a tower before 10,000 people and tell them that twice two is four."

In his brilliant book *The World After Communism*, Robert Skidelsky concedes that the question of how best to make significant cuts in state spending bristles with technical and political difficulties. He goes on to argue correctly that "at root the issue is philosophical. We need to answer two kinds of question. Are the welfare responsibilities which the state has assumed over this century [in most Western countries] any longer appropriate in privately wealthy societies? And what, in such societies, is the appropriate division of responsibility we would want to see between the individual and the state?"

This is a profoundly liberal issue. It assumes a goal of lower taxes and the banishing of envy as the motor of fiscal policy—a notion largely unknown in Hong Kong and other successful Asian societies, where doing well for yourself is regarded as a matter for commendation rather than carping. I do not advocate the crasser sorts of individualism, in which men and women are regarded as culturally rootless and devoid of a sense of duty and responsibility. Nor do I argue that everything the state does is wrong and that we need an ideological assault on public services. I believe strongly in the ethic of public service. In Britain, certainly, we get highly professional public service on the cheap. I favor, as I have said, a smaller but much better paid public service, looking after a more narrow range of responsibilities. What we require in Europe, both in the European Union and in those fellow European states to the east—and the same may apply in other richer countries—is what Skidelsky calls "state repair." We shall be able to restore the authority of states only by shrinking what they do. Today they are muscle-bound but weak, ambitious but derided. To do a lot better, they must do a little less.

How much do they try to do today, and how much has their appetite grown over recent years? The share of national income consumed by the state in the rich, industrialized countries has grown sharply during the postwar years, especially since the superconfident 1960s. By the early 1990s, public spending took 42 percent of GDP in the OECD as a whole. In France, the share was 55 percent; in Germany, about 50 percent; in the Netherlands, nearly 56 percent; in Britain, 43 percent; in the United States, 34 percent. Most of the increase resulted from a hike in social spending, which rose from 10 percent of GDP in the OECD in 1960 to 21.5 percent by 1990. In France, the figure went up from 13 percent to 26.5 percent; in Germany, from 18.1 percent to 23.5 percent; in the Netherlands, from 11.7 percent to 28.8 percent; in Britain, from 10 percent to over 22 percent; in the United States, from 7 percent to 14.6 percent. Taking the northern member states of the European Union together, the rise was from 12 percent to 28 percent. If we want to trim state spending, we have to focus principally on welfare reform. State repair is above all a matter of *welfare* state repair.

The growth in welfare spending reflects a number of factors. After two world wars, the depression, and the bitterly extremist politics that those events helped to engender, politicians agreed that an extension of the state's responsibility for mitigating need and hardship, for smoothing over the rough edges of economic life, was essential to the survival of capitalism and to the cohesion of society. This understandable sense of obligation was supercharged by the feeling of effortless abundance in the 1960s and by pressure from the growing number of clients that the state had created for itself. Each new social program produced a new vested interest, and each vested interest proved effective at lobbying for the growth of individual programs and benefits for whose aggregate cost the increasingly restive taxpayer had to foot the bill. Any elected politician will testify to the effectiveness of targeting by interest groups. At my own constituency advice office, when I was a Member of Parliament, I would regularly see groups or individuals who wanted more money spent on whatever good cause most affected them. They could be intellectually convincing and emotionally heart-rending. Affordability was not their concern, since it stood to reason that a society as affluent as our own could find the money for such a modest and overwhelmingly well intentioned cause. I rarely saw anyone who wanted to complain that taxes were too high, even though (a point to which I shall return) the level of tax became everywhere in the developed world an issue of growing electoral salience in the 1970s and 1980s.

The rise in Europe's levels of unemployment since the mid-1970s, to double-digit figures unimaginable in the confident years that went before, has certainly pushed up the total welfare bill. This is not a question solely of direct payments to the unemployed but also of spending on those poverty-related programs that alleviate the needs of the families of the long-term jobless. Yet what is striking, certainly in Britain, is the extent to which it is the other components of the social security bill that have absorbed the lion's share of resources. In the mid-1990s, 44 percent of social security spending in Britain went to the elderly (including their pensions); 25 percent went to the sick and disabled (though the nation's health was improving); 19 percent was committed to family support; and 10 percent of the budget was devoted to the unemployed. So it is untrue to argue that the surge in spending is entirely the result of economic breakdown—of the rise in unemployment in the last two decades—even though that increase in unemployment may itself have been partly caused by the results of soaring expenditure.

The development of the welfare state was justified in terms of economic efficiency as well as social compassion. A workforce whose welfare requirements were more than adequately met was thought more likely to behave responsibly as a so-called social partner; industrial harmony would be preserved, and pay demands would be moderated. This argument was carried to a slapstick conclusion in the "social contract" that underpinned the sputtering social democracy of the Wilson and Callaghan governments in Britain in the 1960s and 1970s. Under this empty accord, the government undertook to do things that it should never have agreed to do (on tax, spending, and union rights), in return for the trade unions' signing up to promises (on pay restraint and productivity) they had no intention of keeping. The social wage—benefits, pensions, and so on—rose, and so too did actual pay. Growing welfare spending was not accompanied by pay restraint. Nevertheless, some economists also argued that loading costs on to the employment of labor, the overheads of welfare capitalism, would ensure that employers made the maximum productive use of their most precious commodity—a modern, welfare state workforce. Expensive energy made employers more efficient in its use, and it was said that they would become equally efficient in using expensive labor, investing in productivity gains to get the most out of their costly employees.

What actually happened was that just as cost-conscious employers used less energy, so they have used fewer workers. With spending on the welfare state growing more rapidly than the economy overall, deficits and hence interest rates have risen and taxes have gone up as well. Higher taxes have meant less saving and investment; they have penalized entrepreneurial activity and reduced the incentive to work. High welfare costs and the deficits and taxes that go with them have slowed growth, and a deteriorating economic performance has increased the demands on welfare programs. There is a debilitating interaction between overambitious welfarism and a sluggish economic performance with much higher unemployment.

Within the OECD countries as a whole, and certainly in any comparison between them and the East Asian economies, higher rates of growth and employment are associated with lower ratios of taxation and spending. Skidelsky and others argue that what might be called with some justice the golden age of Western economic performance in the 1950s and 1960s saw public spending ratios of between 30 and 35 percent, sustainable figures that allowed budgets to be balanced with low inflation and little borrowing. It would be an exaggeration to pin all the blame for slower growth, and the social and economic problems associated with it, on the crisis of the welfare state. Yet there is plainly some relationship between the two. Ironically, because of higher unemployment and lower growth, we now see the rise in Europe—less so perhaps in Britain, where the 1980s saw some reduction in public spending ratios—of precisely that political extremism and social alienation which higher welfare spending was designed to prevent.

It would be surprising if we did not feel obliged to look anew at the relationship between modern governments and their citizens given the other changes that have taken place in society. On the brink of a new century, why should our assumptions about the government's role be determined by the ideas that were in vogue in the first half of the present one? There are also profound moral arguments for a fresh look at the role of government. The nationalization of welfare has subverted local and voluntary effort and has hence circumscribed pioneering and innovation. It has also sapped the local community's sense of responsibility for dealing with the need in its midst. This is not a sentimental view of a Poor Law past of amateurish networks of Lady Bountiful care. Voluntarism has always been the cutting edge of public conscience, of cost-effective service delivery, and of the discovery of new needs and of better ways of attending to them.

The loss of both variety and freedom of choice has been another inevitable casualty of the state's assumption of responsibility for every welfare need; without them, the competitive pressures that raise value for money and standards of performance have been lost. But what concerns me most is the effects on individual benefit claimants and their families. We know that benefits often prolong the social conditions from which claimants deserve to be rescued. Self-reliance, motivation, and determination are weakened as economic incentives to work are slashed. Even privacy is infringed as the laudable public commitment to prevent welfare abuse at the taxpayer's expense leads to increasing prying and intrusion into the individual's private life.

The relationship between booming welfarism and family breakdown raises the most worrying moral questions. If you raise the costs for men and women to form families, and if at the same time you increase the benefits available for women to raise children outside marriage, you should not be too surprised when social behavior starts to reflect these penalties and rewards. High male unemployment (partly, as I have argued, a result of high taxes and labor costs) contributes to marital breakdown. In addition, many poorer families that struggle to hang together find that they are dragged down into the benefit system, or that both parents have to go out to work because taxes claw back so much from even a fairly low income. These taxes, of course, go partly to finance benefits for the jobless and for those whose marriages have broken up or never really formed.

All governments are committed to supporting the family; and politicians (whatever their own private lives) regularly sing the praises of family values. Why do they bother? Given what has happened to traditional family structures in the developed world, it is difficult to think of any single political ambition more humiliatingly botched.

Do appeals for supporting the traditional family, accompanied by the introduction of an ever wider range of state-funded welfare facilities, amount in practice to the advocacy of family values without families? In his pamphlet *Beyond the Welfare State* (Social Market Foundation, 1997), Robert Skidelsky suggests that while the welfare state may not have actually caused the breakdown of the traditional working-class family, it has probably deepened the trends that sustain lifestyles and work patterns which undermine such families. As a result, many parents and children are trapped in dependency and poverty from which it is difficult to escape.

The notion of a dependency culture is in some senses untrue. After all, the poor on welfare are rendered independent of their family and friends and their local community. On the other hand, they do become dependent on the state and its officials, imprisoned by forms and regulations and tribunals, pried on and bossed about, a sullen underclass all too often marooned beyond hope, their latent entrepreneurialism focused exclusively, as they wait in line, on how they can get the most out of the official who deals with them from the other side of the counter. A system designed compassionately—and imaginatively in its time—to abate need, and that often still achieves that objective, also today sometimes increases or prolongs need.

Globalization has arguably made it more difficult for governments to continue to fund bloated welfare programs. When their spending goes up and their borrowing mounts, governments seeking loans in international capital markets have to pay an interest rate premium. The cost of their borrowing rises and they have to pay more to service their debt. In addition, globalization—as Andrew Tyrie has argued—reinforces the trends toward what are in reality "tax strikes" of avoidance and even dishonesty. With fewer countries controlling the movement of capital, and with technology speeding capital transfers, it is easier to move money from high- to low-tax countries. This affects corporate as well as personal taxpayers. "Higher tax rates now risk triggering capital flight (and possibly labor movement too) and deter inward investment," Tyrie notes. "Internationalized avoidance and evasion are likely increasingly to prejudice the tax yield in the years ahead."* Shifting the domicile of a company in order to avoid paying higher taxes has even

* *The Prospects of Public Spending,* 1996.

caught on in the small business sector within the European Union. In the spring of 1998, a number of small French firms—from hairdressers to bakers—announced that they were relocating their business registration to Britain, where the taxes and commercial overheads were so much smaller. To the annoyance of the French government, trade organizations advised small firms how to make the switch to the U.K. and ran advertisements detailing the benefits in lower taxes of doing so.

This makes it both more essential and to some degree politically easier for governments to set about the comprehensive reform of welfare entitlement programs. Both the intellectual mood and the support of taxpayers lean in the same direction. In Britain in the 1970s and 1980s, winning the arguments against industrial subsidy and state ownership preceded the cutting out of expensive regional industrial programs and the privatization of previously nationalized industries; now the growing clamor right across the political spectrum against the nationalization of welfare should help to build support for reform. Taxpayers have made themselves heard as well. Even politicians on the left have stumbled over the unpleasant truth that working people pay taxes—often paying higher marginal rates than the super-rich as they come off benefit into work.

I have always been amused by the pundits and pollsters who claim that taxpayers are not really all that concerned about how much they pay, that they prefer to see well-funded government programs than lower taxes, that tax is much exaggerated as an electoral issue. To support these arguments, opinion polls are often cited which purport to show that, if asked to choose, voters would prefer to see more spent on social programs rather than to receive cuts in the taxes they pay. We should perhaps distinguish between attitudes to expenditure on health and education on the one hand and general welfare spending on the other. But even without this distinction, I have never been convinced by these polls and took no notice of them whatsoever when, as Chairman of the Conservative party, I was running the Conservatives' 1992 election campaign in Britain. It always seemed to me that the key question was loaded and could be roughly translated like this: "Are you a selfish bastard, or would you prefer to spend more money on old people, schools, and hospitals?" Those who gave what was presumably a politically correct answer went on to behave in a politically incorrect way, voting regularly against higher taxes. If the issue is in dispute, if voters may be prepared to favor higher spending over lower taxes, why is it that politicians have failed to grasp this obvious psephological truth? Why have politicians increasingly through the 1990s in every developed country campaigned on a ticket of fiscal probity? It is true that they rarely promise to cut spending or to redraw the lines between the government and individual citizens. But it is equally true that they do not offer voters higher spending and higher taxes. To do so would be an eccentric guarantee of life in political opposition.

After its election in 1997, Britain's Labour government trumpeted its determination to carry through a radical revamping of the welfare state, the most thoroughgoing review—so it was said—of the welfare relationship between the government and its citizens since the Beveridge Report shaped postwar Britain. A middle-ranking minister, Frank Field, was given charge of the enterprise. This boded well, though I had better confess to a personal reason for being strongly disposed to think the best of Mr. Field. When we first entered Parliament, he and I used to be "pairs," an old-fashioned arrangement in the House of Commons under which individual members agree together that from time to time they will absent themselves from the less important votes. Field was a bachelor but understood that as the father of a young family, I faced the usual domestic demands. Thanks to our friendship and his sympathy, I was able regularly to go home early and to see more of my wife and children than would otherwise have been possible. Frank Field became a personal as well as a political friend. Brave in the face of hard left pressures in his constituency, iconoclastic, intellectually generous, personally austere, Field was as good a man as there was in the House of Commons, and he became over the years as knowledgeable about welfare as anyone in public life. Tony Blair's imaginative appointment of this Christian Socialist as the point man on welfare reform was widely welcomed, not least on the right of politics, but the first blueprint produced by Mr. Field for consultation was something of an anticlimax. It looked as though Field's radicalism had been blunted. Frank Field had always in the past favored less means-testing (since it increased complexity and encouraged dishonesty) and the reestablishment of a universal insurance principle in welfare. I had always agreed with him on both these matters. Alas, though there was much to praise in his initial plan (proposed improvements in the administration of welfare services, for instance), on these two fundamental issues the government seemed to be heading in the wrong direction, increasing means-testing and further diluting the insurance principle. But it is early days and all those who believe, as I do, that welfare reform on the right scale and the right lines is likely only if it commands support across the parties will hope that Mr. Field can come back more positively to these issues and will offer him support if he does so. He is too good a man to be allowed to fail, and it is too important a subject to be fluffed.

As I said earlier, I do not underestimate the political problems of embarking on state repair. It will be easier if those who commit themselves to it have the authority of a mandate—if they have been elected to carry it through rather than elected to hold on to the status quo. Reform should also be based on clearly articulated principles and should be comprehensive rather than a collection of candle-end cuts. Four principles in particular might actuate change.

First, reform should seek to make it easier for the jobless to gain employment rather than stay on welfare. Disincentives to work should be cut; incentives to stay at home should be removed. Those who are out of work for long lose motivation and forget the disciplines of work. They also feel deeply humiliated, a sad point wittily made in the British film *The Full Monty*. I favor workfare, making the payment of benefit to those who are fit and have never been employed or have been out of work for a long time conditional on working in public schemes. There are significant start-up costs to such a program, but it does deal with the problem of disincentives. It also makes it more likely that those who would otherwise be increasingly damaged by long-term unemployment find their way self-confidently back into the labor market. Reductions in tax and spend ratios—curtailing the preemption of private resources by the public sector—and a fall in the social costs of employment that employers have to bear should themselves in time help to increase job creation and cut unemployment by raising growth.

Second, the government should see its role as the guarantor and regulator of basic standards of welfare, not as their universal provider. Governments should look for those areas (above all, pensions) where private provision could be developed and made mandatory. The state should regulate a mixed market of private, mutual, and public provision. Obliging everyone to insure themselves against adversity and hardship (getting the state to help with the contributions of those who cannot afford them and to insure the uninsurable) would restore the fundamental principle of social insurance, the long-neglected foundation stone of most welfare states. I much prefer the social insurance route toward welfare reform to any other, getting the individual to insure against adversity. It asserts the comprehensive nature of community welfare while using different forms of delivery system; it embraces whatever works best; it redefines the role of government and its relationship with its citizens; it enables those covered by insurance to see the direct relationship between what they pay and what they receive. The alternative involves a major increase in means-testing, with all the intrusive bureaucracy that goes with it. Each new means test turns into another fight. It is reform by trench warfare; better by far to strike out for open country.

The third principle is that, while retaining an overall commitment to reducing the reach of the state, governments should be guided by practicality, not ideology. Alexander Pope summarized this principle in a couplet: "For forms of government let fools contest; Whate'er is best administer'd is best." Deng Xiaoping argued similarly that it did not matter whether the cat was black or white as long as it caught mice. When I was a minister, I recall the existence of all too many cats that never caught any mice at all and even seemed to be in the business of breeding them. As Environment Secretary responsible, among other things, for Britain's housing policy, I wanted to encourage local authorities to put up municipal housing rents to more sensible economic levels. But I was unable to do so. Why? Because a rise in rents would have necessitated a large increase in spending on the housing benefit, paid for by the taxpayer, which allegedly went to poor families, though in practice it was distributed much higher up the income scale. The existence of an unfocused welfare benefit made it more difficult to run a sensible housing policy.

In British social policy, the best case for Dengism is in the health service. Perhaps if we were starting afresh, we would try to avoid creating a largely free, universal service paid for out of general taxation. But it works (for all the grumbles) remarkably well, as I know from my own and my family's experience, providing high standards at a relatively low cost—particularly in comparison with some privately funded health systems in other countries.

While I naturally favor the encouragement of private provision, Hong Kong demonstrated the limits to how much you can accomplish by this sort of promotion when the standards of free public provision are high and rising. Hong Kong had begun with a largely private service with safety net support for the poor, mainly provided by churches and charities. As public taxpayer-funded health care grew, so the attractions of private insurance and private care diminished. The quality of what was mostly free was sufficiently high to make some feel that it would be economically irrational to dig into their own pockets to supplement what they were already paying for as taxpayers.

The cost-effective, high-quality British health service suffers from one main defect—the lack of a perceived relationship between people's ambitions for improved health care and their willingness as taxpayers to pay for it. I have long believed that this is an area in Britain, and elsewhere, where hypothecation (in other words, setting aside the proceeds of a tax for a deemed purpose) has much to recommend it. A health tax would be a clear statement of the relationship between patients, potential patients, and the service, and its level would reflect what people were actually prepared to spend for their health care.

The fourth principle is that where more spending by the state is required and can be justified, it should be invested. An enthusiasm for reducing the tax and spending ratios does not presuppose that every spending program can or should be cut or reformed. I subscribe to the now-fashionable view that we should invest more in education and training, both because it is in our national interest to have a well-educated and skilled workforce and because there is a unique, liberal value in trying to equip every citizen with the ability to make the maximum use of his or her talents. Governments should guard people's safety, impartially enforce their laws, protect the integrity of their currency, and guarantee that there are services to help the poor and disadvantaged. They should also see that parents are able to secure for their children the best possible education.

It is a cop-out to say that there is no exact relationship between the amount countries spend on education and the quality of the education they provide. Of course, that is true. You could spend more money on the salaries of bad teachers, more on the fabric of schools and classrooms in which lessons were ill taught, more on sustaining a curriculum and teaching methods that were hopelessly out-of-date; that would be nugatory expenditure. But I have little doubt that quality education requires substantial investment. In Britain in the 1980s and

1990s, Conservative governments carried through a wide-ranging program of largely sensible educational reforms. It was hamstrung by the underfunding of the educational system at every level (a process that probably began as far back as the 1950s and has continued under Labour as well as Conservative administrations).

Not all funding has to come from the taxpayer. Britain has, for example, lagged way behind other countries in requiring a reasonable contribution from students to the costs of their higher education. For many years in Britain, we refused to give our universities the money they believed they required, and also refused to let them raise more money themselves from those who wished to study at them. We declined to allow the market to contribute to the solution of a problem largely created by the educational parsimony of the government. In the longer term, higher spending may be almost a condition for any further advance in some crucial areas. All agree for example that good teachers are the key to a good education, and there is at least the makings of a consensus that it should be possible to get rid of bad teachers. But I remain doubtful about any government's ability to recruit and retain more of the former and remove more of the latter without ensuring that over time teaching becomes a better-paid profession. If it matters so much, why not reward it better? I say this despite my own experiences as an Education Minister over a decade ago, negotiating with the leaders of the teachers' unions, on the whole a drab and rather unattractive lot. Is it the same in every country? What enthusiastic classroom teacher could possibly want to spend his or her time arguing about percentage points on pay scales? Teaching is an honorable profession not as well led as it deserves, or maybe it is the fault of rank-and-file members not giving those who try to speak up for sense and moderation in their unions the support they need.

Education brings me from free trade and state repair to the third of the issues touching on my Asian experience and on globalization—the role of the individual. Here my argument becomes more a matter of subjective observation and hunch, not statistics. I have no overarching theory to explain what I am going to say, but I feel it in the marrow of my bones.

In Hong Kong and elsewhere in Asia in good times—and I cannot believe that it is not there (though a little more *piano*, perhaps) in bad—there is something that should be intangible but which you al-

most feel you can touch and smell. It is a belief in progress, the hope—
no, not just the hope, the real anticipation—that things can get better
year by year through the ideas and the efforts of individual men and
women rather than as a result of some chance external intervention.
Perhaps it is the natural result of the stage of economic development at
which Asian societies find themselves; the truly awful days are a recent
lifetime memory, the good days have come with unexpected speed and
unimagined plenty. You can see what individuals can achieve on their
own because you know what you have yourself done with your own talents. It is rather Victorian and wholly admirable. One can laugh behind one's hand at some of its more vulgar manifestations, just as one
is tempted to curl a lip when reading about the Collector, that eventually disillusioned believer in Progress (with a capital "P") in J. G. Far-
rell's great novel *The Siege of Krishnapur,* whose favorite art object is a
marble bas-relief entitled "The Spirit of Science Conquers Ignorance
and Prejudice." But Western cynicism seems today so wearisome and
negative, no longer amusing or chic. I hope that Asia's postcrash difficulties do not give this Western mood a new seen-it-all-before lease of
life. The energy generated by sheer enthusiasm and the potency of
hope are real casualties in Europe (much less so in North America and
Australia), of the feeling that we have had our hours on the stage, done
our bit for humanity, deserve now a break from history. Add to that our
Western indulgence of backbiting as a way of life, and you can understand why something like the Asian buzz has been heard too rarely in
Europe.

I doubt whether economic crises, the collapse of financial empires
based on bad debts and unrealistic dreams, and the reappearance of old
liberal truths about politics and economics will have wiped the Asian
slate clean of that best sort of individualism. Most of Asia will pick itself up and get back to work, having learned (we must hope) some useful lessons from the rout. Once again, before too long, that palpable
sense of the possibilities of human achievement will reassert itself.

One of the most obvious signs of the enthusiasm and self-belief
that I find so admirable is the driving commitment to education; it is
not uniquely Asian, but it is certainly present in abundance in Asia.
Their brilliant test scores regularly place Asian youngsters at the top of
the league tables comparing mathematical and scientific achievement
in different countries. Maybe too much rote learning and drudgery go

into these successes; perhaps Asians need to encourage more creativity and free thinking in their schools and universities. But they certainly do not require to be taught what appears to have been forgotten in too many developed countries—namely, that rigor is at the heart of any good education. Perhaps Asian parents push their children too hard; at least they do push them. I remain surprised that there has not been far more—and far more aggressive—parental pressure in the richer countries of the West for much higher educational standards.

Yet another of the uncelebrated, or at least undercelebrated, boons of globalization is to shine a spotlight on the importance of education in a world where jobs, ideas, information, and knowledge will travel ever faster and (we should ensure) with fewer and fewer restrictions. And if, in Western societies, governments give their citizens a little more room to breathe, ending the public monopoly of welfare and limiting what they themselves do to what they need to do and can do best, perhaps we can ourselves rediscover a few remaining deposits of community adrenaline, a zest and enthusiasm that will help us tackle more effectively the social and economic problems of fatigued success.

8

How to Make Money

Do not sit on a mat that is not straight.
—*The Analects of Confucius,* 10.12

What might this gnomic aphorism mean for someone trying to do business in Asia—or even elsewhere?

I have never myself been responsible for making the tills ring week by week to pay other people's salaries—to keep men and women in a job, to provide them with the reasonable assurance of a stable future, to give them the chance to earn the money to pay their mortgage or rent, their insurance or household accounts. It is the great distinction between life in the public and the private sector. I have run great bureaucracies, a large department of state in Britain, the 180,000-strong government of Hong Kong. Whatever management skills are required for such enterprises, I have never had to turn the figures black at the bottom of the page in order to pay the bills. The taxpayer has always obliged.

That fundamental difference between public sector and private sector responsibilities has not left me in awe of businesses, shareholders, and profits, but it has given me a healthy respect for entrepreneurial skill and the demands of business management. I do not think that the business interest is the only one that matters in society; the business of America—or any other country—is not exclusively business. There are other concerns like social stability and cohesion, national security, the vitality of civil society, and the preservation of the rule of law. If, however, business does not enjoy the conditions in which it can prosper, many of the things that politicians and the public they serve wish to achieve become impossible. That has never persuaded me that politicians should seek to run, steer, or second-guess businesses. The words *industrial policy* make me curl up inside. Nor has it convinced me that the business world's view of its own and society's best interests is always correct. But I am wholly persuaded that one of the highest priorities for government is to provide a business-friendly environment, an infrastructure of law, tax, and public policy that enables all well-run businesses to thrive and make profits.

It was not very difficult to do that in Hong Kong. Though I was occasionally pressed to intervene in the economy—to twiddle like a pseudo-Keynesian with the dials on the macroeconomic control panel, to establish a "winner-backing" industrial policy, to do anything rather than just stand there—by and large there was a political culture that both understood and celebrated the case for government restraint, for keeping bureaucracy's hands off the management of enterprise. So we kept taxes on business and individuals low and cut them when we could; struggled to abate inflation and cost pressures; ensured that public spending did not elbow out private saving and investment; and spent more money on the improvement of education and training. Inevitably, because of the behavior and policies of our neighbors, we looked at whether there should be some closer, symbiotic relationship among government, industry, and banks. We considered whether the government should be doing anything to retain manufacturing capacity in Hong Kong. We looked at the case for an expansion in Hong Kong's research and development budget, which some people claimed lagged so far behind that of our competitors as to threaten our future rates of growth. But always we concluded that the market usually knew best—that it allocated investment far more sensibly than governments, that it secured higher rates of return, that (with some background assistance, for example the provision of government-funded training and retraining) it usually found the best way through the hazards of potentially disruptive economic change, and that it was invariably better to bet on the market than on the latest fashionable business school thesis.

We did intervene in some areas and were mildly criticized for it. I was determined to see that Hong Kong's banks, financial services, standards of corporate governance, and financial markets were properly regulated, and that there was the greatest degree of transparency about our financial statistics. One of my earliest decisions was to publish for the first time the size of our reserves. I believed (and still do) that part of Hong Kong's continuing attraction as a financial center depended on the perceived integrity of its marketplace. I also thought it necessary for government to do more in two other areas—to raise the standards of industrial health and safety and to give the workforce greater basic entitlements in relation to sickness, injury, and redundancy. The first of those policies was a necessary, belated, and not wholly successful response to the city's deplorable record of industrial injuries and accidents. Hong Kong, a first world community in every other respect, still suffered from third world attitudes about safety. I recall that the first reaction of one Hong Kong employer to a particularly ghastly accident was that shareholders should be reassured that it would have no effect on profitability. As for the rights of the workforce, I do not think that enthusiasm for a flexible labor market requires a denial of any fair entitlement for employees on pay, working conditions, sickness and injury benefit, and so on. People are more likely to work better, and society is more likely to be stable, especially during periods of change, if one can avoid factories, shops, and other workplaces being dominated by a sense of grievance.

My enthusiasm for gunning down financial cowboys, for reducing the number of horrific accidents on construction sites and factory floors, and for trying to sign business up to a public code of ethical standards in the run-up to a transition many feared would bring an increase in corruption inevitably led some to charge me with incipient socialism. Would that this were really all that socialism is about! I take these sorts of regulatory interventions as vital to sustaining the moral legitimacy of capitalism, an economic system that properly avoids any flirtation with crowd-pleasing egalitarianism. The pursuit of equality of outcome—as opposed to equality of esteem, of opportunity, and, so far as possible, of access—is a doomed and impoverishing business. But extremes of wealth and lifestyle prick the conscience and raise worrying political questions. I have never lost much sleep over the Gini coefficient and the other statistical paraphernalia of sociology; nor, to their good fortune, have many people in Asia. I strongly believe that growth and the market are better friends of the poor than are well-meaning bureaucracies. Yet they are not by themselves sufficient, and poverty in the midst of plenty remains the greatest moral and political challenge for those who believe in liberal economics.

The darkest side of my responsibilities as Governor was to visit the scene of tragedies, to encourage those who were coping with them, and to try to give some comfort to those who were injured and bereaved. Naturally, what sticks most clearly in my mind is the horror of some of the sights I witnessed—the accident and emergency department of a hospital in the early hours of a New Year's morning with the parents of teenage children crushed to death in a crowd accident arriving wild-eyed with terror and shock to identify the corpses of their children; children, horribly disfigured by a hillside fire, wrapped in bandages like mummies; the relations of men, killed in an elevator accident on a new building project, howling their impotent rage at the world if not at me. While those horrors have left their mark on my memory, what always struck me at the time about the victims of these accidents was how poor and simple they seemed—poorly dressed, poorly educated, comprehensively disadvantaged in a city stuffed to capacity with advantage. I used to make a point of visiting, usually without prior warning or publicity, some of Hong Kong's "black spots," the worst housing projects, private rented slums, rat-infested emergency housing areas, and prostitution- and triad-ridden ghettos. I could not always do very much about the conditions I found—clean up a stinking lavatory in one place, harry a bad landlord in another. But it seemed to me that even an act of presence at a place of squalor by someone responsible for the whole community's well-being was important in a city that so vaunted its success. It also made me understand all the better those agents of capitalism (the Cadburys, Rowntrees, Guinnesses, and others) who comprehend and confront some of the moral consequences of the system that so richly rewards them.

On the whole, politicians tend to make a mess of things when they play at business, and businessmen do much the same when they play at politics. Let me give an example on both sides. The vogue for tripartism, for governments trying to steer the economy through a partnership with employers and unions, is now dated and discredited, though echoes of it still occasionally reverberate, as do the rusty clanks of government policies to reorganize and revitalize industry. We have never quite faced up to the inherent fallacies of this approach to economic management, and have always half believed that it had not worked well in Britain (or really in Europe—America has not been troubled by this nonsense) only because we had never quite learned the secret of sparky, "all-in-this-together-guys" cooperation in the interests of national partnership. If only we had a MITI (Japan's interventionist trade and industry department); if only we could plan for the long term, getting banks to invest where it was in the national interest to do so—building up this or that industry, supporting this or that new technology; if only we could take on the world with the single-minded arms-linked determination of business and government in Japan or Korea—those have been the swooning aspirations of some politicians, bureaucrats, and commentators. One good consequence of Asia's 1997–98 crash, of Japan's long and depressed potter though the doldrums, of America's simultaneous sustained and successful expansion is that we should have finally learned this lesson. Transparency, keen regulation of banks and financial services, responsible corporate governance with boards of directors questioning management, the need to satisfy shareholders with adequate rates of return on investment—this "American model" looks like a sounder investment for politicians than any alternatives. But I hope that Americans will not be too hubristic about this; the moment they are, the failings of this approach will inevitably start to show through the shining paintwork. The American way does require politicians to know their place, which is out of the boardroom and off the factory floor. European politicians, however, do not always like to be confined to the chambers of governance. Perhaps they do not find the basic and limited tasks on which they should be concentrating sufficiently difficult, or maybe they are just too difficult.

For their part, businessmen do themselves few favors when it comes to lobbying governments (sometimes to get governments to do things they should do, sometimes to get governments to do things they should not even think about doing). Some businesses, to be fair, are very good at putting their case. They are the companies you would expect to be professional advocates of their own cause, because they are good at the rest of their business too. They take the job seriously, decline to cut corners, behave entirely aboveboard, and treat those they lobby as intelligent and informed interlocutors, which is sometimes an accurate reading. So the job is sometimes done well. I was surprised as a politician and minister, however, by the low quality of a great deal of corporate lobbying and by the naïveté of the approaches that many made. A quick read through the register of the declared interests of British Members of Parliament used to reveal some breathtaking evidence of how little many businesses knew about politics. Several politicians with scant influence and less judgment were on an astonishing number of payrolls. All that was legal, if ill advised. The low level and fairly squalid British political scandals about payments for services rendered reinforced the point. I never knew whether to be more surprised by how low a price some people put on their own integrity or by the ignorance of those offering the inducements about the quality and standing of those they were seeking to purchase. Blundering about in the not very sophisticated world of politics, many businessmen looked a long way out of their depth.

The connections between business and politics are given an exotic twist when it comes to business efforts to get into the Asian market. Though its relative size, as we have seen, is smaller than sometimes supposed—a point that helps to explain why the initial effect of the Asian crisis on Europe and America was less marked than many feared—there are still good export markets to win, good infrastructure projects to secure, and the hope of much, much more just around the corner. Asia, of course, is well-known territory to many European and American businesses. They have been active in this market for years; they arrived before the "miracle" and will be there for the long haul. There are European and American managers and salesmen with a lifetime's experience in the region and who know far more about it than transient politicians. However, because the Asian success story is relatively new, there are many more businessmen who have only recently tested the temperature of the Eastern waters, and they sometimes perhaps have an exaggerated expectation of what politicians can tell them about how best to make a splash there.

What should a businessman want of a politician when he contemplates trading or investing in a market far from home, whether in Asia or elsewhere? The view taken of the responsibilities of governments and their representatives for the well-being of business can be pretty crude. Writing to the British Consul-General in Shanghai a century ago a trader noted: "You are Her Majesty's Consul and you are bound to look to national and permanent interests—this is your business. But it is my business to make a fortune with the least possible loss of time."

Opinions are usually a bit more sophisticated than that. While recognizing the irreducible limits on what politicians can achieve outside their own country, those in business should expect their political leaders to work to secure globally, so far as they can, the same conditions that help business to prosper at home. That does not just mean capitalism. Capitalism without the right software can be a dangerous jungle, as the American columnist Thomas Friedman has argued. We have seen that in Europe since the collapse of communism. Several countries that purportedly embraced capitalism lacked the institutions that enable capitalism to work effectively for the good of the whole community. They did not have independent courts, a clean civil service and police force, a vigorous legislature, or proper regulatory bodies. A notable example is Russia, where capitalism is riddled with crime and dominated by gangsters, a mafia marketplace. Capitalism, like patriotism, is not enough. Businessmen from pluralist societies should press those countries that want to attract their investment to buttress capitalism with the institutions and attitudes that distinguish it from the commercial jungle. "After the Cold War," noted the Dean of Yale's School of Management, Jeffrey Garten, "the assumption was that countries which adopted the hardware of democratic capitalism would inevitably develop the software. But adopting the hardware is the easy part because there's no credible alternative model in the world today. It's getting the software that's the hard part. . . ." And so it has proved in Asia as well as the countries liberated in Europe from the Soviet empire; sometimes the software employed has been straight out of the Middle Ages or borrowed from the Al Capone School of Business Ethics. At its worst, in Albania for example, the arrival of capitalism has been accompanied by financial scams on a truly spectacular scale.

Businessmen invariably say that a primary requirement for them in foreign markets is that ubiquitous piece of turf, a level playing field. Level playing fields are much cited, seldom described. Level for one company is uphill for another. What "level" should mean is that all firms or investors are treated the same, that the market makes the choices between products and prices or at least that the way the choices are made—all other things being equal—gives every firm an equal chance. Liberalization of markets remains a priority for Western governments and has recently received much welcome support from Asians as well. As we remove more tariffs, police intellectual property toughly, open up procurement procedures and the telecommunications and financial services industries, the playing field for everyone will become genuinely more level. The more members there are of the World Trade Organization (which has led the fight to open up markets), the better. But free and fair trade extend beyond these important considerations of international trade policy. There are three other related issues that should concern businessmen and political leaders. The first is buying contracts with what purports to be aid; the second is buying business with bribes; and the third is using political connections to establish a dominant place in the marketplace.

For some years now, the United States has railed against the use of "concessional financing" and tied aid (that is, aid with strings attached) by other countries to purchase market share or mega-projects. The aims include sustaining lame-duck industries, establishing industrial dominance in certain sectors, and creating new jobs or saving old ones. Let me explain simply how these subsidies work. An aid donor country offers a developing country money on very soft terms—well below the prevailing rate of interest—or mixes grant aid with loans in order to achieve the same effect, provided that the recipient country purchases a product or a project from the donor. Imagine a city in India or China that wishes to build a mass transit system. Construction and engineering firms from donor countries would bid for the work, theoretically undercutting the market price they would otherwise charge (if, for example, the project was being undertaken in a developed country) by the amount of the subsidy their national governments are prepared to provide as notional aid.

A huge amount of business is done around the developing world on this basis, and with so much infrastructure investment required in Asia, the future pipeline of such business extends into the furthest distance. There are international rules and regulations governing these deals—prescribing, for instance, the minimum amount of aid that should form part of the financial package in order to prevent aid turning into a thinly spread interest rate subsidy—but most big companies that work in the regions where concessional financing is used believe that countries other than their own twist and bend and creatively interpret these rules. It is an area where the distinctions between government and business, taxpayer subsidy and market price, are fudged and fuzzy. It is an area that, in everyone's interest, should be cleaned up.

Who benefits from this combination of public subsidy and private business? Does the company whose product or project is subsidized do so? I have my doubts. For a number of years in the 1970s and 1980s, Britain—and other countries could point to similar examples in their own programs—committed itself to building large power stations in some of the most demanding locations. I recall visiting one outside Khartoum and another in a remote part of Central India. I suppose someone could justify these as "good" aid. We all knew that an undeclared subsidiary purpose was to try to keep going a second major power generator manufacturer in Britain. The strategy was doomed. Any company that requires business to be won through subsidy in order to survive has had it. Another company, Trafalgar House, must have been one of the largest beneficiaries of concessional financing in Britain. Much money and vast quantities of ministerial time were expended helping to win business for this company, which employed a vast number of Britain's engineers. Ministers went on visits to hot and steamy places; they strained the resources of the Government Hospitality Service entertaining their counterparts from distant continents at Lancaster House lunches and dinners; they signed Letters of Intent and Memorandums of Understanding by the score. The aid rules were squeezed until the pips squeaked. At the end of all this, Trafalgar House was taken over twice, on the second occasion by a Norwegian firm.

Companies that cannot stand on their own feet cannot long stand. There is no salvation in the occasional pickings to be had from OECD aid budgets. Indeed, the hope of securing subsidy can readily become the most zealously pursued entrepreneurial activity in which a company engages; all its vim goes into lobbying its own trade ministry. Some of the biggest projects supported by concessional financing resulted in losses for the companies concerned. The taxpayer lost; the firm lost; so who gained—the recipient country?

No, not always—for two reasons. First, countries are often encouraged to take on too many big schemes, because these are the sort that are attractive to big companies and big donors. It would be grotesque to criticize every project in a developing country for a dam, tunnel, power station, underground rail system, and the like; many are vital and play a key role in economic development. And some do not, a point put with particular vehemence about some of the biggest third world hydroelectric schemes. Second, it is sometimes doubtful just how much real development assistance a recipient country is getting when concessional financing is on the table. From time to time, the concessional financing merely makes acceptable what would otherwise be an uncompetitive price. Let us take the case of a company doing business in two markets, in one of which subsidies are available and in the other of which they are not. Provided the company knows it can build an element of concessional money into the accounts for one project, it is able to overcharge in one country and use the excess made there in order to undercharge in the other. The developing country is benefiting very little if at all; the taxpayers' subsidy is helping to shave the price in the country where the subsidy is theoretically not available.

This is a murky area in which some countries (and governments) specialize. It needs a real spring cleaning. Aid is aid; business is business. They should be kept at arm's length. I cannot believe that this sort of allegedly compassionate mercantilism does any developed country's economy much good in the long run. Companies that compete on real issues of price, quality, design, delivery, and service and win business on those qualities are guaranteed a successful future; companies that need access to the taxpayers' pockets to win business are a much worse bet.

Britain, to its credit, has recently taken a step in the proper direction by abolishing something called the Aid and Trade Provision in its Overseas Development budget. On a dark night, with a following wind, it was just about possible to justify the cash spent under this program as official development assistance. But it was all pretty dubious, and I think the Labour government was right to get rid of it. Now Britain is well placed to join America and one or two others in trying to eliminate such practices.

Government sweeteners are in a different category from corporate bribes, though both distort markets. Corruption is a serious problem in Asia; widespread in some countries, it has reached pandemic proportions in others. Nevertheless, we are not entitled to assume this is some sort of uniquely Asian phenomenon, like the eponymous flu. We know the extent to which corruption has infested some European countries. In Italy, its disclosure on a comprehensive scale brought down the whole postwar party political structure. The Christian Democrat party, which had seemed to be Italy's anchor ad infinitum—the political representative on earth of confessional capitalism—was laid waste; former prime ministers and their senior colleagues were invited to help the carabinieri with their inquiries; a former socialist leader and premier found the North African climate better for his health than the one back home. So do we assume, as we look at what has happened in the cradle of Western civilization, that corruption is culturally European? Is that our assumption when we hear the tatty stories of parliamentary impropriety in Britain, home of democracy, or the bigger tales of Town Hall sleaze there? (Local councillors have more power than Members of Parliament to make the decisions that are more likely to be subject to corrupt practice, like planning decisions or the award of housing contracts.) What do we make of a former Irish prime minister paid over a million pounds by a supermarket chain for apparently no purpose other than to help him live the life of Riley as was his due? What inherent aspect of European culture is represented by the business ethics of some members of the late President Mitterrand's inner circle of friends and advisers? And what do we make of the fact, on the other side of the Atlantic, that despite rules about public appointment so tough as to deter many from making the sacrifice required to leave their private-sector jobs, most American cabinets contain a scattering of appointees who end up under investigation for this or that impropriety. Corruption may be more prevalent in some Asian countries than in the West. Still, we should be careful not to delude ourselves into thinking that corruption is something alien that happens elsewhere but not in our own backyard, nor should we accept in a sort of resigned man-of-the-world way that its pervasiveness in parts of Asia means that it should be accepted as a normal and permissible condition for doing business there.

Corruption does serious damage in all countries to the standards of public life, the institutions of government, the cohesion of society, and the management of the economy. It does particular harm in developing countries, where the political fabric may be thinner, civic institutions less firmly based, and the economy by definition more fragile. Corruption in a developing country is a heavy tax on economic activity. It raises costs and blunts competitiveness. It distorts the management of the economy, making it more difficult, for instance, to gauge the exact consequences of investment, spending, tax, and regulatory decisions. It also warps policy making in other ways. Just as hefty dollops of concessional financing can entice governments into undertaking too many big projects, so too can bribes. If you are spending the government's money on building primary schools, rural roads, and village health centers, the chances of skimming a large percentage off the top of the price of the work are much less than if you are building a power station or buying a frigate or a squadron of fighter aircraft. The reform of overregulated economies also may be delayed by fear on the part of the regulators that loss of their powers may result in the loss of the income they can make from their exercise.

Venality sometimes surprises even the hard-boiled by its lack of shame. I have never been offered a bribe myself, but have twice been asked in somewhat counterintuitive circumstances to pay one. Both occasions were when I was Britain's Overseas Development Minister. First, after discussing large rail and dam projects on a visit to an Asian country, I was visited in London by one of the ministers with whom I had talked about these matters, who suggested that the two aid ventures could be expedited if he was properly rewarded for his cooperation. I hoped that he had not learned his ethics at Cambridge University, of which he was a graduate. The second time, the finance minister of a legendarily corrupt African country for which Britain had painstakingly put together a large international rescue package told me with a wall-to-wall smile in his hotel suite in the margins of a banking conference that he would naturally need to be rewarded with a percentage of the bailout if he was to accept it on behalf of his government. As investigative journalists of tabloid newspapers write, at this point I made my excuses and left. We went ahead with the rescue, minus the inducement to be rescued. I daresay the minister found some other way of augmenting his Zurich bank account.

This sort of corruption deters sensible foreign investors from risking their money; at the very least, the scale of corruption will be regarded as a hazard that needs to be weighed against any assessment of rates of return. It must be seen by investors as a minus rather than a plus, which is one of the reasons for regarding as a somewhat eccentric proposition the argument heard from some economists that corruption is a sort of lubricant in developing countries that helps to make society there work. It certainly helps the rich and the powerful, though at the expense of much of the rest of the community, particularly the poor. Corruption, therefore, becomes a political irritant, the destabilizer of regimes; it is a principal factor in unrest, riot, and revolution, a point recognized by Chinese leaders, who make occasional high-profile attacks on the corrupt practices of lower-level officials.

Corruption is easier to get away with in authoritarian command economies. But the introduction of the free market and democracy do not necessarily end it. Let us start with the liberalization of hitherto heavily socialized economies. Deregulation and privatization are early items on the agenda. Carried out in a half-baked way, they can and sometimes do result in more corruption, not less, which is naturally a reason for pressing them to their appropriate limits. First, when you are selling off state-owned assets, or franchising what were previously state-dominated activities, the potential pickings are very large. At the very least, the purchaser or holder of the franchise may be induced to pay for this commercial privilege. Second, if the government retains discretionary powers in the sectors that it is selling off, the chances of pocketing bribes continue and conceivably increase. Every act of discretion can prove lucrative. To begin changing the economic environment does not necessarily do more than change the opportunities for and the scale of graft. This has plainly been the experience with, for example, the liberalization of telecommunications in India and other Asian countries. A scandal involving the bidding for licenses to run basic phone services featured prominently in the 1996 Indian general election campaign.

Similarly, it does not automatically follow that the introduction of democracy ends graft. We have already noted the existence of corruption in some of the older democracies. More recent ones, like Russia, heavily underscore the point. Democracy has not prevented corruption in India or South Korea. On the other hand, corruption is more likely to be exposed and fought in a society where there are free elections. Allegations of corruption regularly lead to the downfall of governments in India; and in South Korea, as we have seen, the democrat Kim Dae-Jung is having to scour a society where crony capitalism spawned graft free of any democratic restraint. So liberal economics (if pursued wholeheartedly) and democracy are more likely to see corruption exposed, restrained, and rendered more difficult. South Korea has been out on the streets condemning corruption. What happens in more authoritarian societies when people try to do that?

Western business executives working in Asia should look to their governments back home for one very explicit piece of assistance in resisting being drawn into deals entangled in graft; it would help them as well to avoid losing contracts to competitor businesses with lower ethical standards than their own. We may hope that all businesspeople selling and investing abroad would behave, if not exactly like angels, at least like Phileas Fogg, of whom Jules Verne wrote: "The way in which he got admission to [his] exclusive club was simple enough. He was recommended by the Barings Brothers, with whom he had an open credit. . . . His account . . . was always flush. . . . He was not lavish, nor, on the contrary, stingy; for whenever he knew that money was needed for a noble, useful or benevolent purpose, he supplied it quietly and sometimes benevolently."* Such a model Victorian gentleman would never have regarded a 10 percent markup for a prime minister's political party or the private account of a purchasing director as a "noble, useful or benevolent purpose." In the real world, nobility has to be encouraged by sanctions.

For twenty years, the United States has had the Foreign Corrupt Practices Act on its statute book. It bars American firms from paying bribes overseas. Have some of them lost business to French, German, or Japanese firms as a result? Perhaps they have, but they have also had a sheet anchor to hold on to that must make commercial life and decisions a great deal more straightforward. Now, after years of American pressure, all twenty-nine OECD countries plus a few others have completed a treaty that will oblige all the signatories to put in place their own versions of the U.S. legislation. That marks significant progress. Business should now lobby these nations to be true to their word as swiftly as possible. It will require some significant changes of attitudes. Both the French and German governments, for instance, have been accused of allowing their national companies to treat overseas bribes as authentic business expenses and deduct them legitimately from the taxes they pay. How much easier it would be for French and German businessmen, along with others, to avoid the expense entirely—an outcome that we must hope follows swiftly on the heels of their governments' undertakings. If governments behave sensibly and legislate comprehensively and quickly, businesses will be able to greet every hand extended not in greeting but in a financial demand with a simple rejoinder: "Even if we thought it was right to do what you wish, we cannot, because it is against

---

* *Around the World in Eighty Days.*

our law." I also favor boards of directors publishing, so that their executives and shareholders can be in no doubt, broad statements of ethical behavior making plain their opposition to any form of graft. I doubt whether good firms, which do not pay bribes, lose any business overall as a result.

The third of the issues relevant to ensuring a level playing field for business is the use by some firms of political contacts to gain unfair market access and market share. This poses obvious problems for those businesses whose political connections are less well developed, whose chairmen do not have the right telephone numbers in their Filofaxes. This was becoming an issue in Hong Kong in the months before the transition to Chinese sovereignty. Hong Kong prides itself rightly on being an open, international financial center, playing strictly by the rules of the market. Whether justified or not, suspicions were inevitably raised when mainland Chinese companies with exceptionally strong Peking political connections bought their way on the cheap into Hong Kong companies with dominant positions in the aviation and telecommunications sectors. This was described as "facing reality," the reality presumably being that Chinese firms should have a share in the revenues from profitable franchises owned by companies in which there was a majority British stake. During the summer of 1997, Chinese state-backed corporations went on what the *Asian Wall Street Journal* called a "shopping spree" in Hong Kong. They bought stakes of at least 10 percent in several Hong Kong listed companies from banks to retailing to engineering. On this occasion, what caused most concern was not any implication that the purchasers were using political muscle or promises of future favors to come to secure sweetheart prices for what they were purchasing, but the pattern of stock trading that took place around the actual purchases. Weeks before deals were announced, the share prices of the companies concerned soared; in one case the price of shares in a company went up by almost 70 percent in the ten days before it announced its deal with a mainland company. The chairman of Hong Kong's Securities and Futures Commission gave a salutary warning that Hong Kong should not allow itself to become "the Wild West" of the Far East. The commission undertook once again to crack down on insider dealing, market manipulation, and breaches of the Takeover Code. All this underlined the importance of protecting Hong Kong's reputation. There are of course other Asian markets where investors and businesses have had to make allowances for financial irregularity and political fixes. That affects the attractions of those economies. Hong Kong has had a better name than that. Were it to appear that its commercial life was not proof against political manipulation, sharp practice, and fraudulent greed, Hong Kong's standing would suffer and the chances of two different systems working in one country would begin to look much slimmer. The new Hong Kong government and its regulatory authorities need no lessons on this point; businessmen in Hong Kong may need to be reminded about it.

A marketplace free and fair to all and an economic system purged of or at least resistant to graft are incomparably more likely where there exists the most important of all the software in a free society, the rule of law. What does that mean? First, it means that everyone is subject to the law, however mighty he may be. The rule of law is not some convenient justification for coercion by the powerful, a legalistic cover for locking up or shooting people that the government does not like. It applies equally to those who govern and those who are governed, to lawmakers and law abiders. In a free society under the rule of law, with a fairly elected legislature that itself makes the laws, the ruled are also the rulers. It is vital to understand this. Rules and laws that may or may not apply impartially to everyone are different from the rule of law, majestic, comprehensive, and wholly impartial.

This comprehensiveness was seen in ancient Athens, where one of the most important things meant by democracy and freedom was that any man at all could take his neighbor to court. The law covers or should cover everything—the acts of the president and the party secretary as well as those of the citizen or the corporation. The law is not there merely to police commercial life. You cannot limit its scope or shrink it. One person's law is sooner or later everyone's law. In China, the law that applies to Wei Jingsheng is the same law that applies to Standard Chartered Bank; Harry Wu is dealt with under the same law as Ronald McDonald. It is the gravest of errors to believe that Citicorp, Disney, or Deutsche Bank can find a corner of a foreign field where benign and fair laws will cover them, applying to all *their* operations, even if they do not apply to others. If might is right in dealings with ordinary citizens, there is no guarantee that exactly the same will not apply in dealings with foreign companies from time to time. There is a continuum so far as the law is concerned—as many businessmen in Asia have discovered. There are notorious cases, like that of James Peng (an incarcerated Australian businessman) in China, where politics have infiltrated commercial disputes and the victim has finished up on the wrong side of the powerful and on the wrong side of the prison gates.

The law is not a ceremonial hulk. It lives and breathes. Without it, there is no market economy but a jungle economy, every one for him- or herself, a bracing environment for the brave but not a place where most of us would want to invest much if any of our pension funds. The rule of law underpins prosperity and sustains the most acceptable and profitable way of doing business which is why, as Mr. Lee Kuan Yew has pointed out, so many mainland Chinese companies set up in Hong Kong before the transition. The contracts they signed were governed by Hong Kong law; disputes could be resolved through the courts or by arbitration; and judgments were easy to enforce. Companies found the law predictable, reasonably clear, and relatively easy to understand.

The law constrains just as it enables. It acts as a brake so that liberty does not slide and slither into anarchic license. It draws lines in the sand, protects the weak from the strong, defines the public interest in an orderly and balanced way, and ideally acquires the moral authority to do all that by the extent to which it can demonstrate its own evenhandedness and by the manner in which it is made. If the process itself is suspect, who will obey the law? If you distort the making of the laws, you undermine the rule of law. A free parliament makes the laws; independent courts and judges arbitrate; an uncorrupt police enforces—those institutions provide the core software in any society where it is safe and profitable to do business (and safe and enjoyable to bring up a family).

Businesses can do themselves a favor by constantly stressing that and arguing the case for it. They should try to see that there is an informal market premium on societies which benefit from the rule of law—the equivalent of several plus signs in a rating by Moody's or Standard & Poor's. Those who wish to attract investment into their developing countries should know the emphasis placed by business on rule-of-law issues. This is yet another area where we should not dive for cover behind a heap of arguments which suggest that the rule of law somehow does not have a home in Asia, that it cannot quite fit into Asian cultural habits and attitudes. It is true that Chinese history, to take the most prominent example, has not known or benefited from the rule of law. On the other hand, there are today two wholly Chinese societies that enjoy the rule of law; they are plural and open. They are Taiwan and Hong Kong. If the rule of law can work there, can it really be true that it could not take root in Peking, Shanghai, or Tianjin?

Businesses should also press countries to make good governance issues a higher priority in their overseas development and technical cooperation programs. Western governments can help to train judges, policemen, and prison governors; assist with the translation and drafting of laws; suggest ways in which international agreements and covenants can be turned into domestic law; offer financial assistance for the administration of justice; and ensure scholarships and exchanges for lawyers, young and old. It would be much more in the interest of business to lobby for more to be spent on these things than on concessional financing.

Whenever these desirable conditions for doing business—open markets, the rule of law, and so on—are listed, the word *transparency* takes its place in line. One person's desirable transparency (openness, access to the maximum amount of information, the free exchange of ideas) is someone else's ardor for opacity and obfuscation. What the genuflections to transparency recognize are the relationships between a free market in goods and a free market in ideas. With modern technology, it is difficult to sever those links; and success in knowledge-based economies demands their assertion. But when it comes to free speech and a free media, many of us in business and politics both at home and abroad start to equivocate.

There are two main reasons for this. The first is human nature. As Winston Churchill observed, "Everyone is in favor of free speech, but some people's idea of it is that they are free to say what they like but if anyone else says something bad, that is an outrage." One reason why as a politician I always refused to keep an album of press clippings was that I assumed that like others I would only keep, and presumably believe, the ones that were flattering. But if you take those seriously, then you have to take some account of the others as well. Being no more virtuous and humble than the next person, it seemed to me that the easiest thing to do was not to collect any clippings at all, and then you could regard everything said about you, good, bad, or in between, with at least a pretense of detachment.

The second factor, particular to politics though not necessarily to business, is that in an open society there is a proper and desirable tension between public officials (especially those who are elected) and the media. The absence of such tension is a hallmark of societies that are neither open nor free. Democratic politicians may not think that media criticism of them is informed or fair, and it may not be informed or fair, but they should recognize that it is part of the process that makes them accountable and that reins in those too voracious for power and advancement. I would much prefer a society in which the great are occasionally humbled to one in which they are allowed to bask unchallenged in their triumphs, virtues, and omniscience. That is why I rather care for Britain's no-nonsense disinclination to revere its political leaders (or at least not to revere them for long).

Politicians vary in the interest they show in the press and broadcasting. Few are as uninterested as Britain's postwar premier Clement Attlee, who could only be persuaded to agree to the purchase of a news agency tape machine for No. 10 Downing Street by the seductive prospect of being able to keep a regular check on the Middlesex cricket scores (those were admittedly the palmy days, when that county's Compton and Edrich took the spectators' minds off postwar rationing). Attlee once emerged from his study saying "the cricket box is just reporting what I said in Cabinet." Most politicians are at the other end of the spectrum, professing sublime indifference even as they feverishly search the newspapers (preferably two at a time) for some "wholly objective" reference to themselves and the merits of their views and policies. Newsprint and television lights are to most politicians what the weather is to farmers: a subject of endless fascination, the currency of success and failure, the arbiters of unknowable chance.

For myself, I start at least with an ardently Jeffersonian belief in free speech, siding naturally with Junius and the jurors against Lord Mansfield. I recall with enthusiasm that when Franklin Roosevelt called, in his third inaugural address, for a world founded upon four essential freedoms, the first that he cited was "freedom of speech and expression—everywhere in the world." While that is my starting point, I soon find myself confronting some tricky propositions. None of us, surely, would argue that the only aim of a benevolent, decent society should be to achieve freedom of expression. Nor are we likely to believe that freedom of speech is the only one cherished by individuals. When we consider the arguments for free speech, we have to remember the arguments for other values too—justice, equality, community, order, and (is it permissible to add?) moral progress. In a good society, therefore, it is inevitably necessary to reconcile free speech with many other aims and values. So freedom of expression is not an absolute.

Yet no one should allow these sort of sensible philosophical limitations on the principle of free speech to be turned by authoritarians into an assault on its very foundations. Three main principles support the case for free speech, and it will be readily apparent that all are relevant to a healthy market economy. There is, for a start, a market case for free speech. It is a means to an end, and the end is truth. The search for truth is best advanced by a free trade in ideas, just as the search for the best plum jam is advanced by a free trade in preserves. The ideas do not all have to be smart and sensible or even worth examination. Most people who have bought Stephen Hawking's *A Brief History of Time* will presumably, like me, at least have read the beginning and will recall the story of the famous scientist who was giving a public lecture on astronomy. At the end of his lecture, in which he described the earth's orbit around the sun and the sun's orbit around the center of our galaxy, a little old lady got up at the back of the theater and said, "What you have told us is rubbish. The world is really a flat plate supported on the back of a giant tortoise." The scientist, smiling patronizingly, replied, "And what, madam, is the tortoise standing on?" "You're very clever, young man, very clever," said the old lady. "But it's turtles all the way down." Much political and economic argument has its ration of tortoises and turtles; they all have their place, shell-backs on the path to the truth.

Second, free speech is an end in itself, not just a means to an end. It is intimately connected to human dignity. In Justice Thurgood Marshall's words, the First Amendment to the American Constitution served not only the needs of the polity "but also those of the human spirit—a spirit that demands self-expression."

Third, free speech is the engine room of a free, democratic society. It augments stability by providing a safety valve for tensions and social pressures. It provides some of the means by which citizens participate in decision making. It helps check abuse and corruption. A free society plainly cannot exist without free speech, though it does need more than that.

Why should businesses bother about any of this? One of the lessons of the Asian *annus horribilis* is the importance of openness in good economic management, and openness is difficult to compartmentalize. Our old friend "transparency" incorporates other things as well as a free media—corporate disclosure of ownership and debt, governmental honesty about reserves, and so on. The more open all the books, the better for the business environment: if only every company everywhere had to provide the information required to list on the New York Stock Exchange. Openness with economic and commercial facts and figures will not necessarily happen just because there is a free press. Yet, once again, such openness is more probable where the media are free, and at least good, uncensored media will pick up incidents of cover-ups and dishonesty and harry those who are trying to hide the truth. The worst problems in securing the acceptable minimum of accurate information occur in countries where the domestic press and broadcasting companies are gagged, are in the government's pocket, or are owned by the very businessmen who are colluding with government to cheat and chisel the market. Ownership of the media raises very difficult issues in several Asian countries, though as a British citizen I should immediately concede that it does exactly the same rather closer to home!

Most business executives working and investing in an Asian country would presumably feel more secure if they knew that they could buy the *Asian Wall Street Journal, Financial Times,* and *International Herald Tribune* at their hotel newsstand, that *The Economist, Forbes,* and *Business Week* were able to report whatever they wanted in the country, that Reuters, Bloomberg, and Dow Jones were operating freely there, and that broadcasts by the BBC World Service and Voice of America were not being jammed. The contents of the hotel newsstand provide quite a good test of whether you want to live, stay, work, and invest somewhere. Anyone sensible will have a limited faith in a government's promises of future openness and disclosure when he cannot read what he wants and listen to or watch whatever should be available. The old myth—featured prominently in the Asian-values debate—that while authoritarian governments might clamp down on political free speech, they would certainly give business whatever information it required to do its job took a hammering through 1997 and 1998.

Even before the crash, there were signs that in the absence of some of the software that has been described, many Western businesses were starting to vote with their wallets and their return air tickets. Vietnam had aspired to "little tiger" status in the early to mid-1990s, but in the last year or two, many foreign investors who arrived in hope have departed in frustration. Promises of reform have been regularly broken. There is legal confusion, red tape, and bureaucratic obduracy. The state-owned banks are heavily in debt, but the figures remain under wraps. State-owned firms have preferential access to land, credit, and trade licenses. The Vietnamese Communist party nervously surveys the consequences for itself of introducing some of the software for which the World Bank, the International Monetary Fund, and foreign investors have pressed. No software, no foreign money—or at least less of it. In Malaysia, foreign companies have expressed their growing annoyance at the system of "negotiated tenders" for big development projects. What has happened in the past is that the government has chosen business groups in secret to carry out particular projects and then negotiated the contract price with them. Even some Malaysian ministers have criticized the expensive obscurity of this method and called for less wasteful, open competitive tendering. Foreign companies have also been having second thoughts about doing business in China, partly because of the opacity and unpredictability of the system. Everywhere it is the same story. Doing business in markets where the rules are not clear, where they do not appear to apply to everyone, where they are arbitrary and uncertain, and where too much is secret is a risky adventure and only for the brave and the very, very patient.

This is an important point for ministers to make, along with all their other representations, on behalf of their national companies. Most Western governments are vigorous and professional in the support they give to business, promoting exports, sponsoring trade fairs, glad-handing, and opening doors. I have seen something of what others do, but most of my firsthand experience is of the British effort. There used to be some criticism that embassies and diplomats were insufficiently attentive to the British commercial interest. This even resulted in the faintly absurd suggestion that businessmen should be parachuted into some of our most important ambassadorial posts. How many volunteers would come forward for this work at foreign service salaries has not so far been discovered. I must say that I have found almost every embassy I have ever visited fully seized of its commercial responsibilities. Unfortunately, British embassies invariably have fewer resources for this work than their main competitors, the result in part of one of the enduring examples of envy in public life—the Treasury's mean-minded and shortsighted efforts to reduce the Foreign Service to genteel global penury. In addition to the English language and the historic connections of the Commonwealth (nine out of thirty-one Asian countries, for example, are Commonwealth members), Britain has two other institutional advantages that should redound to some extent to our commercial advantage. The first is the BBC and the second is the British Council. The British Council is a disgracefully unsung and underutilized national asset. No one else has anything quite like it. It is a highly professional agent for the best of British cultural, educational, technical, and scientific life. It increases the numbers of foreign students at British institutions and opens doors for business and the professions. It is also shamefully underfunded, a victim of the British tendency to exclude value judgments from our decisions on public spending priorities. British businessmen should speak up for it.

Glad-handing, as I have suggested, has its place in helping business abroad. Unfortunately, it can result in real business eliding into show business. This suits some Asian countries, such as China, since, as we shall see in the next chapter, the promise of streets somewhere around the next corner paved with gold lies at the heart of their diplomatic effort. But I remain pretty skeptical about the extent to which the rest of us should really be taken in by business through banquets.

The all-singing and all-dancing version of this approach is the high-level visit to China by a Western leader accompanied by a jumbo jet full of business chiefs. It is difficult to know whose ego is massaged more—the political tour leader or those who follow the man or woman with the flag. The party, whose schedule is finally agreed upon only moments before takeoff (though the precise identity of the "leader" who will deign to receive them may remain a mystery), is driven around Peking and Shanghai in charabancs. They meet vice-ministers and mayors; they drink warm white wine, or small glasses of spirits diluted by melting ice cubes, at embassy receptions; some of the senior members present join the political mentor at a half-hour meeting in the Chinese leaders' enclave, the Zhongnanhai; they hear their politician exchange vacuous pleasantries with Jiang Zemin, Li Peng, or Zhu Rongji; some of the lucky ones may find that long-running negotiations for a contract have been slightly advanced, or that they have gotten access to a ministry or state-owned enterprise whose doors were previously bolted. Some good can certainly come from these grand package tours; they do no harm—except that sometimes the country sending the tour party has to pay a diplomatic price for the Chinese invitation and red carpet.

This will sound a bit crabby to some. They will point to the headlines full of figures about billions of pounds' worth of contracts signed and thousands of jobs saved. These are cracking good stories for presidents, premiers, and trade ministers. But the headlines do not stand up to much close scrutiny, a commodity usually absent from the reporting. That is not a charge anyone could lay against the *Asian Wall Street Journal*. It regularly analyzes in detail the show-business aspects of these high-profile trips. The result is not what the tour leaders want to hear. I once sent a selection of the *Journal*'s clippings on this subject to Britain's Department of Trade and Industry, not to discourage it from trying to get businessmen interested in the China market but to try to get it to go about its work with its eyes open and without any self-delusion (the sort of self-delusion that, for instance, in past days had led to so many high-profile trade missions to Iran—and future heavy losses—just before the fall of the Shah). I have an old-fashioned feeling that it is not very sensible to believe one's own propaganda. Maybe you have to utter it with a straight face. But believe it? I never received a reply to my attempt to be helpful.

I have in my hand several *Journal* clippings about the difference between political trade and real trade. Let me just take two examples, the first a high-profile American trip to China in 1994, led by the then Commerce Secretary, the ebullient Ron Brown (later to die tragically in a plane accident), and the second an equally high-profile trip out of China by President Jiang Zemin to Germany in 1995. The U.S. business trip to China reportedly netted $6 billion in deals. Analyzing these a year later, the *Asian Wall Street Journal* concluded that the main outcome of the visit was paperwork; fewer than one tenth of the alleged deals had been realized. The report ran through a familiar list—

the rounding-up of figures by public relations departments, the signing of joint venture agreements that had never been approved, the raising of expectations about assistance that were subsequently dashed, the photo opportunities to reannounce deals that had already been set up, the deals that turned out to be no more than agreements on prefeasibility studies for projects that had yet to be approved. "Having a Cabinet official witness a deal signing does nothing," concluded the paper, "to clear Beijing's bureaucratic thicket." The analysis of the Chinese trip to Germany noted that many of the contracts signed had a "familiar ring" about them, and this was because they were simply "rehashed versions" of agreements signed the previous year when the Premier, Li Peng, had visited Germany. "There's a lot of gong-sounding going on," said one German official. "These deals don't mean anything at all. They're fully noncommittal for both sides, and nothing more than protocol acts of a friendship visit." Nowadays you can, of course, sign exactly the same deals in several different European countries since so many big companies and big projects straddle European boundaries. During his spring visit to France in 1996, I recall my local French newspaper noting a touch sourly that Li Peng was just signing a deal in Toulouse that was to all intents and purposes the same as the deal signed previously by Chinese leaders in Germany.

These deals and visits are the visible mountain peaks of a world in which political correctness and mood allegedly determine much of a Western country's ability to do business with Asians. For example, political rows with Asian countries—most notably Malaysia—have been followed by threats to the trading interests of the countries concerned. There would be less of this disruptive nonsense if OECD, and in particular European Union countries, stuck together when one of their number was threatened in this way. But this is all pretty small potatoes in comparison with the commercial market where the political game is played most ruthlessly—China. I will deal in the next chapter with some of the political issues raised; for the moment, let me stick to the business and economic arguments.

I was recently carrying out a speaking engagement for an international bank, one of whose executives recalled that during my years as Hong Kong Governor they had once invited me to a lunch with some of their clients which I had unfortunately missed because my plane was delayed by snow at Munich. "What did you do without me?" I asked.

"Oh," replied the banker, "all our clients sat around and discussed how bad you were for their business in China." This went to the heart of the issue. It was frequently argued when I was in Hong Kong that you could not have an argument with China without it affecting your business interests, that a good political relationship was essential to good business contacts, that trade these days followed the flattery not the flag. Standing up for Hong Kong was simply bad for business; ergo we should recognize the cost of our so-called principles and back down. To be fair to British ministers (and to the then Labour Opposition leaders), while they got their ears regularly filled with this sort of talk, it did not really affect their support for me. Britain's trade minister, Sir Richard Needham, the most energetic and effective person in the job for years, was one of my stoutest and most articulate defenders. (Exactly the same was true of Britain's trade commissioner in Hong Kong, Francis Cornish, a tough and sensible diplomat who had to endure with a good grace meal after meal of ill-informed grumbling.) Needham's department, however, invented a figure for the damage our policy on Hong Kong had allegedly done to British business. We had lost, it calculated, between £1 and £2 billion in trade. Heaven knows where this figure came from. It would never say. Presumably, it grossed up all the contracts it thought that Britain should have gotten and assumed that the reason we had not won them was our policy in Hong Kong. It was not surprising that if the Department of Trade and Industry thought this, some business executives did so as well.

All this has encouraged me over the years to take a more than academic interest in the trade figures with China. Can we establish by looking at the figures that a good political relationship is the key to a good export performance? It is difficult to get figures that are quite the same, and there are all sorts of confusing statistical differences between one table and the next. But they all seem to tell much the same story: There does not really seem to be any relationship between political good conduct in China's eyes and trade performance. Indeed, you could argue counterintuitively that bad relations were good for trade, with as much if not more statistical support than exists for the proposition that it is "love-ins" that drive up exports.

Looking at the latest (as I write) IMF trade statistics with China for the last ten years, 1986–96, the country that has seen the biggest increase in its share of OECD exports to China is the United States, the very country that has had the worst and most scratchy political relationship with Peking. Its share of OECD exports has increased from 14 percent to 20 percent. The argument is not just that U.S. exports in the aggregate have increased substantially (which they have) because the China market has grown. The point is that the U.S. share of what all the rich countries sell to China has increased by over 40 percent. The country in Europe with the best political relationship with China is undoubtedly Germany. The Germans work at this at some political cost; and so do the Chinese, at no cost at all. In 1986, Germany's share of the overall market was 13 percent; at the end of the ten-year period, it had fallen slightly to 12 percent. Germany's overall exports to China are high, but proportionately they have not obviously benefited from a pretty cozy political affair. France's row with China over the sale of weapons to Taiwan at the beginning of the 1990s may have affected some sales, but Germany's share of the China market fell as sharply during this period as France's. Perhaps, one concludes, whatever the diplomatic noise or the occasional high-profile deals, the Chinese do business on much the same basis as everyone else, buying the goods they want and need at the best price.

Turning to Britain's case, the figures tell a similar tale. Let us assume for the sake of argument (it is quite a big assumption) that all was sweetness and goodwill before 1992 and that it was ructions night and day thereafter. I have U.K. figures for 1997 as well as for the other years so can come more up-to-date. We signed the Joint Declaration in 1984. From the following year until 1991 (presumably the "golden years" for cooperation and friendship) our exports to China actually fell. For most other OECD countries they soared. We moved from having a surplus with China to having a large trading deficit. Assume that 1992 is a pre-Patten year and 1997 is a Patten year. In the five pre-Patten years, our exports to China totaled £2.052 billion; in the five Patten years, the figure was £4.075 billion. Our exports practically doubled. This had nothing to do with me; business grew for business reasons. Maybe the figures could have been better still. But there is no proof of this whatsoever. The fact that our exports did worse—not least, in relation to others—when we were purportedly being more politically correct with China than when we were not, and the additional fact that no one else's position over a reasonable run of years seems to be much affected by politics, gives additional credibility to my plea of innocence to the charge sheet.

There are one or two other statistics about Britain's economic relationship with China to chew over. Britain now has a substantial trade deficit with China of over £1.5 billion; our exports are only just over one third of our imports. Britain is by far the biggest European investor in China—$2.54 billion in 1996, in comparison with $1 billion by Germany, the second largest in Europe. Britain's share of OECD exports bounces around pretty consistently at between 2 and 3 percent, more or less the same as our share of imports. But if the importance of a relationship is to be calculated in terms of strict pluses and minuses—an unattractive mercantilist notion—then the simple truth is that the pluses are on China's side and they have gotten bigger. Their exports to us are much greater than their imports from us.

I once asked a pretty hard-bitten group of British salesmen whether our policies in Hong Kong (to which, incidentally, Britain sells about three times as much as it does to China and where it invests incomparably more) had made it more difficult for their efforts in China. One of them replied that it was always difficult to do business in China and that he was not sure whether our Hong Kong policy had added very much to the problem. Certainly, no one was ever able to point to a project or contract we had ever lost because of Hong Kong. There was a bit of anecdotal grumbling. If you lost a contract you had expected to win, it was easier to blame Hong Kong policy than to look for other reasons. Some argued that we missed out on a big contract for building a subway in Canton because of Hong Kong policy, and the Chinese implied as much, but it was far more likely that in fact the scale of German concessional financing tipped the project their way. There are other allegations. I remember a British oil company chairman once accusing me of jeopardizing a huge refinery project, which was in fact lost because of financing arguments between the Chinese and the British firms involved.

All that said, our policy in Hong Kong may have had an effect on our trade performance in any of the following ways. We may have lost out on big, highly politicized projects, though no one was ever able to give a good and sustainable example, and Trafalgar House—owned in the mid-1990s, as the Chinese must have known, by the controlling family interests of the demonized Jardine's—went on picking up large contracts in China apparently unscathed. Second, perhaps political correctness would have affected some Chinese bureaucrats and businessmen lower down the system, who would have concluded that they should avoid doing business with the British, who were known to be out of favor. On the other hand, the survey by Lucian Pye of businessmen's experiences of working in China (*Chinese Negotiating Style*, Quorum Books, 1992, to which I will return in the next chapter) suggests how often we make the wrong guesses about the politicization of Chinese officials. "Many American businessmen," writes Pye, "especially during the early phase of dealings with the Chinese, say that they sought to gain favor with the Chinese by manifesting political awareness. In some cases, the effort involved high company policy, such as dramatically ending operations in Taiwan; more frequently, the attempts to curry favor take the form of expressing enthusiasm for revolutionary precepts and Chinese theater and art. Anecdotes abound about American businessmen espousing Maoist themes even after the fall of the Gang of Four and thereby irritating their Chinese hosts. In contrast to this uncharacteristic American eagerness to introduce political notes into business relationships, Chinese officials currently responsible for commercial activities are usually starkly apolitical, concentrating on purely business and technical matters." The third, unfathomable, possibility is that because of the high costs involved in putting in tenders, some British firms may not have bothered to go for the business, fearing that the final decision would be made on political grounds. In other words, we may have been the victims of our own paranoia. The most that I think one can say, returning to the salesman's comment, is that our policy on Hong Kong cannot have made a difficult job any easier. Overall, however, I hope that our experiences will encourage others to test against their own figures the proposition that exports to China and cozy politics go hand in hand.

In Hong Kong, I used to see a lot of businessmen on their way into or out of China. I recall having a breakfast and a lunch one day, separately, with the chairmen of two companies working in the same field; both of them were heavily involved in China. I discovered that they were having dinner together that night, and each of them, unknown to the other, was hoping to be able to sell his company's Chinese interests to his dinner companion. It was not that they were wholly pessimistic about China and the China market. They were impressed by the changes that had taken place there, hoped for the best for the future, and contemplated returning at some future time. But for the moment it just seemed too difficult, above all because of the lack of all that software—and most important, because of the absence of the rule of law. "Whatever the frustrations in India," one said, "at least they have the rule of law there—and so therefore do we. It makes our business easier." As Asia after the crash picks up and puts the pieces together again in the years ahead, that should be a lesson business helps the governments in the region to learn. To borrow from Confucius, Asian governments will need to get the mat straight before they can persuade many Western investors and businesses to sit down again.

9

China and the West

The Master said: "To worship gods that are not yours, that is toadyism. Not to act when justice commands, that is cowardice."
—*The Analects of Confucius,* 2.24

We, by the Grace of Heaven, Emperor, instruct the King of England to take note of our charge. Although your country, O King, lies in the far ocean, yet inclining your heart toward civilization, you have specially sent an envoy respectfully to present a state message, and sailing the seas, he has come to our Court to kowtow and to present congratulations for the imperial birthday, and also to present local products, thereby showing your sincerity. We have perused the text of your state message and the wording expresses your earnestness. From it your sincere humility and obedience can clearly be seen. It is admirable and we fully approve . . .
—The beginning of a letter from the Emperor Qianlong to King George III, October 3, 1793

I t takes a long time to kowtow. I have just tried it on the carpet in my study. There was no particular object of homage, and I was speeded on my way by two attentive and puzzled terriers. So I may have gone a bit fast. But it still took me one minute and fifteen seconds. I guess it is the sort of gymnastic activity that will take longer as the years take their toll. If one was robed and wearing an embroidered crest and ostrich feathers, like a favored Chinese courtier, or even dressed more simply in a velvet jacket with the diamond badge and star of the Order of the Bath, like Lord Macartney in 1793, the pace of the elaborate ritual would be considerably slowed. Bear with me a moment as I describe, as though running through an aerobics class for the middle-aged, exactly what is involved.

You begin by standing up straight, then you kneel down and lean right forward until your forehead touches the floor. Now raise your torso and bow again so that your forehead once more brushes the carpet, and repeat once more. After that, stand up again, then go through the whole business on two more occasions. So you stand, genuflect, bow down to the carpet three times—and then repeat that ritual twice more with appropriate dignity and reverence.

It was this ritual that lay at the heart of the controversy surrounding the mission of Lord Macartney to China in 1793. Macartney, a cousin of King George III and former ambassador to Russia as well as Governor of Madras, had been sent to the Middle Kingdom from his small barbarian country on a far edge of the world to try to persuade the Chinese both to open their market to Britain (which was to become the first country to be transformed by the Industrial Revolution) and to deal with the barbarians just like the barbarians dealt with one another— with treaties and tariffs, ambassadors and envoys. Macartney came with a retinue, gifts, and a message from his monarch. But would he be allowed to deliver it, and if so, how should he behave? For the Chinese the matter was simple. He should behave like the representative of any vassal state, showing the courtesies that were due the august inheritor of the Mandate of Heaven. Macartney saw things differently. To the intense annoyance of the Chinese court, he argued that he could not be expected to show greater reverence and loyalty to a foreign monarch than he showed to his own. A genuflection and bow were good enough for a Hanoverian and they should be good enough for a Manchu. Chinese displeasure at this may have slightly affected the tone of Qianlong's reply to King George. But later students of the art of dealing with China should note that the draft of Qianlong's letter (bowdlerized by its translators so as not to shock Macartney, and further bowdlerized by Macartney and his colleagues so as not to shock anyone back home) had actually been shown to the Emperor more than six weeks before he received the letter to which the draft was ostensibly a reply. The Chinese would have gone their own way whatever Macartney had done, refusing to countenance any of Britain's requests. As for the kowtowing, the Chinese simply behaved—as we see from the Emperor's letter—as though it had taken place. The smooth surface of Chinese history could not be allowed to be ruffled by a boorish barbarian.

Macartney had the good fortune to travel on his diplomatic mission long before the telegraph, the telephone, and the fax. He made his own decision on how to behave. He decided himself not to kowtow. How much more difficult it would have been for him today. He would have had to await instructions from London, and these would have hung on the decisions made by ministers after they had considered a submission from officials. Things may be different these days (though I would not put money on it), but there was certainly a time not long ago when a certain sort of sinologist would have drafted something along these lines:

> The Secretary of State will be aware of a problem that Lord Macartney has encountered in Peking. We need to resolve it urgently in order not to compromise the success of his talks with the Emperor and senior Chinese officials.
>
> The Secretary of State knows we have secured an audience with the Emperor that can be taken as a mark of Chinese sincerity and of their growing regard for Britain's global influence. This doubtless owes much to the Secretary of State's own contacts with his opposite number and his success, much against the odds, in thickening up relations between our countries. France and Germany will be mildly aggrieved that the mission is taking place at all, and Macartney's access will further rub salt in their wounds.
>
> But all this could be put at risk by failure to go through one tiresome formality. The Secretary of State will recollect that the Emperor expects those he receives to kowtow at the beginning of an audience. Lord Macartney has raised with us the political sensitivity of his striking his head on the carpet nine times when he would only bow once, or at most genuflect, to his own monarch.
>
> We have tried to find ways of finessing this; for example, we have pointed out to Chinese officials that a genuflection would be regarded at Windsor as tantamount to a kowtow, and that were a Chinese official to pay a reciprocal visit and be received by His Majesty, we would be perfectly happy for him either to genuflect or (if he preferred) to kowtow, should he believe that this was culturally tantamount to a genuflection. These representations have alas so far failed to elicit the response for which we had hoped.
>
> On foot of this breakdown in discussions, we are therefore faced with an unpalatable choice. Should Lord Macartney kowtow, there will undoubtedly be some uninformed public criticism at home, and there may even be questions in Parliament. We would try to minimize the problem by asking that there should be no photographs of the audience, but on past form the Chinese may well take

photographs anyway and leak them through the New China News Agency. So there could be a storm. But we believe ministers should be able to ride this out.

If we instruct Lord Macartney not to kowtow, on the other hand, the potential fallout is incalculable. It would certainly put his whole mission at risk, would set back a relationship that may be about to bear fruit, and would be sharply criticized by British industrialists. The Secretary of State also will recall that the president of the Board of Trade is hoping to visit China shortly with a two-hundred-strong delegation representing the British invisibles industry, and we are still trying to arrange a visit by the Prime Minister next year. In addition we have a number of high-level incoming visitors from China, led by the Vice-Minister of Barbarian Affairs, who is strongly tipped for promotion at the next meeting of the National People's Congress.

In light of all these factors, while we can see that a colorable case can be made out for declining to kowtow, the balance of advantage is strongly in favor of doing so. We can point out to critics that we seek neither to confront China nor to surrender our principles, and that in this case an understanding of Chinese cultural sensitivities will set our relationship on a more mature and sustainable footing.

While Lord Macartney should be instructed to kowtow, it is important to hold the line firmly on other matters of principle and, for example, decline to accede to the Chinese request to sign a Memorandum of Understanding, which implies that the kowtow is actually being performed by His Majesty. The Chinese must be told very firmly that that simply will not run.

Do I exaggerate? A little perhaps, though on the other hand some will think this an excessively robust draft. I expect that other bureaucracies have been capable of much the same sort of nonsense—much, much less so in the case of the United States; much, much more so in the case of some of the senior members of the European Union. For some, the request to kowtow would have met the response—"Must I only bang my head on the ground nine times? Why not twelve or eighteen or thirty-six?"

The best account of Macartney's mission to China is Alain Peyrefitte's *The Collision of Two Civilizations*. It is much more than a brilliant, detailed account of this doomed enterprise, this "abortive rendezvous." Peyrefitte seeks to place the whole episode at the heart of the cultural, political, and economic standoff between China and the West, and he regards the Qianlong letter as the most important document in Chinese-Western relations from Marco Polo to Deng Xiaoping, an example of "cultural autism," the belief not only in Chinese superiority and uniqueness but in complete Chinese self-sufficiency. So how did the representative of a brash new economic power, confident that its values should suit the rest of the world, behave when confronted with a society and system "as self-contained," according to Peyrefitte, "as a billiard ball"? Macartney's conduct, in Peyrefitte's view, had the effect of seeming to deny the validity of Chinese civilization. By his behavior, Macartney drove the Chinese back into their bunker, provoking them to turn in on themselves, with disastrous consequences as the West outstripped them industrially, militarily, and politically. Peyrefitte concludes, "Had the ambassador presented his offer differently, had the emperor received it differently, China would likely have 'awakened' without the world having to 'tremble.' Its creativity might have diversified; its capacity for progress might have soared. Instead the confrontation between arrogance and self-sufficiency robbed humanity of incalculable riches." Perhaps we should all therefore lament the geostrategic missed opportunity of the refused kowtow.

This goes right to the heart of all the most common arguments about how we should deal with China. And how we deal with China will be one of the defining issues of the next decade. It may therefore be thought that my own rather relaxed view of this question grossly underestimates its significance. For me, there is much to be said for not rushing after China, for not detaching policy from common sense, for reticence, for dispassion. China is neither a miracle about to be performed nor (we must devoutly hope) a ghastly global accident waiting to happen. But it is more than one fifth of humanity, and what happens there—which we can affect only at the margins—will matter to us all.

Peyrefitte's implication is that China would have been more likely to take an outward-looking, expansionist course if only Macartney had treated the Emperor differently, if only he had understood China better, if only he had made concessions to Chinese "face," to the Chinese way of doing things. This is argued by Peyrefitte with exquisite sensibility and scholarship, although of course it is Peyrefitte himself who points out that the Chinese reply to the British request long preceded the row over the kowtow. The suggestion that there is a correct way of dealing with China—humoring China, acceding to Chinese sensitivities, allowing China to rewrite whatever language it is negotiating in, leaning over backward not to provoke or annoy China, playing end-lessly to what (as we shall see) are China's not very awesome strengths—blights the West's attempts to develop any sort of sensible strategic relationship with Peking. Perhaps as important, it is bad for China; it encourages China to think that it can become part of the modern world entirely on its own terms. Were that to happen, it would make the world a more dangerous and less prosperous place.

It is not easy to see how we can construct a stable China policy without a stable China: The thin crust of an outwardly self-confident Leninist leadership covers a society swirling, bubbling, churning with change. In the years since the Communist revolution and the estab-lishment of the People's Republic of China in 1949, those responsible for China policy in Western governments have offered us with rare ex-ception a choice of extremes—flab or flint; engagement or constraint. Lurching from one to the other makes little sense. Until the early 1970s, most of the democratic world followed America's lead and kept China at arm's length, which seemed in any event to be where Mao and his colleagues wished to be. They presided over the years of revolution and hunger in the 1950s, and of ruinous fanaticism during the 1960s Cultural Revolution, truculently mindless of what the Western de-mocracies thought of them. Then in the early 1970s, a mutual ner-vousness about the Soviet Union drove the United States and China into an uneasy and suspicious accord; engagement followed constraint, and to exemplify this Richard Nixon visited China in 1972. Both Mao and his deputy Zhou Enlai died in 1976 and Deng Xiaoping reemerged at the top of the heap two years later, completing the nor-malization of Sino-American relations with a barnstorming visit to the States in 1979. Deng's "open door" economic reforms through the 1980s encouraged greater engagement with the outside world, but his government's murderous assault on the people of Peking in June 1989, witnessed on the television screens of the whole world, plunged Amer-ican and European policy on China back into the freezer. President Clinton was elected in 1992 on a policy of containment; he criticized his opponent, George Bush, for pampering Peking's dictators.

Through the mid-1990s to the present day, the Chinese have neatly picked holes in America's and Europe's attempts to construct a comprehensive strategy that separates politics from economics. The vocabulary of our diplomacy has jumped about from year to year.

What is "coddling dictators" one year becomes the sophisticated attempt to make sense of "a multifaceted relationship" the next. One minute we sell arms to Taiwan and stamp our feet about human rights abuses on the grandest of scales in China, the next we are prepared to eat the humblest of pies and even curtail our own civil liberties (trying to segregate demonstrators, for example, lest they are seen by a visiting Chinese leader) to accommodate Chinese Communist prejudices. Both approaches are infused with an unhealthy obsession with China that distorts policy making. Both approaches, pursued rather randomly though affected to some degree by the extremes of Chinese behavior, encounter an invariably unchanging Chinese strategy of table thumping on sensitive political issues while offering us the prospect of earning through our servility the goodwill that will trigger commercial benefits. Chinese officials must find our responses to this boringly and feebly predictable. When even the unimaginative and plodding former premier Li Peng can read us like a Little Red Book—accurately predicting our reactions to his bullying diplomacy—we really should start to question whether we have things quite right.

The advocates of engagement range from the knowledgeable and well meaning to the ignorant and craven. At its best, the argument goes like this: China is the largest and in some respects—the depth and longevity of its civilization, the potential of its marketplace and creative energy—the most important nation on earth. It presently has a government struggling to make the transition from impoverishing Communist economics to market capitalism. That is a formidably difficult task, given China's size and the former backwardness of its economy. So far, the Chinese leadership has managed the transition quite adroitly. It is terrified of losing power, and that accounts for the unfortunate incident in June 1989. No one can condone that, but it cannot be allowed forever to shape our relationship with China. At least the government did not allow the country to spin out of control and lose the momentum of economic reform. That process is gradually transforming the lives of the Chinese people, bringing them more freedom than they have ever enjoyed before. We should help the reform program along, doing both ourselves and the Chinese a favor—they will steadily become better-off and more free, and we will sell goods in their huge marketplace. By quiet rather than strident diplomacy, we can best help the dissidents and assist China to build the rudiments of the rule of law. China has never been an expansionist power, and provided we understand some of its sensitive border and maritime problems—Taiwan; exploration rights in the South China Sea—we should be able to smooth the way to China playing a constructive role in the region and the world. Whether we like it or not, we have to make some allowance for China; if we fail to do so, we will only drive China in on itself (as Macartney did). This might be a policy that occasionally obliges one to hold one's nose, but that is what life is like in a grown-up world. When we isolated China in Mao's days, look how disastrous the consequences were. We cannot allow our longer-term interests to be distorted by emotional spasms. Let's not find ourselves placing a greater emphasis on freedom than do the Chinese people themselves. We should encourage greater contacts with China; count to ten before reacting to their occasional tantrums; seek to bind them into a network of international agreements; give them the "face" they seek in order to encourage them to demonstrate the global responsibility in trade, environmental matters, and geo-strategy that we all desire.

On the back of this sort of sophisticated analysis ride some rather crude sentiments, most notably the notion that China presents a spectacular trade opportunity and we should not screw that up by getting all misty-eyed about human rights. I touched on this general argument in the last chapter, and there is little need to repeat it save to say that it is invariably at its crudest, silliest, and most offensive when applied to China. I once heard a Eurasian businessman in Hong Kong referring to the "kerfuffle" in Tiananmen Square, and a British politician-turned-businessman arguing that the only people who cared about civil liberties in China were a tiny handful of intellectuals, most of whom were in prison; for the majority of people, he said, full stomachs were all that mattered. I remain skeptical of the proposition that all boards of directors are ethics-free zones; it is just that a few captains of industry work hard to give that impression.

Montagues and Capulets, Dark Blues and Light Blues—against the conciliatory advocates of engagement we find the proponents of containment. For this school, China is the last evil empire, the litmus test of our continuing determination as a bloody century closes to stand up for freedom, in America's case for the values that have shaped its own society and that it believes should best shape its relations with the rest of the world. A brutal and corrupt Leninist clique holds on to power by locking up not only those who disagree with it politically but those who seek to inhabit their own private space through the practice of their religious beliefs. It polices an inhumane family-planning policy. No longer Communist, Chinese society bears many of the hallmarks of early-twentieth-century fascism: The military is very powerful; the tentacles of the Party (a clan of interconnected family interests, not an ideological movement) entwine every aspect of commercial life; nationalism and xenophobia have replaced moral zeal; the state is supreme. Using its easy access to Western markets and Western technology, China builds up its economic strength and uses that strength to bully and barter and break all the customary rules of international trade. While pressing hard for entry into the World Trade Organization, it still subsidizes state industries through state-owned banks, controls trade, maintains high tariff walls, and refuses to recognize property rights. It continues to steal intellectual property despite agreements and reassurances. It has a huge surplus with the United States and most of its trading partners that enables it to pile up vast reserves, part of which are spent on modernizing its military hardware through the purchase of Russian high-performance attack jets and guided-missile destroyers. It lies about the use of imported technology that, while meant for civilian purposes, is diverted to military manufacturing, while we pretend we do not know what is happening. We also usually look the other way while the Chinese armed forces sell the components of lethal military hardware to the rogue regimes of the Middle East. If China has no intention of flexing its muscles in Asia and beyond, why is it secretly increasing its military budget so far and so fast? We should take seriously the remark of General Mi Zhenyu, Vice-Commandant of the Academy of Military Sciences, in 1996: "[As for the United States] for a relatively long time it will be absolutely necessary that we quietly nurse our sense of vengeance. . . . We must conceal our abilities and bide our time." We have already seen the first signs of China's growing international assertiveness with its missile rattling over Taiwanese democracy, its seizure of Mischief Reef from the Philippines in 1995, and its invasion of a Vietnamese natural gas field in 1997. China is rapidly becoming a threat to world peace, as well as an affront to our civilized conscience and an unfair competitor in global markets. We must stop cosseting China; use access to our markets as a carrot for good behavior and a stick for bad; stand unequivocally by Taiwan; keep up our military strength in the region; encourage Asian countries to keep up their own guard; speak out for the oppressed of China and work for freedom there; press China in every international forum to improve its behavior; refuse China "face" until China improves its behavior. And that's just part of it . . .

Using the barbarians to control the barbarians has long been an important part of Chinese statecraft, and one aspect of this infuses—as the tea leaves infuse the water in the pot—the whole of this argument between ring-around-the-rosy diplomacy and the ring-of-steel school. It is the dominance in the debate of OCHs and OFOCs—who are sometimes, though not always, one and the same. OCHs are "old China hands," steeped in the language, culture, and politics of China. OFOCs are "old friends of China," specially chosen by China because they can be guaranteed, usually at the end of, or some way beyond, their political working lives to agree with whatever China does at any one time, or at least to find a plausible excuse for it. They are not always steeped in real expertise, but they are certainly steeped in paid official trips, official banquets, official stays in state guest houses, and official meetings at which mutual flattery is exchanged in prodigious quantities; they are in some cases steeped in lots of money. Let me discuss some consequences of the roles of these two groups in shaping the barbarian view of the Middle Kingdom.

Study of the Chinese language is intellectually tough, and students of Chinese culture and history are often overwhelmed by the scale and richness of what is laid out before them. The sheer size of China adds to a sense of wonder. Today, salesmen marvel at the number of potential customers; yesterday, missionaries blessed themselves at the prospect of the number of souls to be saved. Scale, longevity, complexity, cultural self-containment and confidence, and the successful Chinese rejection over the years of the outsiders' way of doing things—all this bedazzles some of the OCHs and all of the OFOCs. They believe, which is what the Chinese wish them to believe, that China is unique— "nowhere quite like it, old boy." It is totally different from anywhere else, opaque where others can be more readily understood, and its very uniqueness and opacity earn it the right to be treated differently from everyone else.

Now, I have never heard this said to the same extent about any other country. The Soviet Communist system, for example, was opaque as all totalitarian systems have been. But it was never suggested that special allowance should be made for it because we did not really understand its bloody and alcohol-sodden purposes. In what sense is China thought to be more opaque than Japan or India? How lucidly can a Chinese scholar read what is happening in Britain or Germany or the United States? Are we opaque to them? Does the opacity of cricket, a cultural form as much as a game, to an American or Frenchman reflect some unique and incomprehensible aspect of Englishness which should ensure that our friends make allowances for us when we kick over the traces from time to time? Much of Chinese life may well be mysterious to the outsider, and the degree of mystery may be all the greater because of years of Chinese isolation and years of authoritarianism. Yet I find it difficult to believe that the order of magnitude of the opacity renders China in a league, or a world, of its own.

The tyranny and clientitis of expertise make for further problems, much aggravated by China's careful tendency to withhold access to the country from those who have broken the taboos of friendly scholarship. It is astonishing how generous are the interpretations of Chinese history and behavior made by many (though not all) experts and how often these experts seem prepared to swallow, almost unquestioningly, whatever is China's current version of events. Looking dispassionately at the wickedness before the Communist revolution, which punctuated the century, and the wickedness that followed it, how could modern scholarship do other than condemn that revolution as a further, terrible disaster visited on a vastly talented people, who seem to have discovered almost everything in life save, for the past couple of centuries, the way to govern themselves decently? What tender mercy of history is it that has enabled Mao largely to escape (so far) his place on the same pedestal as the world's wickedest villains—Stalin, Hitler, Pol Pot, and the other angels of death? There has even been a cult of "pop" Maoism—a pottery model of the old pervert, capped and blue-suited, to put on the mantelpiece; Andy Warhol silk screens of him to hang on the living room wall. Imagine showing off your Hitler memorabilia to friends. I would not give Mao's picture or pottery figure, surrounded by manifestations of Struggle and Plenty, house room.

Gerald Segal, a senior fellow at Britain's International Institute for Strategic Studies, whose dissident views on China and sinology act as a useful check on the mainstream orthodoxies, has pointed out how often the experts have been wrong about Chinese policy and tactics. Most of them were wrong about China's active involvement in North Korea's attack on South Korea in 1950; wrong about the disastrous consequences of Mao's Great Leap Forward; wrong about Mao's renewed bid for power through the Cultural Revolution; and wrong about Deng's bloody intentions in Peking in 1989 (the ambassador's sophisticated "brown sneakers" analysis to which I referred earlier was in step with the conventional view at the time). These errors of interpretation and scholarship reflect a pretty common feature of OCH and OFOC wisdom not apparent, it has to be said, in the work of the greatest of the historians, like Jonathan Spence; the wisest of the political scientists, like Roderick McFarquar; or the most informed of the journalists, like Jonathan Mirsky. The OCHs and OFOCs so often tell us not only what their Chinese interlocutors want us to believe but what they want us to do—a consequence partly, I suspect, of their deep humility when addressing the affairs of the Middle Kingdom. They tend to assume Chinese superiority and Western shame. The superiority in terms of the achievements of Chinese civilization, at least until the sixteenth century, I can more or less understand; but we should not allow this to push us too far. I was somewhat taken aback when, before embarking for Hong Kong, I was preparing the speech that I was to make at my swearing-in as Governor. The reference in my draft to the shared historic responsibilities in Hong Kong of "two great and ancient civilizations" was scored out on the grounds that China's civilization was much older than the West's and China might feel offended by the assumption of parity. I kept the draft as I had originally written it. As for Western shame—well, imperialistic expansion, the nineteenth-century attempt to carve up China, the Treaty ports (mainland trading bases won by force from China), Hong Kong, opium, and all that are beyond excuse in twentieth-century terms, even if they are explicable by historians. But is not part of the shame, as far as Chinese nationalists are concerned, that Chinese people themselves flocked to the Treaty ports and that Hong Kong was a huge Chinese success under a British flag? It is difficult to reconcile thumping the nationalist drum in any country with a high and pure attachment to ethics and objectivity.

It is the alleged uniqueness of China that most blurs comprehension and mangles policy making. If pricked, we all bleed. I know of no good reason for believing that the theorems of politics and economics do not apply in China as elsewhere. Economic growth has social consequences, some of which may be politically disruptive. Freedom to trade brings political issues in its train. Men and women everywhere yearn to be free and secure. Information technology liberates just as it broadens. People need more in their lives than the prospect of material reward. Corruption creates bitter resentment. Economic breakdown causes social unrest; so do strong nationalist and religious sentiments unless skillfully accommodated. Carbon dioxide emissions threaten all our futures. Leninism has run out of road. The beginning, if not quite the end, of my views on China is that we become so preoccupied with how different it is from everywhere else that we overlook the myriad similarities. We are lured into thinking that there is a special, an exact, way of dealing with China, which turns out on close inspection to be one part correct to four parts mumbo-jumbo. China should be treated just like we would treat anyone else, not on the basis of voodoo or on the assumption that it requires its own rule book.

Western politicians invariably get into trouble when they ignore this sort of advice. Persuaded to try to turn themselves into instant China experts and forgetting their own political instincts—thinking perhaps that these would be wholly inappropriate in dealing with China—they allow themselves to be used by Chinese officials, to their subsequent political embarrassment. It was instructive to compare the visits by Vice President Al Gore and Speaker Newt Gingrich to China in the early spring of 1997. The Vice President is a decent and intelligent man, and no political slouch, but someone had gotten him to think that it was not good enough to go to China as a politician, that he had better become a sophisticated foreign policy analyst—and fast. The result was predictably disastrous, with Mr. Gore strongly criticized at home for appearing to be manipulated by Chinese leaders. Mr. Gingrich went as a politician and sounded like a politician. In the words of columnist Jim Hoagland of *The Washington Post*, he did what Americans expect of their politicians—not speaking like a foreign policy wonk but as someone who could "get the big things right—principles, the drift of history, the contemporary mood and the enduring values of the American nation." One of Margaret Thatcher's commendable virtues, though it rattles the chandeliers in chancelleries and embassies the world over, is always to be herself. On her visits to China in the years after Tiananmen, with her old sparring partner over Hong Kong Zhao Ziyang now swept into some sort of outer darkness (maybe, in his case, just that of the golf course), she always made a point of asking after him. "I want them to know that they can't dispose of him without some of us caring about it," she said. On one occasion, she tried to send him a present—a tie and matching handkerchief. I imagine the ambassador swallowed hard. Thatcher's gesture was exactly what any decent person's instincts would have told them to do; expert advice would have counseled against such becoming boldness.

Where does this lead us? The detachment that I advocate, the focus on our own national interests—individual and collective—in the West, does not go quite as far as was once advocated by George Kennan, the principal intellectual architect of the containment and overthrow of Communism in Europe and of the salvation of democracy and freedom. Kennan did not urge containment of China, but he did think that America should keep its distance. In the second volume of his memoirs, covering the period 1950–63, Kennan cites a memorandum he drafted in 1951, in which he expressed a coolness about both the Communist and the Kuomintang regimes. "[The] less we Americans have to do with China," he argued, "the better. We need neither covet the favor, nor fear the enmity of the Chinese." Kennan did not see China as "a great and strong power." Its industrial and military strength was limited. He noted that if in the postwar years the Soviet Union had been able to choose its ally in the region, it would have opted for Japan, not China. While admiring Chinese intelligence, he thought that xenophobia and arrogance would make it difficult to construct any satisfactory international relationship between America and China even if political antagonisms were overcome. Chinese ruthlessness, the lack of "a capacity for pity," meant that one should respect China, but not idealize her or seek intimacy. In any event, the Chinese insistence that they were in the right and others in the wrong did not augur well for a harmonious partnership. Kennan did not wish to ignore Communist China or to block its entrance into the United Nations, but he opposed formal bilateral diplomatic relations that would only place in China's hands American hostages, who would be "humiliated and made sport of for the gratification of the insatiable Chinese thirst for 'face' and prestige." Americans should no longer put themselves in the position where the Chinese could make fools of them.

This is strong stuff, which would have earned the New China News Agency's customary riposte that he had "gauged a noble heart with his own mean measures." As strategic advice, it is very much of its time—Kennan's and America's real preoccupations lay elsewhere, containing the Soviet Union. The condemnations of the Chinese character are sweeping, unfair, and—no "capacity for pity"—even racist. No one could afford today to have as little to do with China as possible. It is not a remotely viable option. But it seems to me that Kennan's arguments cast at least the shadow of wisdom over current fixations. Do we really need to tie ourselves up in knots trying to get China right? Must we accept the Chinese leadership's view that "a good relationship with China" is a commodity that can be offered or withheld by Peking rather than result from the aggregate of business—agreements and disagreements—that each of us does bilaterally with China?

I should now come clean. It is a grave confession. I am not scared witless of the People's Republic of China or mesmerized by China's might and majesty. I am on balance more scared of things going wrong in China—the splintering of China, the breakdown of governance—than of things muddling through or going rather well. China is at the end of an era. Marxism and Maoism are dead and buried. Leninism is going the same way. What more does the Communist party have to offer than cynicism and decadence? This was brought home to me most forcefully by an anecdote I heard from a Chinese woman married to a Westerner living in Hong Kong. She had been born and brought up in China. Her parents had returned there from comfortable academic jobs in Northern California after the revolution, believing that they should make their own proud contribution to building the new China. Disaster soon struck, though disillusionment never wholly set in. They were assailed first in the anti-rightist campaign of the 1950s and then again in the Cultural Revolution in the decade after 1966. As returnees from America, intellectuals who spoke good English, they were prime suspects during both these devilish periods. The father's health was wrecked by the horrors and humiliations inflicted on him during the Cultural Revolution. Throughout the misery and hardship of all these years, the mother never criticized communism or bemoaned the fact that she and her husband had freely left a good life in California for this hell. And then in the last months of her life, surveying the corruption and harsh capitalism of modern China, the mother lost heart, desperate that she had put her family through all this hardship only to see at the end of her life a society no different, in her view, from that of the warlords and the Kuomintang. Stripped of any pretense of an ethical basis for good government, what was left in modern China? She died, a Chinese patriot shorn of hope, drowned in her own despair. This is surely an insurmountable challenge for the Chinese Communist party. It spent forty years attacking and destroying all that was admirable in China's civilization. What has it now to put in the place of the scientific socialism it has had to abandon in order to cling to power? Its hope is that capitalism will so improve living standards for the majority of the Chinese people as to sustain its authority to govern. But what happens if economic progress stutters, and who has the authority to stand over the deeply unpopular measures required in the next stages of China's reform program?

Who knows what comes next in China? Perhaps we should expect a society like Indonesia became under Suharto, a corrupt ideology-free bureaucracy led by a handful of families, backed by powerful plundering generals, allowing capitalism its head and permitting a growing number of smart, usually Western-educated technocrats to steer a course through the occasional economic shoals. Or maybe we will get a late flowering of Zhaoism, a gradual unraveling of political control (as advocated by Zhao Ziyang) to match growing economic liberty: the belated recognition of Wei Jingsheng's fifth modernization. This would not be an immediate metamorphosis into multiparty democracy. But what if, to take refuge in virtual history, Zhao had not fallen in 1989? Do we really believe that murdering students and their working-class supporters was necessary to sustain China's economic reform program? Was all that blood really essential to keep the Chinese economy irrigated? Zhaoism would have kept economic reform going and given the government more of the authority it is going to need as reform from time to time brings pain and abrupt change.

There may be some other future for China. Chaos, as has happened at the end of other dynasties, is always possible. Indeed, there is a sort of Chinese cycle in which chaos customarily follows a period of authoritarian heavy-handedness. This is what we should most fear—indeed, all that we should probably fear. The spillover would have global, though manageable, economic consequences; it would pose serious problems for regional security; and it would launch a tide of illegal Chinese immigration on the world. So chaos would be by far the worst of the outcomes.

Anything else that happens to China is unlikely to cause us terminal anxiety. China is not an economic superpower today and is a very long way from becoming one. It will not be playing in Japan's league—or Germany's or Britain's or France's, let alone the United States'—for as far ahead as any of us can usefully predict. (And those who make predictions about Asia should have learned a thing or two about humility in 1997 and 1998.) In China, the veneer of end-of-the-century technology and know-how is eggshell-thin. China confronts huge problems as it continues on the path to modernization—social, political, and (as we saw in an earlier chapter) industrial. It has a large military capability, but its arsenal is not even sufficiently menacing to take out Taiwan. It can bully its way around the region as long as it is allowed to do so, but what more could it presently do? Would it fare any better against Vietnam today, for example, than it did in February 1979, when it had to retire with a bloody nose? Geo-strategically, what sort of threat does China represent? None to the West (at least for a long time to come). Perhaps Japan, Russia, India, and Southeast Asia can be forgiven for seeing things differently; after all, China has invaded three neighbors since the Second World War—Korea, India, and Vietnam. But there seems little present cause for anxiety outside the region. I very much doubt whether this has been changed by China's recent rapprochement with Russia. Russian interest in arms and energy sales and a quiet border is not going to bury its suspicions of China's uncertain prospects and inscrutable intentions, in Central Asia for instance. In short, the Chinese government may still be able to terrify its own people when necessary. But I see no reason why the rest of us should wake up in a Sino-sweat in the middle of the night.

What is the Western interest—America's and Europe's—in dealing with China, and what, for that matter, is the interest of China's neighbors? First, we should all want to see it continue its program of economic reform, opening its market to the products of the rest of the world, joining those economic organizations whose rules ensure that trade flows freely and fairly, signing and keeping international agreements, becoming a responsible member of the global economic community. Second, we should want to see an equally responsible China, constructive at the UN and in regional groupings, restrained in its dealings with its neighbors and Taiwan, reliable in its acceptance of international rules and standards on weapons proliferation and nuclear testing. Third, we should want to see China a signatory of the appropriate international conventions and agreements on civil and political rights and implementing their provisions. In case there is any doubt about the desirability or relevance of this last consideration, let me spell it out simply.

The pertinence of ethical considerations—freedom, democracy, the abolition of torture, imprisonment without trial, religious persecution, and so on—to foreign policy and the pursuit and defense of the national interest is regularly debated. We are offered, as it were, a rather crude choice between Gladstonian and Wilsonian idealism (Gladstone, incidentally, was Woodrow Wilson's teenage hero) on the one hand and the realpolitik of Metternich and Lord Salisbury on the other. Are we to take our stand with Carter or Kissinger, with high-minded waffle or cynical common sense? The dangers of idealism were pointed out by Lord Melbourne, who advised, "Never try to do good and you won't get into scrapes." Lord Salisbury offered similar counsel: "It's difficult enough to go around doing what is right without going around trying to do good."

In practice, few are prepared these days to denounce the establishment of any relationship at all between ideals and the conduct of a free society's foreign policy. It would be increasingly awkward to do so. More people today live in free societies and assume that, if at all possible, others should have the right to do so too. They see the difference in international behavior between societies that are free and those that are unfree, and they draw the not very arduous conclusion that they will sleep more soundly in their beds when more countries are liberal democracies. Global communications—television in particular—regularly excite their interest in what is happening in other parts of the world, for example the consequences of human beastliness. Gladstone would have had even more support for his views on the Bulgarian atrocities had these been shown live on the BBC World Service and CNN. We have established international networks of organizations and agreements which presuppose that the world is about more than the self-contained pursuit of the national interest. What, for example, do we mean by our support for the UN? Politicians preparing to take what may be controversial action abroad invariably seek to justify what they wish to do in terms of the morality of the action concerned as well as its security or other implications. Appeals to the authority and support of the UN are not just an attempt to drum up the greatest number of reinforcements but an effort to demonstrate that a higher good is on one's own side. Bombing other people is easier if you can plausibly claim that it is not only—to borrow from Lord Salisbury—right but good. No foreign minister these days is likely to argue at all, or at least for long, "Don't give me any of that ethical crap." He or she may be a little cautious in how explicitly ethical considerations are deployed, bearing in mind the imperfectibility of the conduct of any government's policy and the many pressures that need to be accommodated in devising it. But it is unlikely that idealism will be publicly consigned to the dustbin, and very likely that it will be flourished from time to time with appropriate sanctimoniousness in dealing with small countries if not large. It is much easier, shall we say, to wag a finger at nasty Burma than at China.

I do not therefore believe that these days the case for realpolitik will be put all that noisily. Does it make all that much sense anyway? There are extremes of silliness no one should advocate. There is a difference between the conduct of foreign policy and a crusade, between Madeleine Albright and Billy Graham. But the morally preferable course of action is usually in the long-term interest of free (and unfree) societies everywhere. Apartheid was wicked. The world disapproved. Free societies took quite active measures to bring about change in South Africa. Apartheid went. Democracy was given a boost throughout Africa. Whatever its short-term difficulties, South Africa is more likely as a result to be stable in the long term. We fought Hitler because he threatened the freedoms and interests of other countries, but we also fought him because he was wicked. We stood up to Soviet tyranny because we wished to retain our democratic way of life and also because what was happening in Central and Eastern Europe was hideous. At the very least, our moral disapproval strengthened our perception of our national interest.

If we were not to care what happened in the Soviet gulag or in China's labor camps, if we were not to give a damn about what happens to Solzhenitsyn or Aung San Suu Kyi, Mandela or Wei Jingsheng, we would be owning up to a decidedly foreshortened moral reach, a blunted moral sensibility. We also would be rooting for life in a more dangerous world. Societies that treat their own people intolerably, governments whose own laws are a farce, are bad and potentially dangerous neighbors. I want other people to live in liberal democracies; I want other people to live without the fear of arbitrary arrest and torture; I want other people to be able to speak their minds and worship their gods—I want all that because it is what human beings who are joined to one another in the wonderful mystery of Creation deserve and have an unchallengeable right to expect. But I want these things too because they are in my personal interest and my country's interest. Free societies make the best neighbors.

So the human rights of that more than one fifth of humanity who live in China matter to me, matter to those of us who live outside China, as well as to the Chinese themselves. Do I need to parade the horrors of China's repression of its own people? The arbitrary arrests, the beatings and tortures, the mass executions, the regional repression, the organ transplants of criminals, the religious persecution, the suppression of free speech and union activity, the silencing of political opposition, the trading of dissidents, those terrible camps inhabited by the wretched and the desperate—all the horrors that defile Chinese Communism. Perhaps some of the charges are deniable; perhaps here and there some amelioration may have occurred. Who really knows? Whatever may be adjustable at the margins, the full scale and weight of this odious abuse of men and women is a cause of shame for China and shame for the rest of us that it happens and we do so little, think so little, speak so little about it. Burying a friend who died in his camp, the dissident Harry Wu expressed his agony and rage: "Human life has no value here, I thought bitterly. It has no more importance than a cigarette ash flicked in the wind. But if a person's life has no value, then the society that shapes that life has no value either. If the people mean no more than dust, then the society is worthless and does not deserve to continue. If the society should not continue, then I should oppose it."* Where does that leave the rest of us?

Very few of the advocates of minimalism in dealing with the human rights record of China's Communist government say, "It's nothing to do with us." On the whole, their starting point is the assumption that we should wish to do what we can but that our options

* *Bitter Winds*, 1993.

remain limited. Yet the available scope for action is not so limited as is invariably argued. Minimalism offers three justifications. First, we are told—a point on which I have touched before—that the Chinese do not care as much about politics and civil liberties as the rest of us. This racist point appears to be gutted by even the most inattentive study of modern Chinese history. Where has there been more political struggle? Where have there been more dramatic eruptions of outrage about civil liberties? Second, it is argued that more will be accomplished by what is called "quiet diplomacy" than by public protests. Third, it is suggested that the conditions of those who are in prison for their beliefs will be worsened if a fuss is made about them, because Chinese regard for "face" will make the authorities implacably hostile to any amelioration that appears to be a response to outside pressure.

I put these last two points to Wei Jingsheng, probably China's most famous and articulate dissident, in January 1998. He had then been out of China for a matter of weeks, following almost eighteen years in prison with one brief interlude when he was used (unsuccessfully, as it turned out) as a human pawn in China's bid to host the Olympics in the year 2000. Perhaps one should not be affected by appearances, by personality and character. But it is difficult not to be. Wei is warm, graceful, witty, and self-deprecating; but he is also uncompromising and unbiddable. He loves his country and wants the very best for it, which is why he opposes corrupt modern Leninism there. In more than two hours of conversation I heard no abuse, no personal criticism of the Chinese leaders who had locked him up, no self-pity. How is it possible to be like this after the experiences he has suffered? The nearest he came to acerbity was when I raised two of the arguments for minimalism mentioned above. No one, of course, advocates the use of megaphones, yet the case for making an audible fuss has a Chinese dimension as well as an external one. Wei pointed out that the Chinese leadership argued to its people that democracy and so-called liberalism were a sham. Westerners talked a lot about them; they were in reality merely a convenient facade behind which all the strings that mattered were pulled by the rich and the powerful. So when capitalist barons in America or Europe banged on the table, politicians in those countries did what they were told and—in the case of China—kept their mouths shut about human rights. Western Trappism on Chinese freedom therefore had the effect of castrating the case for freedom in China itself. Wei also noted that, speaking for himself, his own treatment and conditions in prison bore a direct relationship to the amount of fuss made about him and other dissidents by the outside world; the louder the noise, the better he was treated. When no one beyond the Great Wall seemed to care, his treatment deteriorated. Next time therefore a Western leader tells you he knows what is best for China's dissidents, and that is to keep his mouth shut about them (or only to raise their plight behind his hand with a suitably junior functionary), you might remember what the dissidents think. They do in this case have the experience, if not exactly the advantage, of being on the receiving end of whatever tactics are deemed most effective by well-meaning outsiders.

We have therefore clear national interests in dealing with China, and they include the way a sunset Communist party treats its own people. How do we pursue those interests? My unshakable conviction is that we currently make a terrible mistake by mixing them up—which means that we do not really secure anything we want—and an even greater mistake in allowing the Chinese to mix them up—which compounds our muddle and our failure. The "we" in this case begins with the United States, the world's leader (or hegemonist, as Chinese propaganda would put it). It is the relationship with America that most concerns China, both because of America's military strength and because of the size of America's market.

American policy is fatally focused on the annual debate about whether China should enjoy what is called most favored nation trading status; "most favored" in this case actually meaning no more than normal. Every spring and summer, American policy is concentrated on and shaped by the discussion about whether or not China should continue for another year to enjoy access to the U.S. market on the same terms as other countries in its position (that is, countries that are not members of the World Trade Organization). The whole gamut of issues—from China's family policy and human rights record to its theft of intellectual property and its weapons proliferation—is thrown into the pot. I see why this happens and respect the motives of those who search for some, for any, way of applying leverage to China. The trouble is that it does not work. It distorts policy. It prevents the clear-sighted construction of a consistent long-term strategy. It plays into China's hands.

Every year we witness the same ritual. In spring, the administration wheels the cumbersome piece of rocketry—the MFN ground-to-hot-air missile—out of its bunker and parks it on Capitol Hill. It is a mighty weapon. Visitors from all over the world stand around, admiring and marveling at its destructive power. This year, we are told, it really may be fired. The Chinese had better get into line, pull their socks up, because Congress is minded this time around to light the fuse. The lobbyists lobby (for which they are handsomely rewarded); the politicians offer sound bites; the administration counsels caution; the State Department and the friends of free trade tell the Chinese that this year it may be different, that the vote looks tighter than ever, that the great weapon could be fired in earnest. The Chinese do not believe a word of it. They announce that they may buy a few Boeings, or alternatively—if there is a deterioration in Sino–U.S. relations—a few Airbuses from Europe; they purchase grain from the western States; they send a high-level mission to the United States to consider a shopping list of possible American purchases (which they anyway needed and were intending to buy). Meanwhile, where once bravado reigned, canny street-wise prudence has become the order of the day. Who knows what might happen if this year the rocket were to be fired? Where might it come down? Perhaps it will hit Seattle; maybe Montana? What will the fallout be? So the rocket is admired for one last nostalgic time, given a final spit and polish, and wheeled back to the bunker for another winter under wraps. As far as the Chinese are concerned, it is an annual pantomime. "Yes, I will"—"No, you won't." They don't.

There are, in fact, several good arguments for separating trade from other considerations. The first is a matter of principle. Trade should be free, and should be used as a weapon only in extremis and where it will work. Trade embargoes or linkages do not usually have the desired effect; South Africa may be one of the few exceptions to this rule, and even here the evidence is pretty mixed. In some places, Cuba for example, embargoes may even have prolonged dictatorship. Second, and for present purposes more important, confusing trade and other interests means that we do not pursue any agenda as vigorously as we should. "Multifaceted" our relationship with China may well be, but I would take each facet as it stands.

This means pursuing economic and trade issues on their own, tough-mindedly and with a bit more common sense. We should negotiate hard with China, as hard as with anyone else, on trade issues. We should not make special allowances for Chinese transgressions. If China wishes to join the World Trade Organization, that is good news. But it is for China to make the pitch, not us. We should not bend the rules for China. It is for China to make the changes necessary for membership—to tariffs, state lending, property rights, and so on—and then we can talk turkey. We should drop our Marco Polo–like obsession with the Chinese market, which may or may not one day be a fraction of what it is currently advertised to be. For the moment, it does not matter very much to many of us and we should concentrate not on finding special wheezes and deals for allowing our firms into it (some of which may make money, others of which certainly will not) but on creating conditions in which all can invest and trade there fairly. It would be a great help if we would drop all the vocabulary about the vital importance of China's market to the West and the suggestion that there is such a crucial link between greater trade and future political liberty that we can overlook every example of present political repression. The first of these points is much exaggerated, and the Chinese believe that talk about trade leading to freedom is merely Western code for putting human rights on one side. Let businessmen get on with business in China on their own assessment of the risks and opportunities. A moratorium on high-level trade visits, new initiatives, and all the rest would be a great bonus all around. If the Chinese want our goods, they will buy them. They certainly want our investment and access to our markets. The number of our own trade hustles mounts; the Chinese signatures on letters of intent add up; the Chinese trade surplus with the West soars. Who is kidding whom?

Second, we should pursue our other interests on their own terms, too—from weapons proliferation to human rights. We should table resolutions in international forums and lobby for support for them. We should press China to sign up to international agreements and codes of conduct on human rights and other matters. We should offer China help—if the Chinese government wants it—in areas like the drafting of laws and the training of judges. We should make a fuss about dissidents and Tibet and ignore Chinese petulance. When

China complains that an American or a European leader sees someone who is on the Chinese blacklist or says something that offends Chinese sensitivities, we should behave exactly as we would if anyone else was so impertinent: We should tell them that it is none of their business, that we live in free societies, that we are under no obligation to tread gingerly around matters they may find unpalatable. If "face" matters so much to Chinese Communist leaders, we should deny "face" to them until they give some to us. Prestigious visits, twenty-one-gun salutes, red carpets, diplomatic flattery—all these have their modest place in the world, but they should be carefully rationed. We should, in short, behave normally with China.

Perhaps the worst aspect of the present muddle of objectives and tactics, which appears to most interested observers to leave the idealists without an effective strategy and the engagement strategists without any ideals, is that it enables the Chinese to mix trade and politics so effectively that they win every diplomatic round and almost every political tussle. The Chinese government believes that all it has to do is to crack the whip—threaten a blocked order here, a purchase from a rival there, a withdrawal of its goodwill, a cancellation of good relations until further notice—and we will all jump back into line. And by and large we actually do, especially the Europeans. Sometimes one has to pinch oneself to remember who needs whom most. The Chinese government needs our investment. It needs access to our markets. Without our money and our purchase of Chinese goods, the very future of the Communist regime would be imperiled. We spin the wheels for them. So what are we afraid of losing—a market that represents 1.7 percent of the total exports of the OECD countries? For Britain, 0.4 percent of our exports go to China. The figures for other rich countries are 1.4 percent for Germany; 0.8 percent for France; 1.9 percent for the United States. Britain sells over nine times as much to Belgium and Luxembourg as we do to China, and almost three times as much to Australia. America sells about the same to these countries as it does to China. Does British foreign policy dance to a Belgian folk song? Does American policy skip to the didgeridoo?

Ah, but what about the potential? Mrs. Beeton's advice to those who wished to cook jugged hare seems appropriate: "First catch your hare." In any event, save in certain specific circumstances, there appears as we have seen to be precious little relationship between the warmth of a country's political relationship with China and its overall trading performance, and there would be no relationship at all if we were not mostly so pusillanimous.

In order to have a coherent policy on China—not flab or flint but common sense—we all have to behave the same. Europe has to resolve not to be picked off and used against the United States, and Canada and Australia have to be prepared to act in the same way. At the moment, country after country in the West is prepared to behave with a humiliating lack of any sort of intelligence or principle in order to curry negligible if not nugatory commercial favors. In return for the French or the Germans curbing the rights of those who seek to demonstrate during a Chinese leaders' visit, what special favors do they actually get? As we have seen, the answer is usually a carefully disguised lemon. Perhaps one could understand pusillanimity if it had a payback. Pusillanimity without a backhander or two, without any real bonus to show for it, seems a wretchedly aimless way of pursuing one's national interest or safeguarding self-respect. All that is required is for the OECD countries to say to China, once and together: "Stop using economic and trade threats; you are in no position to do so; it is unacceptable behavior; if you want to get into the World Trade Organization, then we do not wish to have any more threats or promises of politically earned favors." If this was said once, and maybe repeated occasionally if necessary thereafter, we could all start to develop a more civilized relationship with China. A statement from the G7 summit of the major industrial nations or from the OECD would probably do the trick once and for all.

Europe's pretensions to a common and global foreign policy look, alas, especially hollow when one considers recent behavior over China. To its credit, the European Parliament has invariably been sensible and steadfast and the European Commission has behaved well, too. When China blackballed Jardine's in 1993 and threatened to restrict trade with British firms, Sir Leon Brittan, the relevant European Commissioner, went to Peking and told the Chinese this was unacceptable behavior. Other European politicians were not so forthcoming, and doubtless rubbed their hands at the prospect of more pickings for their own national companies even as British exports, as we have noted, climbed steadily.

But the greatest mortification, and the most embarrassing indication of the gulf between European rhetoric and reality, came in 1997 over the tabling of the Geneva resolution on China's human rights record and in the following year. China makes so much fuss about this each year, goes to such lengths to lobby for its defeat, that it is difficult to believe that it is not a lever of some modest consequence. Much of the recent lobbying has been directed at Europe; others have been worked over, too. In the wake of Gareth Evans's departure as Australia's Foreign Minister in 1995, the Australians soon backed off support for the Geneva resolution, arguing that they could achieve more progress in human rights through quiet dialogue. (Perhaps they would like to give Wei Jingsheng a call.) Then Canada made its excuses. Lloyd Axworthy, the Canadian Foreign Minister, had been told in Peking by Li Peng, so it is reliably said, that if Canada went ahead and supported the resolution, the Chinese would take power station projects away from Canadian firms. Mr. Axworthy, to his credit, was outraged. So were several of his cabinet colleagues when he reported this back to them. But with Mr. Chrétien, the Prime Minister, arguing on the other side, the decision went against Axworthy. Game, set, and match to Li Peng. Canada, too, then opted for quiet dialogue. France and Germany had already been suborned. At every European meeting at which the subject came up, they counseled dialogue and delay; they flourished a Chinese promise to sign (though not yet to ratify) the International Covenant on Economic, Social, and Cultural Rights. Political rights would inevitably come later, they argued, if only we would all behave with a bit of understanding. Spain and Italy went along with this, and the European Union was fatally divided. Eventually, though the Chinese warned that it would be like "a rock on their own heads," Denmark tabled the motion in the spring of 1997, with strong support from the Netherlands and with Britain and others (including the United States) giving tacit support. Then what happened? Denmark is a small country and China saw the perfect opportunity to act on the old adage of killing the chicken to frighten the monkeys. Several Danish contracts were canceled; Denmark and the Netherlands were scolded and sent to the doghouse. Here was a permanent member of the UN Security Council taking economic sanctions against another prominent member of the UN for using UN machinery perfectly properly to call attention to China's abysmal human rights record. And what did anyone do? Nothing. What in particular did members of the European Union do? They looked the other way. There was not a squeak from anyone. Why on earth should European governments think they can carry any sort of collective authority in the world when they will not even stand up to this sort of bullying, which could be prevented by nothing more heroic than a smidgen of resolve and the drafting of a firm communiqué? No great sacrifice was required in this case.

In 1998 Europe went one step further, or as Human Rights Watch called it, "a major step backward." Rewarding China for its behavior the previous year, the European foreign ministers threw in the towel. They announced that "in view of the first encouraging results of the EU–China human rights dialogue they would neither table nor co-sponsor the Geneva resolution in 1998." "Encouragement" seemed to lie in the eye of the beholder. The European Union's representative in Peking, Endymion Wilkinson, praised China's recent "concerted attempt" to address human rights problems as "enormously encouraging." The president of the European Union's Foreign Affairs Council, the British Foreign Secretary, Robin Cook, gave Wei Jingsheng's release as an example of the results of dialogue, a proposition roundly denounced by Mr. Wei himself. The Chinese were told that it was now up to them to show that a policy of dialogue was better than confrontation. If there was no improvement, Europe would—would—? Well, precisely. Europe would perhaps get Mr. Endymion Wilkinson to tell the Chinese that he was not quite as encouraged as he had been before, or more likely we would take our cue from the Endymion of Greek mythology and Keats's poem and carry on sleeping. The timing of this change of policy was unfortunate, coming as it did in the same week that China rounded up more dissidents (who must have been enormously encouraged) in the days before the opening of the National People's Congress and just before the arrest in New York of Chinese officials who were running a bespoke service in the sale of the organs of executed Chinese prisoners. It was also the week of the launch in London of a new foreign-policy think tank, one of whose aims was apparently to help the Labour government to keep human rights at the center of its foreign policy.

Some justification for Europe's new policy (and the United States shortly followed suit) was found in the subsequent statement by China's retiring Foreign Minister, Qian Qichen, in March 1998 that China would now consider signing the International Covenant on

Civil and Political Rights. Hats were tossed in the air. This may have been a little premature. Signing covenants has no real force; it is ratification that binds governments to compliance with the covenants' provisions and that enables other UN members to examine a country's record of compliance. Now, here is the chance for Europe—and America—to show that we are really interested in these ethical issues and not just engaged in a charade. We could say to China's leaders: "We are encouraged that you are proposing to sign the covenant; we hope you will do so quickly and then ratify equally promptly; if you do so, there will be no need for us to table Geneva resolutions anymore, because the Human Rights Commission itself will examine your record; but should you delay ratification, then we will have to think again." Would this be too provocative? At least it would demonstrate that the British government and its European Union partners are genuinely concerned about human rights, that we are not just being strung along by China. When Mahatma Gandhi was asked what he thought about Western civilization, he reportedly replied that he thought it would be a very good idea. I find myself responding similarly when I hear British and European foreign ministers talking about their commitment to an ethical foreign policy.

"Does Europe matter in Asia?" I am often asked. "Can Europe matter in Asia and elsewhere?" I would like to think so. But for what reason should Asians listen seriously from time to time to European governments as well as to the administration in Washington? Who has the gumption to stand up for anything? Too often, unfortunately, Europe plays its "Ode to Joy" anthem around the world on a pennywhistle. We should take some comfort. With any luck, the European Union will continue to be able to say something strong and principled about Burma every now and then. That should keep up morale.

Within an overall policy of relaxed but determined normality, free of sticks, carrots, and toadyism, the problem will remain of negotiating specific issues with Chinese officials for commercial contracts and political agreements. There is plenty of good advice on the subject—the excellent book by Lucian Pye, to which I have already referred, and more useful tips from Dick Solomon (*Chinese Political Negotiating Behavior*, RAND, 1985), Oguru Kazuo (*The Chinese Quarterly*, 1979), and several others. There is no shortage of wise guidance, but most of it seems to be ignored, especially at the very top. No company chairman (or minister for that matter) should be allowed to go to China without reading Mr. Pye's book or, if at 111 pages it is too long, a summary of it. The principal problems, as Pye says, really do start at the top. Let me summarize four straightforward ground rules and then suggest a few tactical considerations. The ground rules are: (a) do not under any circumstances let the chairman go first to set the ball rolling; (b) do not allow the outcome to be constrained or determined by apparently harmless initial agreements on general principles; (c) do not allow yourself to be boxed in by the calendar; and (d) do not leave any loose ends or ambiguities that can be used to reopen the argument.

Let us begin with the chairman (or the minister with suitable modifications to the example). The boss of company X reads a couple of articles in the business press about the China market. "There's a lot happening over there," he says. "Why haven't we got a share of the action? I'd like to go over and have a look around." The visit is fixed. Intermediaries arrange for him to see a couple of senior officials—maybe a vice-premier (there are quite a lot of them) or a vice-minister (there are scores of them). He is impressed. There is a large banquet. Everything is very friendly; everyone gets on very well. Expressions of mutual esteem are exchanged. It is agreed that company X and ministry Y could and should do a lot of business together. There is a natural synergy. "These guys are born entrepreneurs; they really want us in there with them; I don't know why people think they're difficult; we've agreed upon the big picture, now just sort out the details." The chairman gives his instructions and gets on the plane. He has created the mood; the atmosphere is good; the rest is plain sailing.

Now, hear the story from the point of view of the middle-level executive who is required to do the substantive negotiations. Pye, whose book is based on interviews with businessmen, quotes one who speaks for so many:

The president and the chairman of the board went home from Beijing as instant authorities on China, and ever since they have assumed that they are completely knowledgeable about how to do business with the Chinese. With respect to any other part of the world they defer to the specialized knowledge of the man in the field, but not on China. When I report problems in the negotiations, I sense that they are impatient with me rather than with the Chinese. They have no sense of how stubborn the Chinese can be over terms. Their memories are filled with enjoyable encounters with the Chinese when all the talk was about how good it was going to be working together. When I try to report problems to the home office, their first reaction is always that I must be the cause of the difficulties; that it is my fault that I have not got the hang of how to have agreeable relations with the Chinese. The truth is that at every turn I have to bend over backward not to offend the Chinese. I have to keep my side of the record perfect or I'll be criticized by New York or by the Chinese or by both. Above all I cannot call upon my boss to step in and back me up at key points in the negotiations. He wants to come back out for another visit, but only after everything is in order.

This surefire way of doing bad deals and losing money is compounded by the assumption that because a senior leader has been seen and has smiled his approval on a proposed project it will roll forward smoothly. But the senior leader in question may have no clout to make things hum in the area concerned, or else may be far too cautious to commit his political authority to a scheme that he may not be able to guarantee or control. How often is a half hour with Jiang Zemin, Zhu Rongji, Li Peng, or another senior leader assumed to be as good as a signature on a contract? And how often does it turn out to be no such thing?

There are similar problems with ministerial visits. You have to be very careful that you do not pay a price for such a visit—a compromise on policy here, a precautionary silence or refused meeting there ("It may not be quite the best week for meeting Mr. Wei, Minister, as you are hoping to get approval shortly for your Peking visit")—and then have precious little to show for it except an alleged improvement in the atmosphere and a thickening up of the relationship, whatever those things may mean. In the run-up to the handover of Hong Kong, hours, days, weeks of time went into negotiating the precise arrangements for the meetings between Britain's new Prime Minister and Foreign Secretary and Chinese leaders. I think that Mr. Blair and Mr. Cook may have been a little surprised, after all this to-ing and fro-ing, at the largely content-free nature of the meetings. But at least these encounters could be hailed as a gradual warming of relations. In my experience, it was about even Stephen that a minister after the event would regret having made a much planned and carefully arranged visit to China. There was invariably a lot more give than take, and ministers always ran the risk of a deliberate or accidental snub. The reporting telegrams, however, could usually be depended on to celebrate an un-qualified success.

The other ground rules can be dealt with relatively quickly. It is a grave error to allow yourself to be under time pressure when negotiating. The Chinese will use this against you. If the length of a negotiation is out of all proportion to the benefits of an agreement, or if you feel obliged to settle by a given date, forget about it. The Chinese will do a deal with you if they feel strongly enough about it. Have the gumption to pack your bags if necessary and go home. But if you have time on your own hands and if it is all worth it, then be very patient and let the game come to you. You should under no circumstances allow the Chinese to know what your real time pressures are, and should try to convince them of deadlines that may not be real. As the same points go back and forth over the table, you should occasionally comfort yourself with the recognition that others have had to endure similar frustrations. The Catholic chaplain at a convent once described hearing nuns' confessions as like being pecked to death by ducks. This is very unfair to nuns but quite a good description of some Chinese negotiations.

At the outset of talks, commercial or political, the Chinese (who learn these tactics when they are taught to negotiate) will try to get you to agree to some general principles that appear relatively innocuous. Look at these very carefully. They are probably framed to help shape the outcome and the endgame. At the very least, they will be played back against you during the negotiations, when you will be accused of departing from their "spirit," a largely meaningless concept designed to shame you onto the back foot.

Finally, under no circumstances allow any ambiguities or loose ends in the final agreement. They are likely to be exploited to reopen the deal or reinterpret it in the best interests of your Chinese interlocutors. Something else to watch out for is a little creative fiddling with the terms of the deal after it has been negotiated and after success has been announced. Between the smoke-filled negotiating room and the celebratory, champagne-swigging press conference the odd additional clause may suddenly appear from nowhere. You have to be prepared to sacrifice the champagne and walk away from the agreement. Usually, you will discover that it was only a "try-on."

Within those general guidelines, I also would argue that it is sensible not to allow all the talks to take place in Peking; you become too much of the "demandeur." There are advantages in playing sometimes on your own field. Western negotiators in China can feel awkward and isolated. Try to play some of the games on your own ground. Begin toughly and do not give any hint of moderation or compromise, since this will be taken as a sign of weakness. The Chinese will wait for you to move and to make the first—and subsequent—proposals. You should put pressure on them to show their hand first. George Shultz was a master at this. He was prepared to stonewall his way through meetings until his interlocutors showed a card. You should never admit a mistake or apologize, never be discourteous or rude, and always, always stake out your position on the moral high ground. If you do not do this, you can be sure that the Chinese will. You will then find yourself battling uphill at every meeting. It also helps if you appear, whatever the reality, to be enjoying yourself, and the Chinese are more likely to think that you are if you can dissimulate as much as they undoubtedly will.

One of the very best British negotiators with the Chinese in Hong Kong, a young man with a sinuous intelligence and an astonishing capacity for soaking up tedium, nonsense, and harangues without allowing a flicker of impatience or annoyance to cross his face (I always thought the Chinese must have regarded him as very inscrutable), used to describe his opposite numbers as being like guerrilla fighters. It was a point meant generously to describe the difference between Chinese and most Western negotiators. The Chinese system meant that their negotiators would have no room to question their instructions, would not always know the overall strategy behind the negotiations, and would have only one order and that would be to attack, to surrender no ground, and to come back with a clear-cut victory. By contrast, most Western negotiators—commercial and political—are themselves part of the policy-making process, are trained to try to persuade the other side to see their own point of view, to seek compromises and solutions. These cultural and political distinctions were naturally much exaggerated by the subject matter in Hong Kong. We were dealing with some of the most sensitive and difficult issues for China in terms of both nationalism and politics. It was revealing and a little worrying to see how the Chinese reacted on subjects like freedom, openness, diversity, and pluralism, which were going in time to shape their relations with the rest of the region and the world.

Because the system obliges them to behave like guerrillas does not mean that all Chinese negotiators are untrustworthy, hard as nails, and unpleasant. I venture to believe that attractive human beings are scattered randomly in more or less equal proportionate numbers across the surface of the globe, and unattractive ones too. As the present doomed Chinese system of government cracks and changes, I suspect that this will become more apparent, though enough of the Middle Kingdom may survive to mean that it is unlikely ever to be easy to negotiate with China. But then, ask a Briton what it is like to negotiate with a Frenchman, or the other way around, ask an American whether dealing with Europeans is a pushover. We are always likely to believe, come globalization, the end of history, or whatever else the future may have in store, that our own kind, our own compatriots, are blessed with a native-born integrity and straightforwardness denied to others. The nation-state survives in our hearts as well as in the atlases.

Is there, I wonder as I look back over these arguments, some woeful lack of sophistication, some supercharged anti-Communist zealotry, some innately prejudiced hostility to China in the approach I advocate? Even as I frame the questions, I observe again how concepts and value judgments that would apply wholly naturally in discussing relations with other countries are simply deemed inappropriate to any discussion about China. But why is it sophisticated to think that we should always do, by and large, what the Chinese government wants us to do, even in some Western democracies covering up what we know about Chinese behavior (in weapons proliferation, for instance) and requiring our own elected leaders to run political risks lest Chinese Communist leaders should have to run them themselves? Why is it savvy to make assumptions about the connections between political behavior and commercial benefit for which there is no sustainable evidence? Why is it unpardonably ideological to be outraged by China's human rights record and to wish to say so? Why is it anti-Chinese to deplore the past record and present repression of Communist leaders? My arguments lie with them and with what they do, not with the people of China. I suspect that my gravest and greatest crime in OCH and OFOC eyes is that I think they should advance some other argument for their approach to China than that it is different, indeed allegedly unique, and must be allowed to play according to its own rules. They are obsessed with China, and their obsession encourages China's Communist leaders to think they can cheat the fate of every tyranny. For my own part, I do not wish the rich democracies to contain China, but nor do I believe that we should—implicitly or explicitly—condone its government's past record and present behavior. I am quite content to let China take its turn with history, discovering as it does so that economics and politics interweave and interact in every country in much the same way. I will keep my fingers crossed for my Chinese friends that it works out all right—it probably will, in the end. That is what has kept Mr. Wei and countless others like him going, through black nights and desolate days: that faith in a free future for China. I hope they are right, and—every finger firmly crossed—I think they are right, too.

10

Back to the Future

A year before she died, [Queen Victoria,] returning on her yacht from a visit to Ireland, was disturbed by rough seas. After a particularly strong wave buffeted the ship, she summoned her doctor, who was in attendance, and said, in unconscious echo of a distant predecessor, "Go up at once, Sir James, and give the Admiral my compliments, and tell him the thing must not occur again."

But the waves would not stand still.

—from *The Proud Tower*, by Barbara Tuchman

The Master said: "Riches and rank are what every man craves; yet if the only way to obtain them goes against his principles, he should desist from such a pursuit."

—*The Analects of Confucius*, 4.5

I sometimes think that I have lived my politics the wrong way around, not quite long-haired, placid teenager to balding, animated middle-aged man—but not far short of that. A political life is supposed to take you from the thrill of the chase to the mellow deliberations of the chamber, from the spirited clash of principles and ideals to the wordly-wise management of accommodations and reality. You are supposed to begin by wanting to change the world and end by aspiring to administer it.

So as I trudge today toward what seems to me to be the front line in the battle of political ideas, hearing the distant rumble of the guns, I find myself fighting against a stream of well-heeled refugees heading in their overloaded limousines in the opposite direction. "Who is that lunatic?" they mutter as I pick my way forward among the abandoned clutter of retreat—the family piano, the birdcage, the matrimonial bed, the collected works of all the Great Unread. "Where does he think he's going? What's his game? What's he up to? He used to be such a sensible fellow." So what happened to him?

I drifted into politics, a casual embodiment of the contingent factor in history. I had taken no part in politics at university, at that stage having really no interest. The scholarship boy, son of loving, middle-class parents who had not themselves been to university, I spent my three years at Oxford enjoying myself in a rather cautious, laid-back way. I halfheartedly pursued a girl, did just enough work to fail to get a First, acted a bit, played a few games, slept a lot. I made no mark on Oxford, and Oxford's main mark on me was the later realization of all that I had missed.

From my accidental political encounter in New York, I came back to London undecided about my future but persuaded that I might be able to postpone a career choice by prolonging my campaigning adventures. I applied for a job in the Conservative party's Research Department, having decided that I was instinctively a Tory and not a Socialist, and slightly to my surprise was accepted in 1966. The Research Department was the party's parliamentary secretariat and—especially in opposition as we then were—its "think tank." It enjoyed the cachet of having been associated intimately with the Conservative party's intellectual renewal under Rab Butler after the 1945 electoral defeat, and some of the most glittering stars in the subsequent Tory years were alumni—most notably Iain Macleod, Enoch Powell, and Reggie Maudling. It was a comfortable and amusing common room, full of people who were clever in that undemanding British fashion, slightly eccentric in its habits, handsomely dowdy in its appearance in a couple of Westminster's Queen Anne houses, unpushily influential. I joined and I stayed, excepting two years at the Cabinet Office after the Conservative election victory in 1970 and almost two years working for Lord Carrington, party chairman from 1972 until the coal miners routed us in the "don't ask silly questions" election of 1974. (Question: "Who rules Britain, the miners or us?" Answer: "We elected you to rule Britain—come back when you've learned how to do it.")

Lord Carrington, like Douglas Hurd—they are the two most likable and wise people I have ever worked for—had the self-confidence to delegate and cheerfully to accept the consequences. He had a mind like a steel trap, behind an urbane manner that eschewed the vulgarities of enthusiasm. After two years working for him, and a few months for his successor and friend Willie Whitelaw, I toyed with the offer of a job in Brussels with Christopher Soames, one of Britain's two commissioners there. The job interview took place in the main salon of Claridge's, where Soames, on hands and knees, pursued a large and cheerful mouse under the little gilt tables in between asking me my views, or rather telling me his. In the event, and with some regret (he was in every sense a big man), I turned him down and accepted instead the job of director of the Conservative Research Department, just in time for the backbenchers' revolt that swept Margaret Thatcher, somewhat improbably at the time, to the leadership of the party on the votes of the ignored, insulted, unpromoted, and unremarkable majority of Edward Heath's Conservative parliamentary colleagues.

I was back where I had started, running at the age of thirty what one of my predecessors had called "a splendid little destroyer" as it began the job of helping to harry a Labour government with a majority as small as its purposes to eventual defeat in 1979. It was in the following five years that the penny began its long and, such is the law of gravity, accelerating drop.

My political friends were, on the whole, on the left of the party and they did not like Margaret Thatcher one little bit, thinking or at least giving the impression that our brand of moderate conservatism could survive only by being smuggled at dead of night from one safe house to another, like the sacrament in the hands of recusant priests. What the best of them, like Ian Gilmour, disliked about Thatcher was her *ideas*, which she put with some vehemence and a great deal of intellectual energy, especially (in those days) in private. My friends were not without ideas themselves, but one of their ideas was that there was not a single Big Idea, except precisely that. You could, we thought, only nudge political argument a little this way or a little that. The dimensions of the political battlefield were largely predetermined; you had to find the middle point on it and there pitch your tents. Thatcher believed you could shift the battlefield in your own direction; you could fight over terrain of your own choosing provided you could convince people that your own—perhaps currently unfashionable—ideas were right and relevant to their conditions and to their hopes. If you achieved that, then you could do things that had previously been deemed politically impossible. Cometh the hour, cometh the woman. She won the battle of ideas, and then—like Ronald Reagan—this critic of the very notion of government made decisive government seem possible again. The unions were disarmed, inflation was abated, nationalized industries were privatized, a foreign military campaign of breathtaking daring was successfully completed. Yes, ideas mattered. Politics was not just about Buggins-turning your way to the top and then managing whatever you found when you got there. The greatest excitement of politics was to have a view of how the world works, or should work, and to convince other people that it was the right one. The politicians who really mattered were those who did this. This was the sort of political leadership that really left an imprint on history.

Over the years I have found myself out of sympathy with some of Margaret Thatcher's ideas (on Europe and on the relationship between the individual and the community, for example) while recognizing that exaggeration is an inherent part of her style and perhaps an essential component of her intuitively conceived strategy. In a conservative country like Britain, you probably have to run out ahead of the pack, make a scene, shout a bit, in order to move things forward a few paces. But I have always been more in tune with the ideas associated with the late Rab Butler, my political hero for over thirty years, who helped to fashion postwar Britain.

Butler is most frequently remembered these days for what he did not accomplish—that is, become Prime Minister—rather than for a lifetime of public service almost literally unparalleled in twentieth-century Britain for its length and creativity. Only Churchill was a minister for longer. I began by admiring Butler's supreme talents as a political administrator and policy craftsman. He epitomized my earliest notions of the political trade. It was only later, as I read more about him, that I came to realize that he was only as good as he was because his actions as a politician were rooted in a clear political philosophy—in ideas—and that those ideas were wrapped in a remarkable generosity of spirit. Butler believed in market economics, began as Chancellor of the Exchequer to liberate Britain's economy in the 1950s after the socialist rigor of the 1940s, and would have gone further (floating the pound, for example) if Churchill had not stopped him. His belief in the possibility of using the authority and resources of the state to promote the interest of the many and to balance the diverse interests of the community in a program of social improvement was reflected most clearly in his major educational reforms. Like all sensible Conservatives, he believed, in the words of Giuseppe di Lampedusa's *The Leopard*, "If we want things to stay as they are, things will have to change."

Butler once told a friend and admirer, William Rees-Mogg (later to be the editor of *The Times*), that "it is more important to be generous than to be efficient." That is not a literal description of his economic views but an attempt to convey a sense of the moral dimension of his politics. There are many examples of it. In the 1930s, he had been associated as a young minister with the early moves toward self-government in India. This was not a popular policy in those days in the Conservative party. But he used to remark that certain consequences flowed from the fact that Britain had given the Indians a literature of liberty that told them of Hampden, Burke, Fox, Shelley, Mazzini, and Lincoln. As for economics, he believed that "untouched by morality and idealism, [it is] an arid pursuit, just as politics is an unprofitable one."

So, having begun by thinking that Butler was the consummate decent, sensible political manager, I came to realize that he was all this and much, much more. He was what Margaret Thatcher might have called "a conviction politician," albeit with convictions rather different from her own. He was moderate, certainly, but he also had a deep attachment to ideas and to principles.

My increasing recognition of the centrality of ideas to politics, rather than simple managerial careerism, was deepened by my years in Hong Kong. This must have been the result partly of the peculiarly exposed and emblematic nature of my job and responsibilities there, and partly of the extent to which our concerns and perceptions about our own future touched on broader international debates. Discuss the prospects for democracy in Hong Kong, and you soon found yourself arguing about economic growth and political freedom throughout Asia and beyond. Talk about freedom and the rule of law in the Colony, and it was not long before you were arguing fiercely over whether values were relative and civil liberties a Western export. William Rees-Mogg, with the exaggeration that helps to enliven the work of the best commentators on public affairs, once divided the world between Hong Kong types and Harrogate spa-town characters—the one group sparky, fast on their feet, unafraid of the future, in awe of the market not government; the other, defensive, protective of present interests, fearful of change, believing that it is the market not government that is more likely to be imperfect. The best of Hong Kong certainly corresponded to his characterization, infusing traditional ideas about economics and governance with its own vitality. Hong Kong should represent what Asia's future can be, though its citizens might sometimes reflect on the dark fact that all the great cities in history fall as well as rise, and that success is not a birthright. A little humility and just an edge of nervousness should help to keep Hong Kong on top of the world.

As I have argued throughout this book, Hong Kong obliged me to think hard about the nature and causes of economic success, and the relationship between that success and politics. Economic growth, as the wise American diplomat Morton Abramowitz has argued, produces more than just more economic growth. It both engenders and requires greater political pluralism. Technology, economic choices, personal prosperity, education, travel—all these help produce a political agenda. Men and women who scan the Internet for information and news, who save and want to invest their money wisely, who see on their television screen and at first hand how others live, are not content for long to be denied the right to argue about and decide their own future. Defending these ideas brought me into contact for the first time with that world of slim academic periodicals read by elites that tell us how the world is or should be run, the world of the gurus of the Davos World Economic Forum (from which I have always kept an irreverent distance) and of that whole great caravan of captains of this and high priests of that which circles our planet in restless search of the last missing piece in the perfect network. The main theses against which my own opinions have brushed all point us toward millennial predictions; two are individually crafted and the third is—or was—a more widely shared though not systematically argued proposition. They are, first, Francis Fukuyama's almost ten-year-old argument that we have seen the back of history (by which he means ideological struggle, not interesting times) with the victory of political and economic liberalism. The second is Samuel Huntington's contention that our future will be dominated by the clash of cultures, Western, Islamic, Confucian, and so on. The third is the notion, shattered for the time being by Asia's recent financial hurricanes, that the next century belongs to the Pacific Rim. Let me come at my final thoughts by taking these arguments in reverse order.

The Pacific or Asian century should not have been regarded as a serious runner even before the crash of 1997–98. Whatever Asia's unquestioned achievements, there remains—as we have seen—some way to go before Asia makes up the ground lost over the past century and before it comes close to catching the coattails of the richer countries. Japan and some urbanized parts of Asia (most notably Singapore and Hong Kong) will admittedly be as rich as any community anywhere; others have much further to travel. Moreover, why should we assume that the next century's leadership will be claimed by those with the fastest present economic growth (the main presumption behind Asia's claims) or that globalization and interdependence—from travel to trade to television—will permit any country or continent to dominate? The only global superpower remains the United States, whose strength and influence in the present century have depended on the idea of freedom as much as on the economic power created by that idea and the military might that has helped sustain it internationally. Asia will confront many problems of political and social transition in the years ahead, from the reunification of Korea to the fight for democracy in several countries. The two greatest powers in Eastern Asia—Japan and China—are still nowhere near reaching the sort of historic reconciliation that has brought France and Germany together at the heart of Europe and shaped that continent's political destiny and institutions. Japan remains reluctant to play the role in Asia and the world that its economic weight should support. For the indefinite future, it will be American military power that provides the guarantee of security for most Asian countries. Asia has shown the rest of us how much can be achieved by energy, commitment, and hard work, but it does not offer some new idea for the age, least of all the case for authoritarianism, whose delusive and presumptuous bluster has recently been comprehensively repudiated by events.

I considered some aspects of the Huntington thesis in the earlier discussion of Asian values. I am not convinced that a future of global conflicts and clashes between impermeable civilizations can be constructed out of the undoubtedly disturbing world aggregate of ethnic struggles and religious tribalism. At the heart of Samuel Huntington's brilliantly sustained argument lies a proposition that is both true and also devoid of useful meaning. "Western ideas," he wrote in 1993, "of individualism, liberalism, constitutionalism, human rights, equality, liberty, the rule of law, democracy, free markets, the separation of church and state, often have little resonance in Islamic, Confucian, Japanese, Hindu, Buddhist or Orthodox culture."* "Often have little resonance" is a shaky foundation for an overarching theory that seeks to explain the future. But let us try a slightly different formulation, which may make the case against Huntington just as well. "Western ideas," we might equally well assert, "of individualism, liberalism, constitutionalism, human rights, equality, liberty, the rule of law, democracy, free markets, the separation of church and state, often have little resonance in Western cultures and political histories." True or false? What respect for individualism, liberalism, constitutionalism, the rule of law, and democracy do we find in Europe's twentieth-century encounters with fascism and communism? Not much resonance there. What respect for human rights and equality was there in America's Southern states before the victory of the civil rights movement? What free markets do we discover in much of Europe for much of the century? What separation of church and state can we see in liberal Britain?

The allegedly adamantine and aggressive resistance of one culture to another is challenged by the economics and technology of globalization and by the results of economic growth. Demography plays its part, too. As David Hale has pointed out, "Two thirds of all the people who have ever lived to the age of sixty-five are alive today. With birth rates falling and life expectancy still increasing, the ratio of retired people to working people is poised to rise dramatically during the next few decades. . . . The great challenge which every society will have to confront is how to develop effective retirement funding systems for the elderly which do not undermine private savings and investment through crippling levels of taxation on the young."† Hale argues convincingly that the irreversible aging of the world's population will lead to the universal introduction of pension funds, with a huge increase in the number of equity owners around the world and a consequentially substantial impact on the shape of every economy and every society whatever their cultural roots.

---

* "The Clash of Civilizations," *Foreign Affairs*, Summer 1993.
† *How the Rise of Pension Funds Will Change the Global Economy in the 21st Century*, Council on Foreign Relations conference, November 1996.

The young, too, play their part in the assault on cultural stereotypes. They listen to much the same music everywhere, watch many of the same films, share some of the same idols, wear similar clothes. They go abroad to study. In the mid-1990s, Morton Abramowitz reckoned that there were about 450,000 foreign students in the United States and that almost half of them were Asian. He estimated that about 200,000 Thais alone had graduated from American universities. It would be surprising if American or European campus life affected footwear and eating habits but not mind-sets. I remember on an official visit to Japan being ushered with great ceremony on to a bullet train at Tokyo's main station by a phalanx of uniformed, white-gloved stationmasters, bowing their courteous good wishes for a safe and comfortable journey. As we got into our carriage, we bumped into a young Japanese, wearing denims and sporting pink dreadlocks. It was for me a small example of the way in which Japan is a free society that has managed famously to become modern and part of the world while retaining its own sense of cultural identity.

The ideas of the high nineteenth century have more than any others shaped our own modern identity in Europe, though it has sometimes been a close-run thing. We turned the corner into the present century with an ascendant belief in free trade, liberty, and representative government—and a commitment to cooperate internationally in order to secure those values as widely as possible. Not everyone, of course, faced the new age with confidence. A. E. Housman, to whom I referred at the very beginning of this book, was not alone in hearing in 1895 the tap of distant drums:

> *On the idle hill of summer*
> *Sleepy with the flow of streams,*
> *Far I hear the steady drummer*
> *Drumming like a noise in dreams.*
>
> *Far and near and low and louder*
> *On the roads of earth go by,*
> *Dear to friends and food for powder*
> *Soldiers marching, all to die . . .*

But on the whole, as one century elided into another, there was a broad sense of optimism in Europe. As Hugh Thomas has argued, "A widespread expectation was that representative democracy would become the characteristic form of government in much of the world, within the foreseeable future."* H.A.L. Fisher's *A History of Europe*, written in 1936, took it for granted that before the First World War, "there were good reasons for believing that parliamentary institutions would supply the sovereign formula for the coming age." More than that, the closeness of the relationship among liberty, democracy, and free enterprise was widely accepted intellectually, even though the pseudoscience of class-based history had begun to question it. John Stuart Mill argued the point in his essay "On Liberty": "If the roads, the railways, the banks, the insurance offices, the great joint stock companies, the universities, and the public charities were all of them branches of the government; if, in addition, the municipal corporations and local boards, with all that now devolves on them, became departments of the central administration, if the employees of all these enterprises are appointed and paid by the government, and look to the government for every rise in life; not all the freedom of the press and popular constitution of the legislature would make this or any other country free otherwise than in name."

"Glad, confident morning" did not last long. Free trade, liberty, and representative government were almost buried in Europe and by Europeans. Now here we stand a hundred years later with the same hopes that we had before. I agree with Fukuyama that the case for political and economic freedom has indeed been won. But there is much history still to be made in securing those freedoms and no guarantee, in Asia (and particularly China) and nearer to Europe as well, that their future is wholly assured.

The prosperous countries of Western Europe, the core of the European Union, have been so obsessed with preventing repetitions of the past that we have shut our eyes to some of the awkward challenges of the future.

First, Europe's institutional development has focused, understandably and probably inevitably, on lashing France and Germany together at the heart of Europe, so closely joined as to be incapable again of dividing the continent in war. The intensity of concentration on this endeavor has produced worrying distortions. Fearful of the impact on the existing balance of the European Union's interests, we have dragged

* *An Unfinished History of the World,* 1979.

our feet over welcoming the restored democracies of Central and Eastern Europe to our club. This was not a mistake we made when Spain, Portugal, and Greece broke free from tyranny. Instead, we have initially offered Eastern Europe the protection of our military alliance, NATO, against a threat that no longer exists. Once again, as we did with perhaps more reason after the First World War, we seek to shut Russia out of Europe, arousing her nationalist instincts by the bizarre aims of our diplomacy.

Second, we press ahead in Europe with an economic project for monetary union that is bound sooner or later to expose the exiguousness of political authority and democratic sanctions at the heart of our community. What thought have we given to the development of democratic institutions, of checks and balances and legitimizing instruments in Europe? When interest rates rise and growth falls in France or Spain because the German economy is overheating, how exactly will that be explained to French or Spanish voters? How will they react if they are told that it will make no difference even if they change their own government? Europe has to find a convincing and sustainable institutional answer to questions like these.

Third, because of our history, our civilization, and our self-approbation, we aspire to play some role in the world. But what are we for, what do we believe, what are we prepared to do? When we speak of the West—America and Europe—as though of some organized view of mankind's best future, what is it that we in Europe are prepared to contribute now? Admittedly, the soldiers of some European countries have been sent abroad from time to time in recent years to fight and die for the well-being and freedom of others, but what are we prepared as a whole in Europe today to risk for the sake of decency and liberty elsewhere? Does Europe really have any collective sense of how it can and should stand up for the principles and ideas that (with American help) shaped our current destiny? Do we have in Europe any remaining value-driven vision of the world? What help, for example, will we give to those in Asia who think that freedom matters more than cell phones, who do not see any contradiction between democracy and good government, who believe that more sophisticated economies require more open societies?

I do not say any of this because I believe that Europe can make the future in the way that it undoubtedly helped, mostly for better rather than ill, to make the past. If it is true that the next century will not "belong to Asia," because the world has moved on from that sort of history, then it is true also that it will not be stamped with a European hallmark. But whether the twenty-first century will carry indelibly the imprint of the ideas that shaped Europe's rich and free heartlands—the belief in market economics, representative government, and the rule of law—will depend at least a little on whether Europe joins America in continuing to uphold those ideas. The European Union has been recently too slow and too myopic to safeguard those values on its own doorstep. What confidence should we have that Europe will do better further afield? But demands for Europe's help and understanding will assuredly be made elsewhere, are already made elsewhere. We can no more stop the waves than could Queen Victoria.

What almost forfeited freedom in this century? Certainly, we can point to the clash of national interests, to economic and ideological struggles. But should we not also catalog a thousand, or a million, little acts of cowardice, dishonesty, treachery—not just governments doing wrong, but you and I doing wrong, the treason of clerks as well as chiefs? In his book *The File*, Timothy Garton Ash asks what it is that makes one man a hero, a Claus von Stauffenberg, and another an Albert Speer, the sort of survivor who though not himself evil becomes evil's accomplice. How many decent people connived at and contributed to the near triumph of wickedness? What most cheered me about the people of Hong Kong was the number of men and women who were not prepared to make those tacky little compromises that pave the road to hell. And what most depressed me were those inside and outside Hong Kong, inside and outside Britain, who should have known better but trimmed and trespassed, betraying the values of pluralism.

They are the values that lie at the heart of the book that has marked me most. Sir Karl Popper's *The Open Society and Its Enemies*, written in the 1940s partly as an attack on Plato, was also an assault on totalitarianism and its philosophical inspiration. It must have had a thrilling resonance when it was first published; we were in the final months of a bloody war against one tyranny and faced the baleful prospect of trying to make and share peace with another. Popper knew where the battle lines had to be drawn, the trenches dug. For him there was no doubt what was required to pursue reason and truth and all that is best in humanity. This is how he concluded the first volume of his book: "If we are tempted to rely on others and so be happy, if we shrink from the task of carrying our cross, the cross of humaneness, of reason, of responsibility, if we lose courage and flinch from the strain, then we must try to fortify ourselves with a clear understanding of the simple decision before us. We can return to the beasts. But if we wish to remain human, then there is only one way into the open society. We must go on into the unknown, the uncertain and insecure, using what means we may have to plan as well as we can for both security and freedom."

Half a century later, is that still relevant, still a text for our times? Well, the liberal democracies won the war; we did not return to *those* beasts. We in Europe, where the beasts had been bred, put together again the shattered west of our continent. We benefited from American help, from Marshall aid, from privately invested American dollars, from G.I.s by the ten thousand. We set up NATO—we *did* plan for security and freedom. We all of us saw the world divided into "isms." We in Britain emancipated our empire, and many of its newly independent countries—if not as many as we would have wished—survived in freedom and prospered in peace. We also contributed our mega-tonnage of potentially awesome destruction to the serene balance of terror. With our European neighbors we built open welfare economies—more or less free markets, more or less socially responsible. We created together in Europe (Britain coming late to the party) a successful community of traders, regulators, and subsidy beneficiaries, bickering but—unlike in the past—not fighting, and we scratched our heads to discover what it was for not just what it was against. And whatever the headlines, the Sputniks, the U2 spy planes, the SS20 rockets, the crises from Berlin to Cuba, the sad and bitter wars from the Middle East to Vietnam, the threat or the promise that our world would always be menaced by an alien ideology and its warheads, whatever happened, we—feeble, irresolute, inherently inefficient, and all the other pejorative adjectives—we liberal democracies led by the United States kept our nerve. And then one day we woke up and—hey, presto—to borrow from Adlai Stevenson, the most intimidating "ism" had become a "wasm." No Berlin Wall. No evil empire. No world split irredeemably between good and bad. No spikes on helmets or on walls. Had we won, then? What were we to do next? No need to plan any more, perhaps, for freedom and security; no need to carry our cross.

In C. P. Cavafy's poem "Waiting for the Barbarians," written in 1898, the people of an ancient city go out to its gates, led by their emperor, to await the arrival of the conquering barbarians. But the barbarians fail to appear. What can have happened? What can be done?

> *Why this sudden bewilderment, this confusion?*
> *(How serious people's faces have become.)*
> *Why are the street and squares emptying so rapidly*
> *Everyone going home lost in thought?*
> *Because night has fallen and the barbarians haven't come.*
> *And some of our men just in from the border say*
> *There are no barbarians any longer.*
> *Now what's going to happen to us without barbarians?*
> *They were, those people, a kind of solution.*

So they were for us also. Without that kind of solution, it may be more difficult to say what we support, not just what we oppose. Yet it is vital to define our purpose today if we are not to drift aimlessly on the tide, knocked about by the elements, carried hither and yon by expediency and opportunism. There are still principles, ideas, and ideals, hard as flint and clear as crystal. They are the principles of Adam Smith and Karl Popper, of Tocqueville, Burke, and Mill, the principles that uphold political freedom and economic liberty, the principles that helped create and sustain open plural societies, prospering mightily, trading freely, treating their citizens decently. Those are principles that we must hold on to and fight for, East and West, even when the barbarians appear to have melted away from the city's walls, because we know from all history that the barbarians always, always return.

Postscript
June 1999

Use your head, can't you,
use your head, you're on earth,
there's no cure for that.
—Samuel Beckett, *Endgame*

For forty-some years, ever more perspiration,
And we just circle back to before Liberation;
And speaking again of that big revolution,
Who, after all, was it for?
—a popular saying in China

The barbarians did return, rather sooner than even the pessimists had feared—though not exactly where we had worried they would appear. Europe celebrated the last spring of the passing millennium with a further outbreak of ethnic cleansing, this time by Serbs in Kosovo, and with the launching of an air war against Slobodan Milosevic and his Belgrade government. It was said to be a new kind of war, fought with "smart" weaponry for old-fashioned moral purposes, the sort of humanitarian cause of which Mr. Gladstone would have approved. Critics denounced the damage and the casualties that do-gooding with bombs brought in its wake; their ritual denunciation of the rape and murder of the innocent was hollowed out by man-of-the-world qualifications and much wise display of strategic hindsight. Others worried rather nervously that things had ever come to this grim pass, and worried even more about the consequences for Europe and its alliance with North America if the war were to be humiliatingly lost and evil triumphed. But it was not lost; the bombs appeared to do their job—at least for the time being.

Whatever might be the precise long-term outcome in the Balkans of this particular encounter with politics on one of the continent's traditional fault lines, it seemed certain that Europe would never be quite the same again. The obsession with an agenda formed by the rhetoric and aspirations of recovery from the Second World War, and by the politics of instant gratification created by successful welfare capitalism, would need to change. If the countries of the European Union were to preserve and extend their own liberal order, they would need to display a moral commitment to enlargement and a passion for change and reform of the way they conducted their affairs that would demand political leadership of a high order. Sacred cows would have to be herded to the abattoir; electorates would be faced with tough choices and even with modest sacrifices. What price would voters in the European Union—who spend over 6 billion pounds a year on ice cream—be prepared to pay for a peaceful and stable continent whose boundaries of law, democracy, and civility need to be extended so that they become more or less coterminous with its geographical frontiers?

War, improbably, in the West—but the slow and patchy advance of the liberal cause in Asia. There is a story about the former Irish Prime Minister Garret FitzGerald, a gentle intellectual, who was once confronted by his civil servants with a difficult policy choice. "I can see," he responded, "that it works in practice, but does it work in theory?" Those of us who lived in the democratic West had been brought up to believe in the successful marriage of more or less free economics and pluralist politics. Economists, historians, lawyers, and constitutionalists—Bloch, Dobb, Postan, Schumpeter, Pollock, Maitland, Stubbs—had explained the rise of the West in terms of our development there of an efficient economic organization that combined the guarantee of rights—for example, to property—with an institutional infrastructure that encouraged the individual to efforts whose rewards enriched the whole community. These structures grew into representative government, the rule of law and civil society. Economies invariably flourished where those arrangements obtained.

The theory was challenged, as we have seen, by Asian authoritarians who claimed that such notions were culturally alien to the East and that their own economic success showed there were other, and perhaps better, ways of governing. The argument that authoritarianism was not the reason for the boom years but was part of the cause of their abrupt termination became an accepted platitude remarkably quickly after the crash in 1997. I was struck by the speed with which those in politics and business who had previously hymned tiger values learned to sing from a different song sheet. Did their swift Pauline conversion signify a genuine shift of sentiment—recognition that the theory of liberal order worked in practice, too—or were they just parroting the latest conventional wisdom overheard in the bar at Davos and at other gatherings of global networkers? And how could they apply their new comprehension of liberal values in some parts of Asia but not in others, such as China?

What did Asians think of the West's partial rediscovery of the universality of human rights, and of the efficacy of democracy and liberty? While I was filming a television documentary in Jakarta in July 1998, I noted the number of European and American central bankers and foreign and finance ministers who were arriving in Indonesia to give lectures on civics to President Habibie, just installed in office by a nervous army in the wake of riot and arson. The President, until recently at the right hand of Suharto, was told firmly that he should waste no time in introducing democracy and liberal reforms. What, I wondered, had they all been saying to President Suharto a few months before? What did the Indonesians make of these homilies, delivered only after bloody events that might have been avoided if they had been uttered and, more important, heeded rather earlier? Few of these latterly candid friends admitted to any past weak-kneed weakmindedness. But one organization that did own up was the World Bank. Bank officials conceded that during Suharto's final years, they had ignored corruption and growing repression as well as a crumbling financial system, partly because of their huge financial investments in Indonesia and the substantial progress that the country had undoubtedly made with their help in some social and economic areas. It may be that in the light of this experience, the World Bank will revisit some of its optimistic assessments of China.

Indonesia had been devastated by the Asian crash. Violence accompanied collapsing living standards. I visited a burned-out shopping center in Jakarta where Chinese shopkeepers had died in the looters' flames. It was a reminder of the difficulty of securing peaceful political transitions in countries where authoritarian regimes throttle civil society. Tear gas, rubber bullets, water cannons, and barbed wire were inadequate to the task of securing peaceful Indonesian acquiescence for policies that brought pain, misery, and, sometimes, hunger. With its economy in ruins and the tardy introduction of financial and structural reforms, Indonesia saw the social advances of recent years wiped out almost overnight. The number of people living in poverty soared—the Asian Development Bank calculated that the figure had doubled. Children dropped out of schools; mothers, out of health programs. Yet there was no significant populist agitation to shut the world and all its works out of Indonesia's life, no threat by the government to slam and bolt the door against globalization and its comet's tail of economic disciplines. What Indonesians shouted and demonstrated for was democracy and an end to corruption. They prepared for fair elections and kept their fingers crossed that those elections would produce a stable democratic government able to close the book on the Suharto years, when the old general and his brood had given new meaning to the concept of family values.

Remarkably (at least for some Western critics of free trade and open markets), the noisy demand for an end to liberal economics and globalization was the Asian dog that scarcely barked. In his book *False Dawn*, the British political scientist John Gray rants with more enthusiasm than coherence against the alleged shortcomings of international capitalism. But in Asia his arguments found few followers, perhaps because of the difficulty of recognizing his economic caricatures and perhaps as well because no one—not least Professor Gray—has been able to suggest anything much better for maximizing happiness, stability, and prosperity than liberal economics, sustained by open markets and by balance sheets that pour black ink all over the page.

There was, admittedly, some criticism of the wreckage caused by rapid flows, this way and that, of short-term capital—the hot money that gives some bankers and investors their exclusive and expensive tans. Even George Soros, who has bet and won—and sometimes lost— so much in the currency casino, tried his hand at designing a new and ambitious architecture for international finance that would bring order to a brutish world. Mr. Soros demonstrated that, nice man, currency hotshot, and generous philanthropist though he may be, he did not have the ingenuity to design a practical system for regulating the world's marketplace. But then, neither did anyone else. Some Asians were louder than others in denouncing unrestricted financial flows, including, a little surprisingly, the representatives of Hong Kong, bruised by their experiences of doing successful but expensive battle with the hedge funds. Perhaps new workable proposals on these matters will emerge in the coming years. They are likely, however, to be modest and directed toward an increase in transparency and the association of competent domestic surveillance and regulation of financial services and banking with the availability of internationally supported crisis lending. Most sensible financial managers are leery of anything more ambitiously interventionist, an attitude that was not even changed by the sight of two Nobel Prize–winning economists coming close to bringing down the entire American banking system with the allegedly foolproof application of their theories on derivatives trading to the real marketplace. Very clever people offering untold riches through incomprehensible schemes should be decked out in consumer-health warnings.

For all the occasional fuss about footloose money and pillage at the touch of a fund manager's mouse, there was little else by way of sustained challenge to the growing global economic orthodoxy. Suggestions that it was all some wretched American neocolonialist plot were shredded by the evidence that such Asian economic progress as there was largely depended on access to America's still-growing market. The "importer of last resort," as she was called by some American trade officials, was evidently committed to a hegemonistic strategy that had to be bankrolled by a surging American trade deficit. Only Dr. Mahathir, the irascible leader of Malaysia, sought to liberate his country from the rest of the world; borrowing from the "Asian values" of the late Kim Il-Sung, his motto seemed to be "Ourselves alone." Mahathir's policy of locking money into Malaysia had the predictable effect of deterring further investment in his country. Instructed under threat of sanction to lend to favored local companies, Malaysia's banks saw their nonperforming loans soar. This impoverishing nonsense did not, however, last long. Record falls in output and investment in 1998 led Dr. Mahathir to reverse engines and to set out on a charm offensive in the international financial community to persuade bankers and investors that he did not really hate them at all and would welcome their return to his backyard. Dr. Mahathir survived for the time being, a time-warped authoritarian.

Unfortunately, his one-time deputy Anwar Ibrahim fared less well.

The advocate of political and economic reform in his own country and in the region, Anwar fell foul of his boss's paranoia. I went to interview Anwar for a television series in July 1998. When the interview was completed, Anwar dismissed my crew and his officials from the room and told me how worried he was about his position. His attempts to reform the economy and his espousal of political pluralism were regarded by his Prime Minister as signs of treachery. Suspicious and vengeful, Dr. Mahathir resented the favorable publicity Anwar received around the world. Anwar was clearly worried, and unfortunately, it soon turned out that he had good reason to be. In the autumn, Mahathir and his supporters turned against him, filing a series of trumped-up charges—from sodomy to corruption. In prison, Anwar was beaten, and in the courtroom he and his defense lawyers were harassed by a judge who would have given luster to a Soviet show trial in the 1930s. It was a deplorable episode, redeemed in part only by the bravery of Anwar's wife and children and by the willingness of a number of the region's leaders (led by President Estrada, newly elected in the Philippines) to break the normal row of *omerta* on one another's behavior and to condemn Anwar's political martyrdom. From his prison cell, Anwar continued to speak out. "There cannot be an Asian renaissance without social and economic justice," he argued. "All over Southeast Asia we see the political landscape changing with an awareness of the need for democracy and civil society growing, especially among the young."

Patchy signs of a recovery, if not yet a renaissance, first appeared in those countries that seemed to understand Anwar's argument and the need to construct political institutions that were open and representative. In Bangkok in the summer of 1998, I saw both the wreckage of the go-go years and the first halting steps toward sustainable recovery. Muang Thong Thani was a privately owned and built satellite city, with a planned population, bigger than Boston's, on the edge of the Thai capital. It had risen from the fertile plain on wave after wave of cheap foreign credit. When I was there, it looked like a three-quarters-finished ghost city, with empty streets and tower blocks, the occasional builder's truck and developer's Mercedes a grisly reminder that property speculators can lose fortunes as large as those they sometimes make. But there was good news in Bangkok, too. The most democratic government in Thailand's history, under the plain-living Chuan Leekpai, had emerged from the debate about constitutional reform to set in hand an ambitious program of financial, political, and economic reform, covering subjects such as freedom of the press, bankruptcy, and corporate restructuring. During the course of the year, the Thai economy started to claw its way back; the currency strengthened, with the baht rising by almost a third. The stock market picked up by 40 percent; interest rates fell, and confidence and would-be investors started to return. The economy, which had shrunk by 8 percent in 1998, began to expand once more in 1999.

South Korea's sudden economic collapse in the autumn of 1997 had scared bankers and the international financial institutions. It looked as though Korea Inc. had been demolished. But Koreans themselves hoped that over the following year they had begun to create a more open, flexible, and internationally competitive economy. The government of the democratic Kim Dae-Jung did not go as far and as fast as some wanted in liberalizing the labor market and breaking up the chaebols, yet its progress should not be belittled. It had the moral authority, despite union resistance, to make some labor reforms and to press the biggest of the chaebols to start restructuring and unloading some of their subsidiaries. Foreign reserves rose during 1998; the currency stabilized and strengthened, with the won recovering to more or less where it had been at the onset of the crisis; interest rates were cut; the stock market rose through the year by almost 70 percent. The IMF, often unfairly criticized during the early months of the crisis, was able to secure the successful implementation of much of its reform program, leading to a rebuilding from the ruins.

One or two economies seemed hardly affected at all by the calamities all around them. Taiwan, an increasingly raucous democracy, actually grew by 5 percent in 1998. Singapore only contracted by a percentage point. Even here there was, however, a characteristically restrained acceptance of the necessity for some change. In a few areas of overregulated economic activity, the government relaxed its know-it-all grip, and more generally, Singaporean leaders spoke of the need for a more relaxed atmosphere in order to promote greater creativity. There is a joke in Singapore—or perhaps it isn't a joke—that university lecturers are now teaching their students the three ways to think freely. Reports of a government initiative to stimulate nongovernmental activities also suggested that Lee Kuan Yew and his colleagues had not yet quite mastered the new plot. The Senior Minister—or SM, as

Singaporeans call him—continued to give the world the ubiquitous benefits of his wisdom, though the words *Asian values* no longer featured prominently in his *tour d'horizon* tutorials.

The most nervous attention focused on Japan's struggle to relaunch its sinking economy and on China's continuing bravura display of political bullying and economic defiance of the laws of gravity. Japan's position was crucial to that of the whole region, above all because its economic weight represents over two thirds of that of Asia as a whole. After the 1985 Plaza Accord—an international agreement on currencies—the U.S. dollar had lost about half its value relative to the yen, and it dragged down those Asian economies linked to it. To protect their competitiveness, Japanese companies invested substantially in the region, building factories and buying up property and retailing outlets. But as the Japanese currency weakened in the mid-1990s, that flow was reversed. The once all-conquering yen scuttled for home.

Japan's economic travails reminded us that the word *credit* comes from the Latin word meaning "to believe." The Japanese simply lost belief and confidence in their own currency, and as prices sank, there seemed no point in spending money at home when postponement of consumption would lead to better future bargains. The cash was hidden away under the futon. To the traveler, it seemed that the Japanese were doing most of their spending abroad, touring the world's most famous beauty spots in large and usually disciplined numbers (though I did witness in late 1998 a group of Japanese youths skimming Italian coins across the waters of Rome's Trevi Fountain). Japan's banks were weighed down by bad loans to property companies (the values of whose assets had plummeted) and to industrial and commercial conglomerates that had sacrificed profitability to growth and market share. Debt chased yet more debt as the economy spiraled downward. The Japanese government and financial bureaucracy, obsessively worried about the future costs of providing for Japan's rapidly aging population, were reluctant to give the sagging economy the revitalizing stimulus it required; indeed, some budgetary measures—particularly ill-judged tax increases—further depressed activity. When reflationary packages were produced from time to time, they appeared to involve substantial amounts of double counting and discredited infrastructure investment largely composed of handouts to construction companies that had bankrolled the political parties.

To the surprise of most observers, the new government formed in 1998 by Mr. Obuchi—a career politician whose charisma had been unfairly compared to cold pizza—gave a more decisive impression of coming to grips with Japan's problems. A fiscal stimulus on a scale that looked sufficient to really stimulate, an opening up of sectors hitherto largely closed to foreign competition—such as telecommunications—and the beginnings of a restructuring of Japan's banks and some of the larger corporations gave some foreign investors the impression that corners might actually have been turned, or were at least in the process of being turned. Other observers, such as the American economist Paul Krugman, were more skeptical, believing that Japan was still deep in its liquidity trap and would need far more radical measures if it were to stand any chance of escape. What was certainly true was that strong political leadership was in short supply in Tokyo, a consequence perhaps of a system of corporatist governance developed after the war in which powerful bureaucrats and businessmen had made all the decisions that mattered, leaving the political class to the diversions of political fund-raising of varying degrees of dubiety and of the musical chairs of briefly enjoyed political preferment. It was not surprising that when Japan needed to be able to whistle up strong political leaders, they were not easily to be found.

Imperturbable as they are famously said to be, even the Japanese must have been surprised to hear from Washington in 1998 that China was now America's strategic partner in Asia. These extraordinary tidings may only have stretched credulity in Tokyo and sapped morale in Taiwan. But in democratic India, they confirmed the worst fears of politicians and the media, and encouraged the Indians to look more vigorously to their own defenses against potential Chinese aggression. The Indian decision to "go nuclear," regrettable though it was, owed much to the West's neglect of Indian concerns and its increasingly ill judged coddling of China.

Nineteen ninety-eight was a sort of *annus mirabilis* for China, the high point—one must hope—in China's spectacularly successful campaign, first, to bury memories abroad of the repression of dissent in 1989; second, to cover up the nature of a regime that would still, if and wherever necessary, kill its own people to hang on to power; and third, to write pretty much its own rules of engagement with the rest of the world. In the wake of the Hong Kong handover, and increasingly in the following year, Western leaders went on pilgrimage to Peking, the Santiago de Compostella for global businessmen, the Lourdes for flatulent strategists. Deploying every known self-deluding cliché about China, and ingeniously inventing some new ones, the Presidents and Prime Ministers and their caravan of corporate bigwigs came and saw and were conquered. The attempt to engage China—drawing this great country into the international community—was wholly correct. But there was no reason why such a dialogue should be largely values-free on the Western side

Some visitors went to Peking in pursuit of business—an insurance franchise here, a joint venture there. Some argued that a more intense dialogue would encourage the Chinese government to treat its own people better. Some suggested that if we showed that we understood the Chinese and cared about their worries, they would be encouraged to behave more constructively on the world stage. Some were, as ever, simply besotted, discovering like many before them the narcotic intoxication of China—grace, delicacy, and languor on the one hand, and danger, melancholy, and hidden cruelties on the other.

Even the wisest of public officials could suspend some of their rational faculties when discussing China. Robert Rubin, the outstanding American Treasury Secretary, praised China as "an island of stability" in an otherwise turbulent world. Not even the Chinese Politburo would be likely to make this sort of claim with a straight face. To be fair to Mr. Rubin, he doubtless had in mind China's continuing growth while other Asian economies floundered and the promises made by China's economic leaders that they would not devalue their currency, the renminbi. But even here, such stability as there was had been partly secured by the refusal of the Chinese to countenance the sort of market openings, especially for capital flows, that Mr. Rubin and his colleagues had pressed on other Asian governments. As for the renminbi, it had seen an earlier devaluation that had helped put pressure on other Asian currencies in the mid-nineties, and a devaluation in 1998 would have doubtless triggered a competitive round of devaluations elsewhere in Asia and raised the costs of China's dollar-denominated debt (almost certainly larger than the figure conceded in official statistics). So the Chinese government was lauded for doing what was anyway in its own best interest.

How stable was China, economically and socially? The growth figure of about 8 percent looked healthy enough, though it was almost certainly exaggerated. Mr. Zhu Rongji, China's Premier and economic czar, was given to expressing public doubts about the reliability of the economic statistics reported to him. The figures for the consumption of electric power, for freight transport, and for foreign trade and imports all suggested that official growth figures were much inflated. China's main problem was that the state-owned enterprises continued to absorb far too much of the limited money available for new investment. They built up inventories of goods that consumers, nervous about the increasing costs they now had to bear for hitherto free social and community services, were unwilling to buy. The Chinese have a high propensity to save. These savings are laundered through the technically bankrupt commercial banking system and loaned to the state industries, which have an equally high propensity to lose money. You do not have to be an economic genius to know that this process cannot go on forever.

Reform of the state industries was inhibited by political nervousness about the social costs: an increase in unemployment (already high in towns and cities as well as the countryside) and the smashing of "the iron rice bowl"—the industry-based housing and welfare programs that helped sustain the living standards of tens of millions of people. A rising budget deficit and declining tax revenues also limited the government's elbow room, further narrowed by the corruption and incompetent management that curtailed the effectiveness of Keynesian-style attempts to boost the economy through infrastructure investment.

Foreign banking and business confidence in China was hit by one spectacular bankruptcy and a thousand and one commercial frustrations. The bankruptcy was that of the Guangdong International Trust and Investment Corporation—GITIC—one of the many provincially based channels for investing in China's economic miracle and in the private exploitation of previously public assets. Ironically, GITIC had been regarded as one of the better run of these quasi-governmental trusts, but liabilities of £2.6 billion torpedoed it in 1998. Foreign banks and investors had foolishly lent money to "red chip" companies like GITIC, assuming that "letters of comfort" from regional and municipal authorities were adequate guarantees for their loans. They were rudely disabused of this idea as the trusts sank with all hands, and were given lectures by Chinese officials about prudent assessment of risk and moral hazard that had not been part of the script when they had been encouraged to open their bank vaults to Chinese borrowers. It was not the only time that bankers made fools of themselves in Asia.

Declining foreign investment—estimated this year at $15 billion, one third of the 1998 figure—reflected a growing disappointment about the business prospects in China. This was not true of every firm or every sector. But as I talked to bankers and business leaders in America and Europe through 1998, I encountered a growing number who told me with a sigh that they were in China for the long haul, which I took to be a euphemism for the fact that they were not making any money. Some companies had clearly had enough and went home— for example, Royal Bank of Canada, Fosters of Australia, Marks and Spencer of the United Kingdom, and Southwestern Bell of the United States. Others, like Unilever and Motorola, cut back their operations. Many seemed anxious about the favoritism shown to local companies, worried about the hostile regulatory environment in areas such as pharmaceuticals, mobile telecommunications equipment, and power-generating machinery, and concerned about the general slowdown in the economy. Some of those who stuck it out enthusiastically, hoping for a windfall just around the next bend, were given a banquet in the Great Hall of the People and a pat on the back. Mr. Rupert Murdoch, trying to secure a broader distribution into China for his News Corporation's Star TV satellite programs, met President Jiang Zemin, who, according to the New China News Agency, "expressed appreciation for the efforts made by the world media mogul in presenting China objectively and cooperating with the Chinese press." Praise indeed for this champion of uninhibited press and publishing freedom (elsewhere). As has been well said by some of his employees, the Murdoch empire—like the British, before it—has no permanent friends or foes but only permanent interests.

The social costs of economic change in China were set out in *China's Pitfall*, a book by a young female Chinese economist, He Qinglian, which was published in 1998. In the words of Liu Binyan and Perry Link, writing in *The New York Review of Books* on October 8, 1998, this writer "forces us to reconceive what 'reform' meant." She chonicles the dark side of China's recent history: the plundering of state-owned assets by powerful public officials and their friends, the capital flight (as great during most of this decade as the inflow of foreign investment), the financial deception that sustains a bankrupt banking system, the waste of private savings, the nonpayment of wages and the oversupply of consumer goods, the environmental hazards (that helped to cause the terrible floods in 1998), the growing inequality, the corruption, the rip-offs, and the wasting away of what Liu and Link call "the moral basis of society." To borrow from the saying quoted at the beginning of this chapter, who had China's revolution been for? No wonder there were urban and rural riots; no wonder religious cults claimed ever more followers; no wonder the Chinese Communist party leaders cracked down even harder on dissent. They were scared stiff.

The Western visitors in 1997 and 1998 told the world that they had gone to Peking to witness and encourage the first signs of a political spring. Clinton, Blair, Jospin, Santer, and the others were there for the warm breezes but not for the subsequent chill. While the Chinese government said that it would sign (though not ratify) the international covenants on political and economic rights, while it welcomed a visit by the UN's human-rights supremo Mary Robinson, while it allowed Presidents Jiang and Clinton to debate on television, albeit in a pretty perfunctory way, issues of democracy and freedom, anyone who took all this at face value and behaved as though spring really had come was swiftly woken from such a naive dream. Several dissidents were locked up; the best known, Xu Wenli, was given a thirteen-year sentence for trying to form a political party dedicated to democracy. New rules were brought in to curb film directors, singers, and software developers. One Shanghai computer entrepreneur, Lin Hai, was jailed for two years for selling thirty thousand e-mail addresses that could be used to spread the message about freedom. With the number of Chinese Internet users almost doubling to 2.1 million in less than a year, Chinese security officials became increasingly nervous about the threat to totalitarianism from information technology.

Economic unrest and the plethora of politically significant anniversaries in 1999 (for example, the tenth anniversary of Tiananmen) saw the political crackdown increase in severity. China's leaders had plainly found unconvincing President Clinton's advice that a government could not "purchase stability at the expense of freedom." The American administration was embarrassed by China's resiling from all the implicit and explicit promises that the human-rights situation in the country would improve. It supported once again in 1999 the tabling of a resolution condemning China's human-rights record at Geneva. But for the moment, European countries seemed beyond embarrassment. Their behavior gave credibility to Wei Jingsheng's charge: "The Chinese government's human-rights concept has not moved toward the universal standard of human rights. On the contrary, the human-right values of Western politicians actually have moved closer to those of Communist China."

No one could sensibly deny that in many respects conditions for the majority of the Chinese had improved since Tiananmen. Living standards had risen for many as GDP, foreign trade, and investment soared. Materialism replaced Maoism and socialism, and a consumer culture brought greater personal independence. Provided they avoided politics, the Chinese had more social freedom and suffered less interference in their daily lives. But that was not true for all. There were still appalling human-rights abuses that would have earned unqualified condemnation if perpetrated elsewhere. In some respects, things were getting worse in 1999, and the whole political edifice was constructed on quicksand.

With communism's ability to attract commitment and loyalty a thing of the past, the regime encouraged a crude nationalism to try to bind society together. This nationalism was at odds with China's constant promise that it was opening up economically to the world, but it was very much in keeping with the growing assertiveness of China in international affairs. China built up its military threat to Taiwan, deploying new missiles against what it still insists on calling a renegade province. It vetoed UN peacekeeping in the Balkans when Macedonia recognized Taiwan. It continued to court a rogue's gallery of international friends—the Khmer Rouge, Iraq's Saddam Hussein, North Korea's Kim Jong-Il, the Burmese junta, the Yugoslav leader Slobodan Milosevic. It started to throw its weight about in and around the Spratly Islands, intent on establishing first claim to the energy resources that might be found there. When a NATO airstrike on Belgrade hit the Chinese embassy in that city and killed three Chinese citizens, nationalist outrage and protest were whipped up against America and Western Europe, ignoring the sincere apologies for this tragic mistake. The terrible accident was portrayed as part of a Western conspiracy to damage China, incorporating the alleged orchestration of the student protests in 1989 (though presumably leaving out of account China's huge trade surplus with America and most Western countries).

Alongside these examples of rampant nationalism and crude muscle-flexing, there were other developments in America that were aborting the latest attempt to construct a closer, more understanding relationship between the U.S. and China. There were allegations, first, that the Chinese security services had sought to buy influence through contributing to American political campaigns and, second, that they had actually managed to purchase an inside track through the policy-making machinery of the Clinton administration, enabling them, for example, to secure the transfer of sensitive technology to China. Then a bipartisan congressional committee established without much doubt that China had been sedulously involved for years in the theft of American nuclear secrets, with who knew what effect on China's own nuclear capacity. The combination of all these factors—from human-rights abuses to espionage—poisoned the political atmosphere in Washington, with paradoxical consequences. American officials had long pointed to the huge imbalance in trade between their own country and China. American imports from China have outpaced their exports to that country by 5 to 1; China has a trade surplus with the U.S. well in excess of $50 billion. America is China's largest overseas market, the destination of 20 percent of all China's exports. America was keen to challenge new restrictions in China on key sectors for America's exports—from agriculture to telecommunications—and to get the Chinese government to scrap rules that were harmful to all exporters, covering local content, technology transfer, and equity requirements. The best way of dealing comprehensively and conclusively with all these matters was to negotiate successfully China's membership in the World Trade Organization, and to this end the long-stalled negotiations on this issue were given a new impetus in the run-up to the visit to America by Premier Zhu Rongji in the spring of 1999. To the genuine surprise of his American interlocutors, Zhu arrived in Washington with a package of sweeping concessions that he had bravely wrung out of the resisting Chinese bureaucracy. But substantial as they were, the political mood in Washington was so hostile to China that President Clinton declined to give the available deal his stamp of approval. The possibility of an agreement with the Chinese in an area where they were behaving constructively was done in by understandably hostile reactions to Chinese behavior in areas where Western fecklessness had encouraged the Chinese to think they could act without much fear of condemnation or political reprisal. It was a familiar story: Feebleness interspersed with occasional displays of principled outrage is no way to construct a sensible long-term relationship with China.

In his excellent history of America's relationship with China from Nixon to Clinton, *About Face* (Knopf, 1999), James Mann notes that the most successful and businesslike period in Sino-U.S. relations was in the early to mid-1980s, when George Shultz was Secretary of State under President Reagan and Paul Wolfowitz was his Assistant Secretary of State responsible for East Asia. Unlike some of their predecessors in the cold war years, they did not overlook the dark side of life in China, on the questionable grounds that China was a crucial strategic counterweight to the Soviet Union. Nor did they take the view that what appeared to be the short-term commercial interest should always prevail. They would not have been regarded as "Old Friends of China." But they did more business with China that was in both sides' interests than most of the OFOCs have ever managed.

Shultz and Wolfowitz would not have countenanced any attempt to contain China and nor should we do so today, however badly the Chinese government has recently behaved. But in my judgment, everything that has happened in 1998–99 argues for the firmness, clarity, and openness in dealing with China that I called for in an earlier chapter. We should do trade deals when we can, remembering that China needs us much more than we in the West need China. In this respect, as in others, we have played a strong hand extraordinarily ineptly. As I have already argued, we should tell China exactly where we stand on issues sensitive to us and to China and not allow ourselves to be pushed around. We should condemn human-rights abuses, making clear that we agree with the imprisoned Xu Wenli that "China is no different from any other country in terms of human rights. All nations are made up of human beings." We should express our strong disapproval of China's attempt to change the military balance in the Taiwan Straits, point out that unless China reconsiders this policy we will be obliged to sell defensive technology to Taiwan, and tell China's leaders that while we are not going to support Taiwanese independence, it is inconceivable that today's free and democratic Taiwan can ever be anything else. In other words, reunification depends on political change within China. We should press China to negotiate on Tibet face-to-face with the Dalai Lama and his representatives. We should curtail military contacts with China and ration red-carpet treatment of China's leaders to reward real rather than imaginary improvements in behavior. We should refuse any more invitations to conduct diplomacy secretively with China: Our relationship should be out in the open. Above all, we should be less obsessed with China. We would do ourselves and Asia a good turn if we spent more time thinking about our relations with India, Japan, Korea, and Indonesia and rather less puzzling about the meaning of every Chinese mood and the best way of humoring every Chinese whim.

But at least, so far as outsiders could judge, the Chinese leadership appeared to leave moderately well alone in Hong Kong. Battered though it was by Asian economic storms and marauding speculators, Hong Kong remained an indisputably free society. This was not wholly welcome to everyone. Demonstrators demonstrated; newspapers criticized; democratic politicians lamented the truncating of their powers, though not of their moral authority; and tycoons lamented the wickedness of a world which did not comprehend that its principal purpose should be to care for and augment their own fortunes. One Hong Kong property developer, Ronnie Chan, spoke for many others when he remarked, "People used to say, before the handover—'The communists are coming.' But the local community are the communists." This attack on the alleged socialism of Hong Kong's democrats—their arguments, for example, in favor of improved welfare benefits at a time of economic hardship—came ill from the representatives of a business community that had successfully pressed the government to remove land from the market when prices were falling, subsequently urged the resumption of land sales to help developers boost their land holdings, and welcomed the government's $15 billion intervention in the stock market that had helped prop up real estate prices. Democratic critics could be forgiven for thinking that any socialism on offer was being doled out prodigally to those who were already living stratospherically high on the hog. Once again, it was businessmen who seemed less than keen on free-market principles, showing in the process scant understanding of the important distinction between special pleading and cronyism.

Where did these same tycoons stand on the rule of law, the foundation and guarantor of their fortunes? The most worrying controversy in Hong Kong's first two years as a Special Administrative Region in China went right to the heart of what most distinguished the city from the rest of the People's Republic, and of what would continue to signal most clearly that it was a lot more than just the richest city in the country. Some thought that the survival of the rule of law itself had been challenged by this row. The facts can be easily assembled. Hong Kong's constitution, the Basic Law, imposed by China with a veneer of local participation in its drafting, gave the right of abode in Hong Kong to the children of permanent residents there who were presently living on the mainland. In an early legal battle to assert this right, the Court of Final Appeal—Hong Kong's highest court, it will be recalled—handed down a judgment inconvenient to the government, which interpreted the Basic Law as it had clearly been drafted. Critics alleged that the government responded, first, by massively exaggerating the scale of the potential immigration threat to Hong Kong and, second, by asking the rubber-stamp Chinese parliament to give its own overriding interpretation of Hong Kong's laws. It would have been open to the Hong Kong government to seek a change in its constitution (to bring it, incidentally, into line with Macau), but the method chosen of circumventing an administrative inconvenience appeared to usurp the Hong Kong court's power of final adjudication. One Hong Kong legislator, the barrister Margaret Ng, who represents the legal profession, argued: "The Basic Law is the arbiter of all Hong Kong's laws. Take away our court's authority to interpret the Basic Law, and what authority is it left with? Where indeed is the rule of law?" But whatever the disquiet aroused by this incident, at least it was encouraging to see so many people in Hong Kong—led by lawyers, democratic legislators, and some journalists—fighting hard for a fundamental principle. Clearly, not all was lost, but the dispute raised serious apprehensions.

There were smaller and larger challenges such as this to liberal ideas in Asia. On the whole, however, the case for pluralism, the rule of law, and open markets continued to thrive, despite the survival of some authoritarians and the occasional faithlessness of a few who should have known much better. Economic woes strengthened this case; those who argued that the reverse would prove true were proved gloriously wrong. The cause for which leaders like Anwar Ibrahim and Aung San Suu Kyi had sacrificed their freedom made steady headway.

It remains to be seen how much European leaders will be interested in the cause of liberal order in Asia when they face so many challenges to its preservation in their own continent. How much is the rich Europe of the Union now prepared to do to share its prosperity and stability with its neighbors, and how much will it be prepared to change in order to invigorate continental economies grown flabby and complacent?

With the defeat of communism and the discrediting of the more extreme forms of state regulation and public ownership, two main recruiting sergeants for conservative parties in Europe have been demobilized and the center left now finds itself in government across much of the continent, although if the results of the 1999 European elections are a guide, their position may be less impregnable than they and the pundits assume. So for the time being, the challenge is one for incumbent leftist leaders, some of whom have sought an intellectual mantle for the accommodations they have been obliged to make with markets and fiscal prudence. Called the Third Way by Britain's Tony Blair and the New Middle by Germany's Gerhard Schröder, it is in reality no more than a political loincloth to give some discreet cover to the abandonment of socialism's failed orthodoxies. But converts should always be welcome: Better, surely, left-wing governments with a few right-wing views than left-wing governments with only left-wing views.

As they scratch around for a politically credible alternative to all this, some center-right politicians in Europe suggest that because their opponents have embraced their ideas on the grounds that they are sensible and popular, the only choice is to make conservatives seem as different as possible by advocating policies that are presently neither sensible nor popular. This is not an obviously wise strategy. There is quite enough that is relevant, bold, and potentially attractive for Europe's political conservatives to say without abandoning moderation. The European Union, for example, requires a recommitment to markets, free trade, and liberal economies, and it needs, too, a strong political and moral lead to confront its responsibilities in the rest of the continent.

The center right should also be able to make a distinctive contribution to the biggest of all the problems of governance facing us. It is a truism that global economic forces have increased anxieties about the ability of individuals to shape and govern their own destinies. The reach of the nation-state, to which we have been accustomed to direct our primary loyalties, has been threatened from above by global economics and from below by the empowerment of individuals through electronics. The suggestion that we should therefore learn love and loyalty on a broader canvas runs foul of the fact, as the Harvard political scientist Michael Sandel has argued, that most of the time we live our lives by much smaller solidarities. We cannot expect people to pledge their allegiance to large and distant organizations, however necessary and important they may be, unless those entities are linked somehow to a political arrangement that we can readily understand and with which we can easily identify. In the age of globalization, the politics of neighborhood matter much more than ever before.

The best hope for continuing to govern ourselves is, therefore, to disperse sovereignty—to bring it, wherever possible, closer to the people—not to try to make a Custer's last stand for a nineteenth-century notion of sovereignty nor attempt to relocate sovereignty somewhere more distant than it is (insofar as it exists) today. But all this—global markets and media, the permeability of national boundaries—should make us realize that weak governments should be smaller governments, that smaller governments require—as I argued before—bigger citizens, and that in order to encourage the emergence of such citizens, smaller governments need a more daring and ambitious project than that of merely trying to grow the economy and distribute its fruits. All of which brings us back to Tocqueville and the central task of the liberal order—getting men and women to accept the obligation of governing themselves, practicing a more extensive political activity in a smaller area. This is what globalization and modern technology should impel us to do if we are to be content and well governed and take a larger role as citizens on a smaller stage. What politicians will dare to say this against a chorus of sneers at such an antique vision and against a backdrop of dismay at the refusal to restrict political rhetoric to the offer of materialist bribes?

The two years since I left Hong Kong have only confirmed my intense and growing millennial sense of déjà vu. A century ago we thought that liberty was safe, secured at least in Europe by democracy and capitalism, the two great shaping ideas of the late nineteenth century. We spent the next half century almost losing freedom entirely on Europe's battlefields and in our bombed cities, gulags, and gas chambers. With America's generous help and leadership, we held on to freedom by our fingertips and witnessed its triumph with the fall of communism and of the wall in Berlin that literally and symbolically girdled its European empire. So, is freedom really safe this time—as safe in Europe as it is vigorously on the march in Asia? Nothing that has happened since I copied out Cavafy's poem about the barbarians in my last chapter in the spring of 1998 has encouraged me to believe that complacency on this score would be justified. But whereas when I first sat down to write this book I was most concerned about how much Europe was prepared to do to help those who share our pluralist values in Asia, revisiting these arguments today, I wonder instead how much we may be required to do to animate and fortify the very same values closer to home. And is that a real worry or just a sign that, now returned to "Dungovernin' " from the colonies, this particular Englishman's worldview has been attenuated by domesticity?

Back in Hong Kong last autumn to sign copies of this book, I was asked anxiously by one friendly customer, "You won't forget us, will you?" How could I? Hong Kong, however, is no longer the Oriental vantage point from which I watch how the world spins. East and West—I now view things from a leafy London borough. Yet it's the same world, with the same values. It's the perspectives that are inevitably different. I was lucky to spend five years seeing things the other way around, as it were—East *to* West—but whichever way we see them, we are, as Hamm in Beckett's *Endgame* points out, "on earth." And, as he goes on to remind us, "there's no cure for that." No cure either for the brightest consequence of globalization: Liberal values, though far from challenged, increasingly shape the world's political and economic agenda, an end to our century better than we had perhaps dreamed, yet an outcome that (as I have argued) we shall need to fight to secure.

INDEX

CHRISTOPHER PATTEN was a Conservative Member of Parliament in Britain until 1992. He held a number of senior political posts including Minister for Overseas Development, Environment Secretary, and Chairman of the Conservative party during its successful 1992 campaign. He was appointed Governor of Hong Kong in the same year and held that post until the handover of the Colony to China in 1997. He is at present heading the Independent Commission on Policing in Northern Ireland, following the peace agreement there. He lives in London with his wife, a lawyer. They have three daughters.